# NETWORKING PRINT IN SHAKESPEARE'S ENGLAND

STANFORD
TEXT TECHNOLOGIES

**Series Editors**

Ruth Ahnert
Elaine Treharne

**Editorial Board**

Benjamin Albritton
Caroline Bassett
Lori Emerson
Alan Liu
Elena Pierazzo
Andrew Prescott
Matthew Rubery
Kate Sweetapple
Heather Wolfe

# Networking Print in Shakespeare's England

*Influence, Agency, and Revolutionary Change*

BLAINE GRETEMAN

Stanford University Press
Stanford, California

STANFORD UNIVERSITY PRESS
Stanford, California

©2021 by the Board of Trustees of the Leland Stanford Junior University. All rights reserved.

No part of this book may be reproduced or transmitted in any form or by any means, electronic or mechanical, including photocopying and recording, or in any information storage or retrieval system without the prior written permission of Stanford University Press.

Printed in the United States of America on acid-free, archival-quality paper

Library of Congress Cataloging-in-Publication Data
Names: Greteman, Blaine, author.
Title: Networking print in Shakespeare's England : influence, agency, and revolutionary change / Blaine Greteman.
Other titles: Text technologies.
Description: Stanford, California : Stanford University Press, 2021. | Series: Stanford text technologies | Includes bibliographical references and index.
Identifiers: LCCN 2020052611 (print) | LCCN 2020052612 (ebook) | ISBN 9781503615243 (cloth) | ISBN 9781503627987 (paperback) | ISBN 9781503627994 (ebook)
Subjects: LCSH: Early printed books—Social aspects—England—17th century. | Authors, English—Early modern, 1500-1700—Social networks. | Printers—Social networks—England—History—17th century. | Book industries and trade—England—History—17th century. | English literature—Early modern, 1500-1700—Data processing. | Social networks—England—History—17th century. | System analysis.
Classification: LCC Z151.4 .G74 2021 (print) | LCC Z151.4 (ebook) | DDC 094/.20942—dc23
LC record available at https://lccn.loc.gov/2020052611
LC ebook record available at https://lccn.loc.gov/2020052612

Cover design: Michel Vrana

Cover illustration: Nova Reperta, Impressio Librorum, print, Antwerp. British Museum Image.

Typeset by Kevin Barrett Kane in 10/15 Spectral

# CONTENTS

*List of Illustrations* vii
*Acknowledgments* ix
*Abbreviations* xi
*Note on Quotations* xiii

INTRODUCTION   1

1 Methods and Data   17

2 A Small New World: Fire, Infection, and Sudden Change in the English Print Network   44

3 Hubs in the Network: Nicholas Okes and the Making of Infectious Information   71

4 Radical Betweenness: Eleanor Davies and Mary Cary   103

5 Weak Ties and the Making of a Strong Poet: John Milton's Early Publishers   143

EPILOGUE: Future Directions in Networking the Past   176

*Notes* 189
*Index* 225

# LIST OF ILLUSTRATIONS

With the exception of the following, the source of all illustrations is the Shakeosphere database, https://shakeosphere.lib.uiowa.edu/index.jsp. The Python code for analyzing that data, the code for the website, and data for the force graphs found throughout the book can be found at https://github.com/shakeosphere.

**Figure 2.1.** Source: Stephen Davis et al., "The Abundance Threshold for Plague as a Critical Percolation Phenomenon," *Nature* 454 (2008): 636.

**Figure 2.2.** Source: Ricard V. Solé, *Phase Transitions* (Princeton: Princeton University Press, 2011), 55.

**Figure 3.4.** Source: Jérôme Kunegis, "KONECT: The Koblenz Network Collection." In *Proceedings of the 22nd International Conference on the World Wide Web* (New York: ACM, 2013), 1343–1350.

**Figure 3.7.** Wenceslaus Hollar's "Engraving of the Trial of Archbishop Laud," frontispiece to William Prynne's *A Breviate of the Life of William Laud* (London, 1644). Source: Thomas Fisher Rare Book Library, University of Toronto. Reprinted with permission.

**Figures 5.4 and 5.5.** John Milton, *Epitaphium Damonis*. Source: British Library, BL C.57.d.48. Reprinted with permission.

## ACKNOWLEDGMENTS

I love acknowledgment pages, because they perfectly illustrate this book's main argument: that agency and authorship are collective and collaborative rather than singular and individualistic. To quote one of the anonymous readers that deserve my thanks for their thoughtful suggestions, "humans are not quite germs or gerbils, but also human agency is never just a matter of a person acting upon a desire: It's a matter of relationships cultivated deliberately and accidentally."

I can never sufficiently thank all those who made this book possible. I simply could not have done the data refinement and analysis without David Eichmann, Christine Moeller, and Brian Hie. I also couldn't have done it without the Stanford Humanities Center, where I met Brian, the ever-generous Mark Granovetter, and Ruth Ahnert, whose editorial guidance made this book better at every turn. Sebastian Ahnert humored my million questions on everything from NetworkX implementation to eigenvector centrality. James Lee and Daniel Shore provided important insights on this project from conception to completion. The University of Cincinnati's Digital Scholarship Center offered a forum to discuss the work, and the Andrew W. Mellon Foundation's Scholarly Communications program made possible the assistance of Anubhav Maity.

The Folger Library's Early Modern Digital Agendas 2017 Institute served as a valuable place to present and discuss my work, as did the University of Iowa's Obermann Center, led by the intrepid superconnector Teresa Mangum. Victoria Kahn, Joanna Picciotto, and Edward Jones provided encouragement and the all-important letters of recommendation that allowed me to spend a year at Stanford. An earlier draft of some material in Chapter 5 appeared as "Milton and the Early Modern Social Network: The Case of the *Epitaphium Damonis*," *Milton Quarterly* 49 (2015): 79–95 © John Wiley & Sons Ltd, and I am grateful for permission to reprint it.

My colleagues—Jon Wilcox, Claire Fox, Adam Hooks, Kathy Lavezzo, Stephen Voyce, and many more—are simply the best and are part of the reason I could not have completed the project without the institutional support of the University of Iowa and the College of Liberal Arts and Sciences. My friends Matthew Barrow and Jatinder Padda provided room, board, and companionship during my repeated trips to the British Library, and James Geary helped me workshop the very first draft of this idea. Above all I owe thanks to my parents, my children—Finn, Jo, Whit, and Beck—and to Mandi, our most enduring link.

# ABBREVIATIONS

C      John Milton. *The Works of John Milton.* Edited by Frank Allen Patterson et al. 18 vols. (New York: Columbia University Press, 1931–1938).

CPW    John Milton. *The Complete Prose Works of John Milton.* Edited by Don M. Wolfe et al. 8 vols. (New Haven: Yale University Press, 1953–1982).

ESTC    English Short Title Catalogue (1473–1800) (London: British Library). http://estc.bl.uk/F/?func=file&file_name=login-bl-estc

ODNB  *Oxford Dictionary of National Biography.* Online edition (Oxford: Oxford University Press, 2004– ). https://www.oxforddnb.com/

SP      State Papers. National Archives, Kew.

STC    Alfred W. Pollard et al., *A Short-Title Catalogue of Books Printed in England, Scotland, and Ireland, and of English Books Printed Abroad, 1475–1640,* 2nd ed. Revised and enlarged by Katharine F. Pantzer. 3 vols. (London: Bibliographical Society, 1976–1991).

Wing    Donald G. Wing, *Short-Title Catalogue of Books Printed in England, Scotland, Ireland, Wales, and British America, and of English Books Printed in Other Countries, 1641–1700*, 2nd ed. Revised and enlarged by Timothy J. Crist et al. 4 vols. (New York: Modern Language Association of America, 1972–1998).

**NOTE ON QUOTATIONS**

For the sake of readability, I have modernized spelling when quoting early modern sources. The only exceptions are in the cases of authors such as Edmund Spenser, whose archaisms were clearly deliberate, or in cases where modernization might remove a meaningful ambiguity or interpretive possibility (perhaps "mistaking of sillables" for "mistaking of syllables" reveals a silly pun?).

**NETWORKING PRINT IN
SHAKESPEARE'S ENGLAND**

# INTRODUCTION

**AS LONG AS WE'VE HAD SOCIETIES,** we've had social networks. Before Twitter and Facebook, telephones connected us, and before that, telegraphs, the postal service, and footpaths linked one village to the next. We often refer to computer programs or communications technologies as "social networks," but this isn't quite right. A social network consists of people and the material objects that unite them, whether those objects are as simple as the stone tools shared by a tribe or as complex as the satellites beaming data back to earth. Some technologies, however, obviously allow us to create larger and more complex social networks than others, communicating further, faster, and more frequently. Networks spread infectious diseases, and they spread infectious ideas and trends, which is why both doctors studying Ebola in West Africa and marketing executives studying teenagers in New York analyze them, employing methods first developed by sociologists and later advanced into a world of big data by mathematicians and physicists.

*Networking Print in Shakespeare's England* employs some of the same methods of digital analysis to examine the technologies and structures of social networks in early modern England—especially the network of printers, publishers, booksellers, and authors who revolutionized communications during the time of Shakespeare, Milton, and their contemporaries. No one in this network would have used the term. To them, a "network" would have implied something woven together like chainmail or the "curious networke" Edmund Spenser's spider Aragnol spins to entrap the hapless butterfly Clarion in "Muiopotmos."[1] But early modern people participated in networked systems of communication, patronage, and citation that have been of increasing interest to scholars seeking to understand the period. And as this book will show, they were aware of and involved in radical structural changes to the print network in the decades leading up to the English Civil War.

Network science has had a major impact on the fields of sociology, epidemiology, and physics, and scholars in these fields have written several crossover books on the power and behavior of networks. Albert-László Barabási's *Linked: The New Science of Networks* and Duncan J. Watts's *Six Degrees: The Science of a Connected Age* helped introduce the principles of network science to a broader audience.[2] They were quickly followed by Nicholas Christakis and James Fowler's *Connected: The Surprising Power of Our Social Networks and How They Shape Our Lives* and Jonah Berger's *Contagious: Why Things Catch On*.[3] Most readers are now familiar with basic network visualizations of dots connected by lines, whether those dots represent people linked by friendship, genes linked by co-expression, or airports linked by flight paths. Some of the basic terminology of network science—such as "nodes" for the dots and "edges" for the connections between them—has now permeated public discussions of everything from terrorist groups to retail supply chains. Although social media have helped drive this interest by turning the connections between people into big business, network science was not "born digital." Many of its most exciting findings and fundamental principles predate the internet, and a brief outline of that history will be useful to introduce the aspects of the English print network that I'll be exploring in subsequent chapters of this book.

In a series of papers published between 1959 and 1968, the legendary mathematician Paul Erdős and his collaborator Alfred Rényi established random graph theory as a branch of mathematics, demonstrating, among other things, that large, interconnected networks do not emerge slowly, as we might expect. Instead, they suddenly and explosively cross a "threshold," at which point adding just one additional link brings the majority of nodes in the graph together in one giant connected component.[4] Imagine, for example, three distinct railway systems, all serving different towns: One serves four towns, and the others serve three towns each. The largest connected component links four towns, but the majority of towns in the three systems are *not* connected to one another. A single link between any two of the stations, however, will instantly reverse this situation, so that the majority of towns *will* be connected. This sudden shift is "one of the most striking facts concerning random graphs," Erdős and Rényi wrote. And they quickly recognized that it had applications "for the evolution of certain real communication nets (railway, road or electric network system, etc.) ... and even of organic structures of living matter."[5] For this project I have been able to conduct the first large-scale network analysis of the English print network from its origins through the eighteenth century, and in Chapter 2 I will show that it experienced a similar moment of phase transition at the end of the sixteenth century. This transition from many small communities to one vast, interconnected network did not go unobserved by the people who experienced it. And it had structural consequences that I will trace throughout the rest of the book. Scholars once referred to the historical period under examination as a "golden age" of English literature and culture, although now we opt for less evaluative labels like "early modern." Whatever the terminology, England's cultural landscape changed with "startling suddenness": In a generation, the first public theatres opened, thrived, and closed; the first English poets presented themselves in print as laureates; the first writers began to make their living as print authors.[6] And these changes came to define the literary tradition in ways that persist. Spenser's *Faerie Queene*, Shakespeare's *King Lear*, Milton's *Paradise Lost*—such works, and the forms of authorship they establish, must be understood in terms of the network that produced them.

Complex, connected networks behave in peculiar, predicable ways, whether their nodes are booksellers or railway stations. One of those peculiarities was dubbed the "Matthew effect" by Robert K. Merton in 1968, in reference to the Parable of the Talents in the biblical book of Matthew: "[U]nto every one that hath shall be given, and he shall have abundance: but from him that hath not shall be taken away even that which he hath."[7] In more secular terms, "the rich get richer," which in Merton's work meant that prominent scientists in authorship networks gained a disproportionate share of new co-authorship credits, making them better connected, more prominent, and more likely to gain new connections via future co-authorship. Merton was a sociologist, and the scope of his inquiry was limited, but he had reviewed enough biological literature to suspect that this Matthew effect "transcends the world of human behavior and social processes."[8] In fact, Herbert Simon showed in a now-famous 1955 paper that the effect holds true whether we are talking about cities or citizens.[9] Cities with high populations tend to gain more people, and people with money tend to earn a lot more, leading to extremely uneven "power law" distributions of resources; within networks, this means a few nodes tend to be superconnected and serve as hubs with unusual importance for the larger system. Recent research has demonstrated that this dynamic lies behind the extraordinary robustness of complex networks. Most nodes can be eliminated from such networks with little impact on overall connectivity or the flow of information. But removing just a few hubs will quickly cause the entire system to collapse. Chapter 3 of *Networking Print in Shakespeare's England* examines hubs in the English publication network. Who are the outliers? And what strategies or structural factors made a handful of printers and booksellers so "rich" in terms of connections, especially since they have been so poorly represented in histories of the period?

As that last question implies, early researchers into network dynamics noticed that a node's number of connections was not the only way of measuring importance and agency. *Who* you know is at least as important as *how many* people you know. Gatekeepers who can serve as conduits between groups or shut off the flow of information between them are especially important, as Alex Bavelas noticed while he was a graduate student at the University of Iowa, researching the interactions between ideologically distinct minority communities, such as rural Mennonites or urban Catholic immigrants, and majority ones.[10] He later founded the Group Networks Laboratory at MIT to develop mathematical models to understand such interactions, proving in 1948 that some of the most structurally important figures in communication may have the fewest connections. To illustrate his mathematical model, Bavelas offered the example of a woman who worked at a garment factory where she was the only one of her peers to speak English: Although she was not as deeply or centrally connected as the plant's manager or its union boss, "relations between this group and the management of the company regarding hours, wages, working conditions, took place through the single English speaking member (this in spite of the fact that the plant was unionized)."[11] She had a unique capacity to facilitate, obstruct, or distort the flow of information, and Bavelas used a series of hand-drawn graphs to demonstrate that such figures could be identified mathematically by calculating the number of shortest paths that crossed between them and other members of the network—a measure that would later become known as *betweenness centrality*. Chapter 4 of this book explores the hidden histories of high-betweenness figures in the English print network, focusing on female prophets who have been largely ignored but whose texts played an outsized structural role in bridging different communities. Their significance is not a simple accident, but like Bavelas's English-speaking factory worker, can be attributed to specific qualities these women cultivate as writers, publishers, and public figures.

A focus on betweenness has the potential to upend conventional assessments of agency and importance, but it probably is not the most radical way that network science has reshaped our understanding of influence and the spread of ideas. That distinction goes to Mark Granovetter's 1973 article on "The Strength of Weak Ties," which was initially rejected for publication but has subsequently become one of the most cited articles in the history of social science.[12] Granovetter's paper had a simple origin: While studying job seekers in a Boston suburb as part of his graduate work, he noticed that when he asked people if they had found their job through "a friend," they often replied "no, just an acquaintance."[13] For Granovetter, this indicated that weak ties, like the ones that bind us to casual acquaintances or distant relations, may be more powerful for spreading information than the close ties of intimate friends and family. Our close friends and family members, after all, know many of the same people that we do, so to learn about a new job, trend, or idea, we need contact with someone outside our close social circle, and such contacts will almost always be "weak" rather than "strong" ties. "This was sometime a paradox," as Hamlet says, "but now the time gives it proof," and the time was right for Granovetter's proof, which drew on newly available empirical data and recent developments in graph theory to show that "except under unlikely conditions, *no strong tie is a bridge.*"[14] Almost all sociological theory before Granovetter was grounded on the study of small, close-knit groups, and nearly all literary and historical scholarship to this day continues to fixate on the closest bonds of friendship and family when assessing intellectual influence and development. But Granovetter's model showed that to understand the diffusion of information or ideas through a network—and especially to understand innovation, infection, or novelty—we need to connect studies of small groups, such as families or literary coteries, to the growing body of large-scale statistical research on social, political, and communication structures. I will discuss that model further in Chapter 5, where I consider the strength of weak ties in John Milton's social network. At the conclusion of a book that has been built on analyzing links between tens of thousands of people, it will be useful to consider the relationship between English literature's ultimate "strong" poet and the weak ties through which his authorial voice emerges.

Phase transitions, superconnected hubs, and weak ties: These are some of the basic components of network science that a new generation of researchers, like Watts and Barabási, extended to an entirely different scale with the aid of computational analysis. Although trailblazers in the field had been able to assert the importance of betweenness or analyze the distribution of links across small networks, in a pre-digital age it had been computationally impossible to do this at the large scale needed to extend network science into some of the areas that Erdős, Rényi, and others had pointed toward, such as the study of organic matter. Famous experiments, such as Stanley Milgram's project that showed it took only about six degrees of separation to link any one person in the United States to any other person, had demonstrated "small world" phenomena in large networks.[15] But with the aid of computational processing and vast new datasets, it was possible to test such findings much more rigorously and systematically.[16] Some applications had serious consequences, such as working to change network dynamics in order to prevent isolated cases of Ebola from tipping into a sudden epidemic.[17] Some, such as using network analytics to target terrorists with drone strikes, have been controversial.[18] And some are just odd, such as the parlor game "Six Degrees of Kevin Bacon," in which participants compete to find the shortest path connecting any given actor in the Internet Movie Database (IMDb) to the star of *Footloose*.[19] But in the age of the internet, the near ubiquity of small-world network behaviors and the utility of network analysis has become increasingly clear.

Although this work has generated much interest and a smattering of articles in the humanities, the field still awaits the books that will apply network analysis to the study of literature and culture, and especially to what John Sutherland has called the "hole at the centre of literary sociology"— the systematic study of publishing history.[20] This is somewhat surprising, since the language of "networks," circles, coteries, and assemblages has been much used in literary studies generally and early modern studies and histories of the book in particular. As early as 1975, the historian Natalie Zemon Davis had already begun to adopt the language of networks to describe the "ways in which printing entered into popular life in the sixteenth century, setting up new networks of communication, facilitating new options for the people, and also providing new means of controlling the people."[21] A generation of scholars and commentators—including Marshall McLuhan, Walter J. Ong, and Elizabeth Eisenstein—explored these networks as they made the case for a print "revolution."[22]

At the same time, literary historians like Arthur Marotti and Harold Love turned their attention to the circulation of manuscripts, which Marotti found "were designed to establish ties of social, political, or economic patronage ... to declare in-group allegiances of various sorts—to family, to a network of friends or colleagues, to a political faction or programme."[23] As I will discuss in more detail in Chapter 2, the persistence of earlier forms of circulation and patronage long into the era of print has gradually led scholars to reject the idea that a new "print culture" emerged with Gutenberg's press; the language of print revolution has now mostly been replaced with the language of print "evolution."[24] But few would dispute Richard McCabe's suggestion that print "fostered a new set of social networks that radically altered conditions for the composition, editing, and reception of letters," and the contours of those networks have increasingly been central to discussions of readership, authorship, and literary patronage.[25] Kirk Melnikoff, for example, makes an excellent case that the "web of sustained bonds between printers, booksellers, and bookbinders" was crucial to the development of English literary forms during the Elizabethan period.[26] But *Networking Print in Shakespeare's England* is the first book to analyze that web using the powerful tools developed by network science—quantifying bonds, describing their contours, and identifying key figures and strategies in their development.

Outside the field of print and manuscript studies, the language of the network has been adopted to very different effects by literary scholars using the terms to invoke the ontological framework of Gilles Deleuze and Félix Guattari or the actor-network theory (ANT) of Bruno Latour, Michel Callon, and John Law. Jeffrey J. Cohen, for example, draws on the former when explaining that "in medieval culture, the horse, its rider, the bridle and saddle and armor form a Deleuzean 'circuit' or 'assemblage,' a dispersive network of identity that admixes the inanimate and the inhuman."[27] This is a networked understanding of being itself: Bodies are organized into systems, systems are combined into assemblages, and this combination is the process of "becoming." Thus various scholars have explored emotions, bodies, and selves as networks, as in Drew Daniel's discussion in *The Melancholy Assemblage* of the "components and relations that persist across time and territory as a material and social network of forces in which melancholy affects, images, substances, and postures, are formed."[28] Actor-network theory is a close cousin of this assemblage approach but turns attention more explicitly toward the actors and processes through which relationships are established, maintained, and altered.[29]

"We follow the actors' own ways," Latour says of actor-network theory, "and begin our travels by the traces left behind by their activity of forming and dismantling groups."[30] Michel Callon identified four stages in this process: *problematization*, in which an actor identifies a problem or a knowledge claim that requires the involvement of others; *interessement*, in which those actors negotiate their roles in the new group; *enrolment*, in which they accept their roles; and *mobilization*, in which one or more actors speaks for the group or makes a truth claim in which the voices of many actors are subsumed into one. The process involves humans and nonhumans alike, with Callon explaining, for example, that "if the scallops are to be enrolled" in a scientific experiment that includes a network of fishermen, scientists, and scallops, "they must first be willing to anchor themselves" to the equipment used to collect and measure them.[31] As that language implies, by tracing the paths whereby various actors become incorporated into a network, ANT aims to understand the ways agency is distributed throughout complex systems, a "shift *from principle to practice*," Latour claims, that "allows us to treat the vague notion of power not as a cause of people's behavior but as the consequence of an intense activity of enrolling, convincing, and enlisting."[32] Michael Witmore, Jonathan Gil Harris, Miriam Jacobson, and others have all drawn on an actor-network theory framework to discuss, respectively, the action of fiction in the world, the "polychronic agency" of anachronistic costumes in early modern plays, and the importation of foreign words and images into English poetry.[33]

Such work usefully shifts our attention to the materials of culture and the labor involved in network formation, but as Carl Knappett has noted, "[W]hile the 'actor' component of ANT has received elaboration in literary and cultural studies, the 'network' side has been more of a sleeping partner" or "a heuristic for encouraging relational thinking."[34] This is not surprising, since Latour specifies that "the network does not designate a thing out there that would have roughly the shape of the interconnected points, much like a telephone, a freeway, or a sewage 'network'"; rather it is a "set of relations."[35] Knappett, however, believes we can "convert network thinking into network analysis by thinking explicitly in terms of nodes and links."[36] I think so too, so long as we are clear about the limitations of most digital analysis for tracing the kind of multilayered networks that are of interest to Latour and others who use the term in his sense. Digital tools help us track and visualize associations that would have otherwise escaped us, and they help us discover and acknowledge the importance of actors who have been left out of existing historical accounts. But as will become clear in my first chapter on this book's data and methodology, most current tools of network analysis and visualization *by definition* require the compression of multimodal networks into unimodal ones in which all of the nodes are the same sorts of things (people connected to other people, books connected to other books, proteins connected to other proteins). Tracing the paths by which those actors achieved their place in the network, as this book will demonstrate, is a slower, more discursive process. But this process is where network thinking and network analysis meet.

Although Knappett heralds the promise of digital network analysis, his own work largely involves mapping the spatial and temporal relationships of objects in the classical world. Indeed, as Ruth Ahnert notes in *News Networks in Early Modern Europe*, "maps have been the dominant mode of representing . . . networks" in early attempts to think in terms of nodes and links by bringing digital methods to the study of literature and culture.[37] This is true, for example, of Lindsay O'Neill's *The Opened Letter: Networking in the Early Modern British World*, as well as projects like Stanford University's *Mapping the Republic of Letters*.[38] It is explicitly the goal of Franco Moretti's "Network Theory, Plot Analysis," which maps character relationships in *Hamlet*. "I had never 'seen' [Horatio's] position within Hamlet's field of forces," writes Moretti, "until I looked at the network of the play. 'Seen' is the keyword here. What I took from network theory were less concepts than visualization."[39]

But Johanna Drucker has usefully called into question the value of such visualizations, arguing that they are "anathema to humanistic thought," since "[h]umanistic methods are necessarily probabilistic rather than deterministic, performative rather than declarative."[40] Drucker's point is not that visualizations are useless, but that we must be cautious about adopting mechanical forms of visualization as if they were interpretive.[41] I often share her unease when I stare at dense network hairball visualizations, which all look more or less like one another but which have threatened to become the avatars for "network analysis" in the humanities. Such visualizations, for example, adorn the covers of both *Macroanalysis* by Matthew Jockers and *Distant Reading* by Franco Moretti. But the usefulness of network visualization and mapping tends to diminish rapidly as the size of networks increases—a problem, since "distant reading" and "macroanalysis" theoretically hold the most promise precisely at such large scales (a human can read a dozen books and draw connections between them but will find this impossible with 50,000 or 500,000 texts). This is why Drucker suggests that the greatest value of digital analysis lies not in the way it produces some graphic representation, which is typically the "result of display protocols" for this or that program, but in the way it "exposes start points for study and permits the investigation of social and cultural issues in texts at a scale no representative single selective exegesis can produce," shifting "from the symptomatic to the systematic as a mode of inquiry."[42]

This shift has been a real challenge, not only for network analysis in the humanities, but also for the field of digital humanities generally, which as Alex Poole writes, seems always to be in "a liminal state, neither fish (discipline) nor fowl (interdiscipline)."[43] Theorists in the field have helped make the important case that new methods are needed to "read" the vast amounts of data now in our archives. But the results, as Jockers is the first to admit, are often "a ringing confirmation of virtually all our stereotypes," as in his own finding that the "themes most indicative of female authorship" in a corpus of 3,346 nineteenth-century books include "fashion," "children," "flowers," and "sewing."[44] Patrik Svensson notes that the field of digital humanities "always seems to fail to deliver on at least some level, whether it be intellectual robustness ... or possibly quality of the work produced." But he concludes that "a solution does exist," precisely in embracing the interstitial space that disturbs Poole, "a way of thinking about the digital humanities that brings together the humanistic and the digital through embracing a nonterritorial and liminal zone."[45] *Networking Print in Shakespeare's England* attempts to inhabit such a liminal zone, using digital tools to produce starting points for an inquiry into early modern book production that is ultimately humanistic in its close attention to individuals, texts, and cultures.

This seems to me a happy space, in part because digital humanities has progressed as a field in tandem with complementary forms of textual scholarship, or sociological bibliography, that turn attention both to the material technologies responsible for producing texts and our analyses of them. In Jerome McGann's hugely influential formulation, "[E]very text, including those that may appear to be totally private, is a social text" because it is "produced and reproduced under specific social and institutional conditions," and it is part of the business of literary analysis to elaborate those conditions."[46] D. F. McKenzie similarly found it necessary to reorient bibliography from the description of texts and variants and toward a "sociology of the text" that would elaborate "the human motives and interactions which texts involve at every stage of their production, transmission, and consumption."[47] The work that has resulted from this shift has put relational thinking about bibliography and textuality at the center of literary study. Histories of the book have generally turned our attention to textual technologies—tablets, tables, title pages, indexes, margins and marginalia—as writing and reading technologies.[48] They have highlighted the interrelations between print and manuscript and the social dimensions of a printing milieu that, Cecile M. Jagodzinski has suggested, permitted "readers to sit in as members of a gigantic coterie," that was in some sense an expansion and continuation of an existing textual culture.[49] At the same time, they have explored in depth the ways that print "unsettled an established book trade," as Joseph Loewenstein has put it, and especially the role that monopoly, privilege, and textual commerce played in shaping the figure of the author.[50]

Some of these works have even flirted with converting their relational thinking into analysis of actual nodes and links, as Knappett suggests. McCabe, for example, collaborated with colleagues to construct a database of print and patronage networks, although he "prefers a qualitative to a quantitative approach" as he attempts "to look beyond the visible markers of dedication to the authorial dynamics that produced them and investigate the role of patronage in literary creativity."[51] Joad Raymond, who has worked extensively on news networks, clarifies that he is "not analyzing data" yet, but instead hopes "to project what network analysis could do on a larger scale."[52]

By taking as its object a distinct dataset, large and complete enough to make such analysis both possible and rewarding, *Networking Print in Shakespeare's England* attempts to show the value of quantitative analysis. This book's data comes from the English Short Title Catalogue (ESTC) of 487,000 books printed in English before 1800. The ESTC is a collaborative project, with over 2,000 libraries submitting hundreds of thousands of records since 1977, and it is the most comprehensive record of the hand-press era. But as I will discuss in Chapter 1, it was also not set up to be used as a database, or even to allow for systematic research of booksellers, printers, and publishers, and I have spent years refining the data and restructuring it as a relational database that can be configured, queried, and analyzed as a network. The book's argument, however, will make it clear that the value of this work lies in advancing qualitative, humanistic inquiry, rather than replacing it or replicating its results. Although I present some graphs, tables, and charts, readers will find the mode of argument and analysis largely (perhaps dismayingly) discursive rather than graphical.

After an initial chapter on methods and data, Chapter 2 explores the evidence that the English print network experienced a "phase transition" during the late sixteenth century that altered its dynamics in fundamental ways. As I have already briefly outlined, subsequent chapters explore the dynamics of this newly complex, small-world network and focus in some detail on the figures who played an outsized role as hubs and bridges within it from the 1580s to 1660s, a period of tremendous social and political change. But before turning to those chapters, it is worth considering the larger story they tell of the network's changing structure, the individuals involved in those changes, and the history of the period.

Although their motives differ, the figures in this book all encounter systems of print production or regulation that they work to circumvent and subvert. In the case of the printer Nicholas Okes, who is the subject of Chapter 3 and the most connected printer of the era, this seems largely to be motivated by an effort to gain market share and turn a profit. Okes was trained to produce quality works in prestigious formats and editions, in a shop that placed control and consistency ahead of speed, volume, and collaboration. When he gained control of his own press, he promptly rejected this model. The new one he forged turned him into a hub in a network that was ideal for spreading viral information, with many partners collaborating to produce and sell smaller, more timely works. He was willing to challenge printing monopolies and to evade licensing restrictions in order to print works both of Protestant satire and Catholic Counter-Reformation. It is tempting to cast him as a figure working for the free circulation of knowledge, but it seems more accurate to say that Okes knew controversy sold books and that he opposed monopolies until he got a piece of them himself. Whatever his motives, he helped build a book production system that thrust him into the center of the era's most monumental political and religious controversies; depending on who you believed, he was either a cynical mercenary who helped engineer the fall of Archbishop Laud or a martyr of Laud's religious tyranny. The one point on which both Laud and his critics could agree is that once Okes produced a book and put it into circulation, it was almost impossible to eradicate its spread. Indeed, other hubs in the network would come to lament their own role in creating this dynamic. Michael Sparke—who sometimes worked with Okes and who was in his own right the most connected bookseller in England between Shakespeare's first folio and the collapse of the licensing regime in 1640— initially cheered the fall of Laud and celebrated his own role in it, but he would end his career renouncing the radical forces he helped unleash as a public wildfire that threatened to decimate English society.

Those forces were most dramatically embodied by some of the figures at the center of Chapter 4: the female prophets Eleanor Davies and Mary Cary. This chapter investigates a surprising dynamic: When we rank texts by their degree, or number of connections, the top ones are uniformly male and mostly "official" publications of church and state, but when we rank them by betweenness centrality, or ability to bridge otherwise distinct parts of the network, texts by these female prophets appear to serve an unusually important structural role. That role is not accidental, I will suggest, but the result of publication and promotion strategies pursued by Davies and Cary. Both women position themselves in a state of radical betweenness, as mediators between God and man, between the world as it is and the world as it can be. And to maintain that position, both take unusual measures to print and preserve their texts from state censorship and misogynistic attack. Their efforts range from furtive smuggling operations to sophisticated invocations of female patronage, and along the way, they cultivate a wildly diverse set of connections—from Samuel Hartlib and members of his circle, to Queen Henrietta Maria and her courtly literary coterie, to Gerrard Winstanley and members of his radical Digger group. Their strategies for establishing themselves as print authors had consequences for the print network; as we explore those strategies we see the potential of network analysis for revealing hidden histories and magnifying the contributions of important figures who have been erased from other historical accounts.

It may seem odd, then, to turn in Chapter 5 to John Milton, an author who has suffered no risk of erasure. In fact, he is Harold Bloom's ultimate "strong poet," the "central problem in any theory and history of poetic influence in English," a figure whose influence threatens to erase his ancestors and warp his progeny.[53] This way of describing Milton began almost immediately: "I saw him strong," wrote Andrew Marvell in the preface to *Paradise Lost*, anxiously suggesting that this poetic Samson might "ruine . . . The sacred Truths to Fable and old Song."[54] But the chapter considers a paradox: This strong poet formed his authorial voice through the cultivation of weak ties to printers, publishers, and others, rather than the strong ties that have been the subject of most literary history. Some of these figures are highly connected and obviously influential; others are remarkable for their ability to leave so small a trace on the print network. In both cases, Milton collaborates with members of the book trade who have their own interests in opposing monopolies, promoting Reformation, and producing his work.

As I conclude the book, I will explore what those collaborations tell us about the ties that bind social networks together and our assumptions about what it means to be a "social" or "anti-social" author. I hope that this analysis of the English print network will not only inform the way we think about English history and culture, but also point the way toward the kinds of work that will be possible with other databases and catalogues, such as the Medici Archive, Early Modern Letters Online (EMLO), the Universal Short Title Catalogue (USTC), and the National Union Catalogue of Manuscript Collections (NUCMC). In the Epilogue, I'll discuss some of the work that is already being done with these materials and some of the ongoing developments in network analysis that could offer new insights into persistent gaps in our historical and literary knowledge. We are at the early stages of using digital methods to analyze historical networks, but as my first chapter will show, this work has exciting possibilities today because of the labor done by generations of archivists, cataloguers, and scholars. This is a powerful network, often rendered invisible, but connecting our work across time and shaping the histories we write.

## CHAPTER 1 METHODS AND DATA

WE SOMETIMES TAKE LIBRARY CATALOGUES, finding aids, and other bibliographical tools for granted, using them without the same critical rigor we'd apply to a scholarly edition or monograph. This is not the case with digital scholarship in the humanities, which we expect to be theoretically justified, transparent, and replicable. But library resources are shaped by the scholarly assumptions, historical conditions, and material resources of the people who create them, and one of the most important outcomes of building new tools for exploration and analysis may be forcing us to think more critically about the other resources we use. This book derives its data from 487,000 records in the English Short Title Catalogue, or ESTC. The ESTC has been called "the most comprehensive record of what has appeared in print in Britain and the English-speaking world for all branches of human experience from the last quarter of the fifteenth century to the start of the nineteenth."[1] It is both a collaborative project—with over two thousand contributing libraries submitting hundreds of thousands of records since

1977—and a centralized one, with a North American office and another at the British Library creating the records for unmatched items and adding locations of copies to existing records. "By the end of 1997, after 18 years of processing contributed entries, the North American office had created nearly 70,000 new records, added nearly 800,000 locations to the file, processed over a million entries, and established some 30,000 name-authority records."[2] Decades of work, at least 9 million dollars in grant funding, and the efforts of catalogues and bibliographers around the world have not only made the ESTC our most extensive record of the English hand-press period, but also one of our best models of international collaborative scholarship. But even during its most controlled phase, the project's long-time North American director and biggest booster Henry Snyder admitted that "catalogers are human, and much of what they enter is a personal decision, often subjective rather than objective," so errors and inconsistencies crept into the files.[3]

Moreover, and surprisingly for a project dedicated to documenting the hand-press period, no attempt was made to extend authority records beyond author and title. While the names of printers, publishers, and booksellers are often included on early modern imprints and were captured by ESTC cataloguers, no effort was made to standardize spelling, to assign roles (such as "printer") and make it possible to search by them, or to create authority records for these names. Although the ESTC has gone through considerable enrichment—with generations of cataloguers and bibliographers supplying missing or incomplete information about printers, publishers, and booksellers—the lack of authority records has meant there is no reliable way to search for or analyze the contributions of a given printer, bookseller, or publisher. For example, a user seeking to discover all the works printed by one major figure discussed in this book, Nicholas Okes, would need to search the publisher field for "Nicholas Okes" (350 publications), "N. Okes" (122 publications), "Nich Okes" (7 publications), "Nic Okes" (3 publications), and so on, to get anything resembling a comprehensive view of the publications associated with him.

In the following chapter I describe the language-processing and database tools we used to make it possible to search for the individuals and communities involved in print production, as well as to conduct more complex analysis on the structure and evolution of the print network. In addition to detailing our workflow, I will address some of the persistent concerns about the ESTC data itself, explain where our process has been able to resolve those concerns and where it has not, and clarify the heuristic value of messy or incomplete data for conducting network analysis.

## I. Data Source and History

Students and many scholars now primarily turn to digitized texts and images in Early English Books Online (EEBO) and Eighteenth Century Collections Online (ECCO) as *de facto* bibliographic databases, so it is first worth explaining why my project uses metadata from the oft-ignored ESTC instead. Both EEBO and ECCO have been critiqued on the cost of access and the pitfalls of using digital images as proxies for physical objects.[4] But they are remarkable resources for those fortunate enough to have access to them, and they have undoubtedly transformed research into the early modern period. A greater issue for scholars of the book trade, as Ian Gadd notes, is that EEBO offers scholars an "illusion of comprehensiveness" that can be deceptive, while "there are, and will always be, items on ESTC not available in EEBO."[5] For scholars seeking to understand the contours of the early modern book trade, the gap is non-trivial: As of September 2017, EEBO had "bibliographic information for more than 101,687" titles from 1473–1700, according to the website.[6] For the same period, the ESTC had 139,577 records, meaning 27% of the records in ESTC did not have an EEBO equivalent. This sometimes creates remarkable distortions, especially when grappling with the impact of non-canonical authors. In Chapter 4, for example, I discuss Eleanor Davies, who emerges as a significant but under-discussed figure in my network analysis; the ESTC contains records for 75 of her publications, while EEBO contains records for 72. In another chapter, I discuss the career of Michael Sparke, an important bookseller who also authored one of the era's most popular works; EEBO lists only 19 of his books compared to the ESTC's 49. ESTC records also contain significantly more bibliographical information. Although EEBO relied on the

ESTC for constructing its own records, it heavily edited that data, removing collation information, Stationers' Register entries, and other notes. Where information about printers, publishers, and booksellers has been supplied by cataloguers drawing on other resources, EEBO has often not included that information in its own metadata. Stephen Tabor turns to a cartographic metaphor to explain the difference in the databases: "Some people prefer to explore the world through books of photographs with occasional schematic maps. ESTC, on the other hand, provides the equivalent of a detailed topographic map, but no pictures. Such technical tools have limited appeal, even to some specialists; but if you want to thoroughly learn the lie of the land, you will need one."[7] My goal here is to understand the lie of the land, using network analysis as a new instrument to map its changing topography. Ultimately, as I will discuss in the Epilogue, our work with the ESTC data can then be linked back to EEBO, ECCO, and a host of resources such as the Map of Early Modern London (MoEML) and Wikidata so that others can use it to construct new tools and interoperable projects.

Yet the ESTC is far from perfect. The primary critiques of the ESTC all derive from a central tension: The project aspires to be both an authoritative bibliography *and* a database—on the one hand a "scholarly project" and on the other "a venture in international librarianship."[8] Born on the cusp of the digital revolution, ESTC originally stood for the "Eighteenth Century Short Title Catalogue," and it was envisioned as a resource that would continue in the line of great bibliographic projects initiated by Alfred W. Pollard and G. R. Redgrave's *Short-Title Catalogue of Books Printed in England, Scotland, and Ireland, and of English Books Printed Abroad, 1475–1640*, continued in Katharine F. Pantzer's definitive second edition of that book, and extended in Donald Wing's later *Short-Title Catalogue of Books Printed in England, Scotland, Ireland, Wales, and British America and of English Books Printed in Other Countries, 1641–1700*.[9]

Unlike these standard bibliographical works, familiarly known as STC and Wing, the ESTC was "born digital," and this brought the promise (and peril) of turning it into both an authoritative bibliography and a union catalogue of libraries around the world. Beginning in 1978, cataloguers at the British Library began keying records onto magnetic tape in machine-readable cataloguing (MARC) format using a Singer 1501 terminal, at the rate of about 24 records per person each day.[10] But this was also an early example of what we would now call crowdsourcing, with contributing libraries tasked with verifying whether books in their collections matched existing records or represented something new, then submitting records compiled by staff. Because the staff had varying degrees of training and resources, the British Library adopted an approach intended to maximize the authority of the records as it began compiling the base file of works for 1700–1800. Librarians throughout Britain would send photocopies of title pages with "a template on which a relatively unskilled trainee could record the format, the pagination or foliation, and any other features judged to be relevant, such as illustrations, marginalia, provenance."[11] These copies were then matched with the authoritative record in the British Library file, and when they could not be matched, a new record was created. These "verified" copies were mingled with others, marked as "unverified" and drawn from sources such as the North American *National Union Catalogue*. The process of verifying these records remains ongoing to this day.

In the early stage, title information was "short" not only because the project was based on existing models, but also because storage space was limited and expensive. In coming years, the project grew in scope as both the perils and promise of the rapidly developing technology became clear. Most significantly, in 1987 the controversial decision was made to incorporate all of the records from the STC and Wing, as well as newly discovered books and editions that were not in those print resources—and by this time advances in digital storage made it possible to move away from "short titles" and include full title and imprint information, as well as subject headings and extensive bibliographical notes.[12] This, as Tabor explains, is one source of lingering ambiguity in ESTC records.[13] For standardized, modern books, it is relatively easy to enter authoritative title information without error. But early modern books have long titles, with erratic spelling, inconsistent typography, and often incomplete or willfully misleading imprint information (such as books claiming to be printed in London that are really printed in Amsterdam, or vice versa). It is easy for cataloguers to introduce small typos or elisions, and when users turn to the ESTC to discover whether a local copy of a book matches the description, this frustrates the process at best, or leads to false reports of variants or new editions at worst.[14] Still more subtly, as David McKitterick has shown, the "untidy border between issues and variants" has sometimes led cataloguers to create entirely new entries for publications that should probably have been absorbed into existing STC entries. These "strays" may simply have a cancel title page or variant spelling, reminding us that "everyday sixteenth- and seventeenth-century book trade practices do not always fit with modern bibliographical classification."[15] This introduces a degree of ambiguity for bibliographers seeking to understand exactly how many new titles, editions, and issues have been added since the publication of the revised STC in 1976–91. Such ambiguities are one reason that the extension into earlier material was viewed by some critics as a disastrous dilution of the project's original focus on the eighteenth century.[16] But even the harshest of these critics noted that "the records for the STC period from 1475–1640 have one significant advantage" over those for the Wing period and later periods: "[T]hey have been the subject of detailed bibliographical scrutiny for almost a century."[17]

Although McKitterick's article points to some real issues with using the ESTC as an authoritative bibliography, it also illustrates just how careful scrutiny of the STC-era records has been. As of 2005, when he wrote it, he identified 295 records marked as "not in STC" and was able to show that a significant number of these designations may not have been fully warranted.[18] By September 2018, when researching this chapter, the number of titles noted as "not in STC" in the ESTC database had fallen to 231, thanks to the continuing efforts of librarians and scholars hand-curating the records over the years. While those records still deserve extra scrutiny by users, and often highlight the need to "verify everything," they represent .005% of the pre-1641 titles in ESTC. For the kinds of network analytics conducted in this book, this is a remarkably clean dataset, which we have enhanced by normalizing and creating authority records for names of printers, publishers, and booksellers. In total, our process added 10,171 such distinct authority records—an increase of 25% over the person records in the ESTC. The Shakeosphere project has invested further effort in cleaning the records from 1641–1700, and I follow the career of Eleanor Davies, Mary Cary, and their printers into the mid-1640s in Chapter 4, as well as discussing some of Milton's later works in Chapter 5. But the largest claims in this book about the print network, and especially claims about the shifting dynamics of the network over time, focus on the STC-era records from the incorporation of the Stationers' Company in 1557 to 1640. The proliferation of material in the later seventeenth century, combined with the finite resources of the ESTC, mean that later records from the Wing era require a special degree of caution, and while it is possible to identify individuals and texts of unusual structural importance during these latter years, I have avoided making claims about how the print network evolved from the pre- to post–Civil War eras. In the Epilogue, I will discuss some possibilities for using network inference, prediction, and Linked Data to verify, clean, and learn from such messy or "heuristic data."

Like the STC before it, the ESTC includes books and pamphlets printed in the British Isles, or its colonies, or printed elsewhere in English or another British language. It also includes works with false imprints claiming to have been printed in Britain. The ESTC does not, however, include the substantial number of Latin and foreign language books imported to Britain. Nor does it systematically include engraved books (rather than those produced using movable type), or some categories of printed ephemera such as playing cards. Expanded information about genres, theatrical companies, and detailed Stationers' Company entries—which can be found in specialized resources like the Database of Early English Playbooks (DEEP)—is also not included in ESTC data.[19] My own analysis of the publication network and book trade is similarly limited by these criteria.

Likewise, we know that some books simply disappeared, and the effects of such missing data must be considered in this or any other type of historical analysis of the book trade. As Joseph A. Dane and Rosemary A. Roberts have explained, statistical models of book loss are bedeviled by two facts: Book copies do not "have an equal chance of surviving," since they are printed in different formats and on different materials, and they do not survive "independently of each other," since patterns of collection and destruction are not random, but influenced by the whims of collectors and authorities.[20] Loss rates for incunables—books printed up to 1500—range from Rudolf Hirsch's rather optimistic estimate that 10–25% of all fifteenth-century editions of books and broadsides have disappeared, to Jonathan Green, Frank McIntyre, and Paul Needham's analysis that suggests the real number may be as high as 50%.[21] A very high loss rate for these early books seems entirely credible if we "follow the curve," since most incunable editions of any size exist only in a single copy, with the number of surviving editions with two, three, and more copies dropping exponentially.

The rate of book survival improves markedly for the years covered by the current study. Alan Farmer analyzes data in the STC and ESTC, looking in particular at numbered subsequent editions for which there is no existing earlier edition. Out of 713 titles printed in 2,496 editions, it appears that 501 editions were lost—a rate of 16.7%.[22] Farmer also makes the point that loss is dependent both on size and genre—schoolbooks, catechisms, and other books made to be used, as well as read, are lost at higher rates than poetry or plays, while publications in one or two sheets are proportionally more likely to disappear than publications in ten or twenty sheets. We know, for example, that sometime after 1606 William Jaggard sought and gained the exclusive right to print playbills; we also know that not one of the playbills he printed survives.[23] Excluding single-leaf publications, which struggle to survive in any genre, this brings Farmer to an estimate of the overall loss rate for the entire book trade of 23.3% from 1580 (when publishers began using edition numbers with some regularity) to 1640.[24]

Questions of data loss are certainly not unique to studies of print. Letters have been one of the most attractive early subjects of network analysis, because it is informative to map their exchange in ways that reveal the distance and frequency of communications between correspondents, and it is intuitive to think of this map as a network. Indeed, Anthony Trollope had already written of a "postal network, which should catch all recipients of letters" long before literary scholars began doing digital analysis, so it makes sense that some of the earliest and best-known attempts to apply network analysis to literary and historical study involved letters.[25] But if we seek to analyze epistolary networks and make any historical claims from this analysis, we will need to know whether most letters were lost, destroyed, or turned into fish wrapping. We will also need to understand that certain types of letter are more likely to be preserved than others, since a passionate declaration of love has a better chance of preservation than a reminder to pick up milk. This does not prevent us from analyzing those works that remain and the connections between them—it simply helps us avoid arguing that people write more about love than they do about milk. In the current study, it seems safest to say we do not have enough information about the printing of ballads and other single-sheet publications to know how their disappearance has impacted our understanding of the connections between booksellers, printers, publishers, and others.[26]

But for codex publication, network analysis is a promising tool even taking into account the high loss of genres such as catechisms, prayer books, and schoolbooks. In fact, this is one area where network analysis has significant advantages over some traditional methods of assessing influence and importance, because the structure of complex networks is remarkably robust when dealing with noisy or missing data. "This robustness," writes Albert-László Barabási, "is rooted in the fact that random failures affect mainly numerous small nodes, which play only a limited role in maintaining a network's integrity."[27] He offers the example of the network of US airports. If you randomly remove nodes, there is a very low probability you will remove one of the hubs rather than one of the vast number of smaller airports—and so you must remove almost all the nodes in the entire network before it fails. This is true whether a network is scale free or random (two properties discussed in Chapter 3), so long as the average number of connections per node is greater than two ($k>2$).[28]

The "nodes" in Figure 1.1 are the 5,890 named individuals in the English print network from 1557–1640, connected through their collaborations on the 31,384 publications for this period we have downloaded from the ESTC. I will detail the process of creating this graph from the ESTC data below, but here I will simply note that the average degree, or number of connections per node, during these years is 2.876, well above the threshold that Barabási has shown correlates with high robustness even in random graphs. Even if we assume a random degree distribution, which is the least robust kind of network to random node loss, we would need to remove 65% of this graph's nodes before its structural integrity would be compromised so severely that it would break apart.[29] In other words, while a given edition may disappear from the bibliographic record, this should not impact our ability to understand which authors, publishers, printers, and booksellers are the most connected; which ones form important bridges between communities; and how the structure of the English print network itself changes over time.

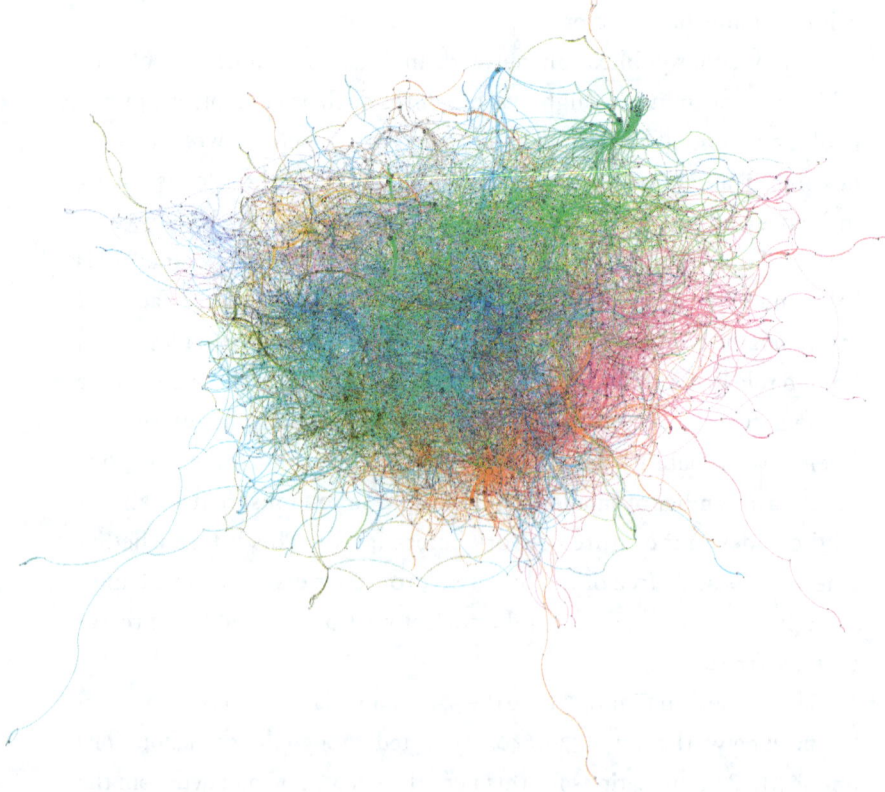

**Figure 1.1**  The English print network, 1557–1640, shaded by community detection algorithm.

As Chapter 2 explains, some of those changes were dramatic, and I should offer the final caveat that the graph illustrated in Figure 1.1 is cumulative, so that if bookseller A has worked with printer B in 1580 and printer C in 1585, we will find a path connecting printer B to printer C. If we slice the graph into temporally smaller units, we will not necessarily find this path, and therefore we need to exercise special caution in making claims about individual years during earlier periods where connectivity is low and data loss is high. Figure 1.2 illustrates the average degree per year, from 1557 to 1640. If we take an earlier year where k<2, we will have a sparse graph with fewer connections, and lost books will have a greater impact on our ability to make generalizations (for 1591, where k=1.15, for example, the critical threshold for a random graph is 0.13, meaning the graph would fail with the random removal of 13% of its nodes). By the turn of the seventeenth century, connectivity is much higher, and our ability to discuss even individual years with greater confidence increases dramatically. I will discuss some of the reasons for this sudden shift, and its consequences, in Chapter 2.

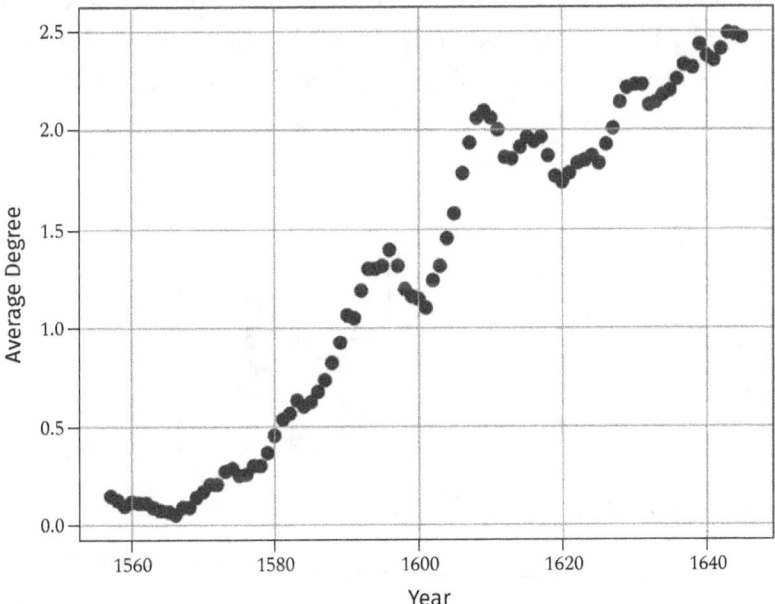

**Figure 1.2** Average individual degree per year, 1557–1640.

One more form of missing metadata derives from what Sabrina A. Baron has called the "underinformed title page," which was sometimes used as "a smoke screen behind which to conduct political and religious battles."[30] For instance, David R. Adams published an article in 2010 identifying 35 works that had been secretly and anonymously published by the radical Leveller Richard Overton.[31] Such texts raise questions about our true knowledge of the early modern print network, since the titles themselves survive, but crucial information about them has been obscured or erased. The ongoing work of librarians and bibliographers around the world has helped mitigate this issue, as they have continually incorporated new research to update the ESTC catalogue—by the time I began work on this book, all of the titles that Adams identified had been edited in ESTC to show Overton's role in printing them. But some 57,663 works in the ESTC still lack part or all of the information about printers, publishers, or booksellers, as indicated in the catalogue with some variant of "s.n." or *sine nomine*—Latin for "without a name."

As Figure 1.3 shows, in some years as many as 36% of publications exhibit this form of data loss, for an average of 9% across the whole ESTC dataset. About half of these texts (20,450) belong to the high-loss categories mentioned above—single-, half-, or quarter-sheet publications,

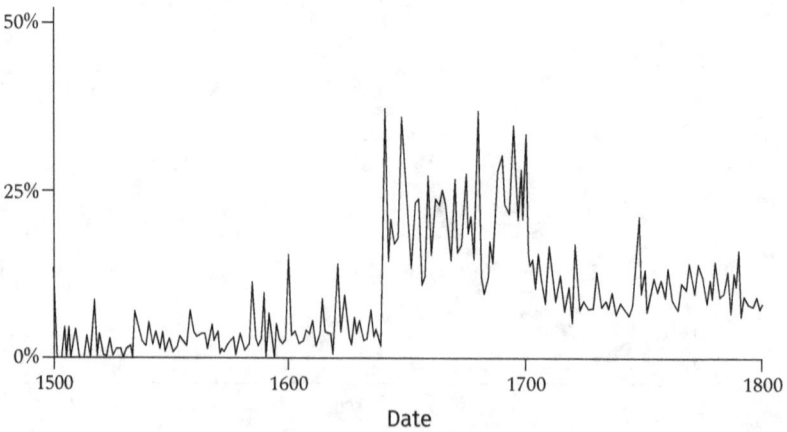

**Figure 1.3** Percentage of books in the ESTC that lack some or all publication information, 1500–1800.

such as advertisements, flybills, and other ephemera. In many other cases, however, the "s.n." designation does not really mean we lack all meaningful publication information—24,037 of these works include an author's name, for example, and were often self-published by that author, as is the case with Milton's *Epitaphium Damonis*, which I discuss in Chapter 5. Hundreds more include at least one bookseller, printer, or publisher. Most importantly, the size and density of the print network means that even if we take the worst case scenario and assume that 9% of all publications have "missing" metadata, this should not meaningfully impact the metrics used in this book—such as identification of the nodes with the highest degree or betweenness.

This is a category of problem common to nearly any kind of historical network analysis. Studies exploring the connections between ancient villages based on co-occurrence of pottery shards, for example, must assume that some percentage of artifacts have been lost or destroyed and qualify their claims accordingly, which is why Matthew Peeples developed a method for testing exactly how much impact such data loss had on various network metrics.[32] His method takes samples from a network at various intervals, removing 10%, 20%, 30%, or more nodes, then replacing them with new, randomly connected ones. It then compares metrics such as betweenness and degree in the new and original graphs. In Peeples's sample networks, which include fewer than 500 nodes, correlation between the original and sampled networks was surprisingly robust: Degree rankings remained more than 90% correlated at sampling rates of 30%, while betweenness remained more than 80% correlated at these loss rates. In my own implementation of Peeples's code for the much larger ESTC dataset, the correlation never falls below 99% for the metrics used in this book, even if we assume that 10–30% of the metadata is "lost." In short, even in years in which an unusually high percentage of works are produced "s.n.," we can draw meaningful conclusions about the people and texts whose names remain.

## II. Data Translation, Tagging, Parsing, and Extraction

To generate the kinds of graphs and analysis found in Figures 1.1 and 1.2, we had to transform the ESTC data. In a 2011 article on "The Limitations and Possibilities of the ESTC," Stephen Karian recounted the many shortcomings that have been documented in the ESTC over the years and suggested that "the only way to improve the ESTC as a database would be to supplement MARC records with another database structure."[33] He went on to suggest that "[a] revised ESTC should do more to situate the book as a product of the book trade," with fields "for evidence from printers' ledgers ... and the Stationers' Register," and noted that "in order to accommodate these multiple perspectives, the *ESTC* would have to be reconceived in such a way as to tap the full power of a relational database ... [with] a set of tables linked together in various relationships."[34] This is what our project, Shakeosphere, has done. Behind the current public interface at https://shakeosphere.lib.uiowa.edu, the project used natural language processing to mine names, roles, and locations from the ESTC publication fields, introduced authority controls and deduplicated variant spellings of names, and structured this information in a relational database that enabled new forms of querying and quantitative analysis of the book trade. Heeding Paddy Bullard's call for "independent but interoperable resources that describe, organize, and analyze the mountains of raw primary material appearing ... in digital media," we built Shakeosphere on a Linked Open Data infrastructure, with IDs incorporated into the Wikidata project, the Map of Early Modern London (MoEML), and elsewhere.[35] In this section I describe that process both for those who are interested in how I make use of it in the book and for those who want to query, download, or link to the data. All the tools we used are freely available on the web. This process was made possible through the expertise, and processing capacity, of David Eichmann, a database specialist, programmer, and professor in the School of Library and Information Sciences at the University of Iowa. When I say "we" in this section, I often mean "Dave," from whom I have learned everything I know about natural language processing and database construction.

We first downloaded 487,023 MARC records from University of California–Riverside, which houses the ESTC database. MARC became the library standard for bibliographical data in 1971, but it was designed for machines with limited tape storage and was encoded as language to be read (as in a card catalogue) rather than to be parsed, tagged, and queried in the ways that would later become common through relational databases. To enable this kind of manipulation, MARC records must be translated to MARC-XML, which we did using the metadata editing tool MarcEdit, developed by Terry Reese at Ohio State University.[36] We then parsed the MARC-XML, loading the individual tags as separate records in a Postgres database. MARC tag 100 contains the authoritative ESTC author entries, and we adopted these as our own author table without additional refinement. MARC tag 260 is a field that provides publication details in unstructured prose. Its non-standard format and complexity made it the focus of our extraction and refinement efforts. In the ESTC records, this field includes the imprint information from the title page, augmented when possible by cataloguers drawing on bibliographical information from the STC, Wing, and elsewhere. For example, field 260 for George Wither's controversial *Collection of Emblemes*, which I discuss in Chapter 5, includes the information "printed by A[ugustine] M[athewes]. for Robert Allot, and are to be sold at the Blacke Beare in Pauls Church-Yard, MDCXXV [1635]." A note in MARC field 500a tells us that the printer's name is "from the internal title pages," while other notes provide the engraver's name from the STC.

We remove all brackets and inject the words "it was" to the beginning of the string, creating an easily recognizable sentence structure ("It was printed"). We then annotate the field with a local implementation of the Brill Tagger, trained for seventeenth-century English. The Brill Tagger is one of the most widely used tools for assigning parts of speech to words, using a two-step process.[37] In initial state tagging, the standard version assigns parts of speech based on a lexicon drawn from the Penn Treebank tagging of the *Wall Street Journal* and the Brown Corpus.[38] In the second phase, it iteratively applies a set of 284 contextual rules to transform initial tags based on context. For example, the most common tag for "print" is NN (common noun), but "print" can also be used as a verb, and to accommodate this possibility the contextual rules transform nouns followed by determiners (definite articles, indefinite articles, numbers, etc.) into verbs. In the phrase "They print a book," for example, the indefinite article "a" would be tagged DT, triggering this rule and transforming the tag on "print" to verb (VB) in the final state. The tagger is 95% accurate, and this rate is improved by a pre-tagging process that can guide assignment of tags. When in doubt, the Brill Tagger labels unknown words as common nouns (NN), and we swept through the most common uncategorized common nouns, to create an additional vocabulary for tagging and extraction of 2,432 words for people and establishments with eccentric or unrecognized early spellings ("wydowe," "ececutrix," "goaler," "vniversitie," "blak-friers," "agaynste," etc).

The next step was to assign a syntactic structure to the tagged text using Carnegie Mellon University's Link Grammar Parser, which we modified with our augmented dictionary. This is a rule-based parser, which approaches each word as a building block that can be linked to other words in different ways—the participle "printed," for example, can be linked to forms of the verb "be" and to various kinds of modifying phrases and conjunctions.[39] The CMU parser includes 105 different types of links. In the publication field for George Chapman's 1634 translation of Homer's works, which was "printed by Richard Field, William Jaggard, and Thomas Harper, for Nathaniel Butter," the parser links "by" to "Richard Field," and "for" to "Nathaniel Butter" by link type "Js," which joins prepositions to their objects.

We store the multiple parses back to the database in the form of constituent trees. Figure 1.4 shows the automated parse for Chapman's *Whole Works of Homer*. Although title pages follow a fairly regular syntax, they do vary, and some publication fields are much more complex. Ben Jonson's *Alchemist* was "printed by Thomas Snodham, for Walter Burre, and are to be sold by John Stepneth, at the west-end of Paules, 1612." The tenth edition of Coke's *Institutes of the Laws of England* (mercifully printed in 1703 and safely outside the bounds of this study) was "printed by William Rawlins, and Samuel Roycroft, assigns of Richard Atkins and Edward Atkins, Esquires. And are to be sold by Charles Harper at the Flower-de-Luce against St. Dunstan's Church in Fleet-Street and J. Walthoe in Vine-Court Middle-Temple, adjoyning to the Cloysters."

We built a program based on Tgrep, which was developed by Richard Pito and is publicly available through Stanford's Department of Linguistics, to extract syntactical patterns that indicated a book was "printed by,"

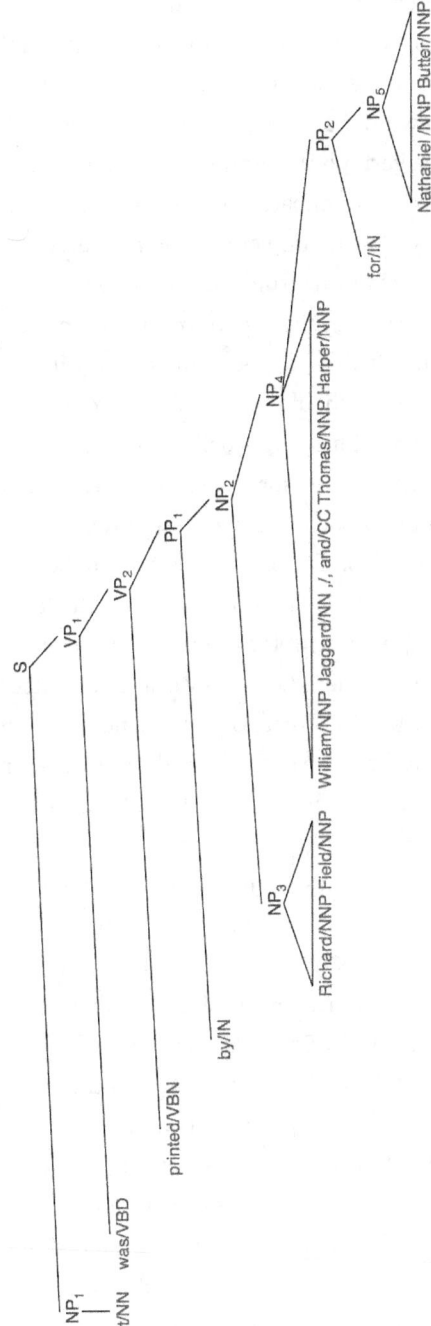

**Figure 1.4** A parse tree of *The Whole Works of Homer* (London, 1634) generated by our extraction process.

"sold by," or "printed for" a person, and to assign printer, bookseller, and publisher roles based on those designations.[40] Tgrep searches syntactically parsed corpora, allowing users to specify a pattern to be matched rather than searching by word. For example, searching "VP < (PP<NP)" returns structures where a verb phrase immediately dominates a prepositional phrase that immediately dominates a noun phrase (i.e., "printed for Nathaniel Butter"). We modified our implementation of Tgrep to retrieve the most common syntactical patterns from the annotated corpus and allow us to assert the roles indicated by those patterns. For example, in the parse tree in Figure 1.4, we specify that the noun phrase following "printed by" is the name of a printer, which should be stored back to the printer table in our database. Working with Christine Moeller, then a graduate student at Iowa and now a librarian and professor at Pacific Lutheran University, we took a low-hanging fruit approach, first working through the most prominent patterns ("printed by X for Y," "printed by X and to be sold by Y," "printed and sold by X," etc.) and moving down through the long tail of variants. We used the same approach for locations, which we matched with entries from the Map of Early Modern London (MoEML) Gazetteer of authoritative place names.[41] Since the ESTC cataloguers did not create authority records for anyone except authors, we deduplicated variant spellings for names of printers, booksellers, and publishers and created authority records based on the most frequent spellings.

As Lukas Erne has put it with no little understatement, when dealing with early modern imprints "their meaning is sometimes less transparent than the modern book historian desires."[42] In training our extractor and assigning roles, we relied heavily on M. A. Shaaber's classic article, "The Meaning of the Imprint in Early Printed Books," which as Erne notes, remains "the best guide to an understanding of the various formulations in early modern imprints."[43] Henry VIII issued a proclamation in 1546 requiring that all books printed in England must include the name of the printer, the author, and the date, and this requirement was regularly reiterated by the Stationers' Company after it was founded in 1557.[44] But these ordinances and customs were often avoided or ignored, and even when names are present on early English title pages, the chains of responsibility for publication are not always apparent. To complicate matters, as Michael Treadwell writes,

> [T]he one word, "bookseller," served to cover any one who engaged in any one, or any combination, of the three activities, now generally separate, which we designate as wholesale and retail bookselling and publishing. This usage was quite natural since, at that time, all but the smallest London booksellers, whether principally retailers or wholesalers, engaged in some publishing, and . . . little publishing was done except by booksellers.[45]

In the most straightforward examples cited by Shaaber and found in our database, printer, publisher, and bookseller are all mentioned in a fairly formulaic way, as in the first quarto of Ben Jonson's *The Alchemist*, which was "printed by Thomas Snodham, for Walter Burre, and are to be sold by John Stepneth, at the west-end of Paules," in 1612. For this pattern, we have designated Snodham the printer, Stepneth the bookseller, and Burre, who had entered the play in the Stationers' Register on October 3, 1610, the publisher.[46] But the most common forms for the STC period mention only one or two stationers: "printed by A," "printed by A for B," and "printed by A and to be sold by B" are among the most frequent. Especially in early versions of "printed by A," the printer is often also acting as bookseller and publisher. In the formula "printed by A for B," Shaaber explains that the Stationers' Company registers "usually show" that B is "the copyright-owner and therefore the publisher."[47] Finally, Shaaber notes that the formula "printed by A and are to be sold by B" typically means that A was a printer-publisher, selling his books through B, although he also explains that in around one-third of the cases it means exactly the opposite, where B is a publisher-bookseller contracting with a jobbing printer to produce his book.[48] For example, the 1605 title page of the fourth quarto of Shakespeare's *Richard III* states that it was "printed by Thomas Creede, and are to be sold by Thomas Lawe, dwelling in Paules Church-yard, at the signe of the Foxe, neare S. Austins gate." The Stationers' Register shows that Andrew Wise transferred this play and several others to Law in 1603, and so he was acting as the publisher here, as he was in the other quartos of Shakespeare's plays where he used this formula.[49]

Our syntax-based parsing makes no effort to disentangle such cases of publisher-booksellers from those of printer-publishers. In the case of this syntactical pattern, Thomas Creede is assigned the role of printer and Matthew Law the role of bookseller. Only when a book is "printed for" someone do we label that person a "publisher." This may mean that the publisher role is slightly underrepresented in our data, but to avoid anachronism we have thought it safest to capture the roles as they are most clearly on display: variations of "printed by," "imprinted by," and "excudebat" indicate a printer; "sold by," "venduntur," "bookseller," or "to be sold at his shop" indicate a bookseller; "printed and sold by" indicate a dual role as printer and bookseller.

I have not used the role of "publisher" for the purposes of quantitative analysis, heeding Peter Blayney's warning that "the early modern book trade had no separate word for what we now call a publisher" and his estimate that 88% of books were published by booksellers, with "a few" published by stationers who were also printers.[50] I have, however, taken "bookseller" and "printer" as meaningful categories for analysis, as well as exploring the impact of all stationers, regardless of role.

### III. Visualization and Analysis

The database allows us to construct a graph that has publications and people as nodes (also known as vertices). If an author, printer, or bookseller is involved in publishing a book, we say there is an "edge," or connection between these nodes. These edges can be plotted on an adjacency matrix, such as the very simple one in Figure 1.5 showing the relationships between the first quarto of *The Alchemist* and two other books published in 1612: Thomas Dekker's *Lanthorne and Candle-light*, and Cyril Tourneur's *Atheist's Tragedy*. In this matrix, "1" indicates an edge between the person and the publication (the person is the publication's author, printer, bookseller, etc.), while "0" indicates that they are not connected in these ways. This is a bipartite graph, meaning it has two different types of vertices: publications and people. We can also represent it as a bipartite network, as in Figure 1.6.

The giant hairball in Figure 1.1 is a bipartite graph of the early modern print network writ large, clustered (and colored) by communities of

|  | The Alchemist | Lanthorne and Candle-light | Atheist's Tragedy |
|---|---|---|---|
| Ben Jonson | 1 | 0 | 0 |
| Thomas Snodham | 1 | 1 | 1 |
| Walter Burre | 1 | 0 | 0 |
| John Stepneth | 1 | 0 | 1 |
| John Busby | 0 | 1 | 0 |
| Thomas Dekker | 0 | 1 | 0 |
| Richard Redmer | 0 | 0 | 1 |
| Cyril Tourneur | 0 | 0 | 1 |

**Figure 1.5** A simple matrix showing the people associated with three publications in 1612.

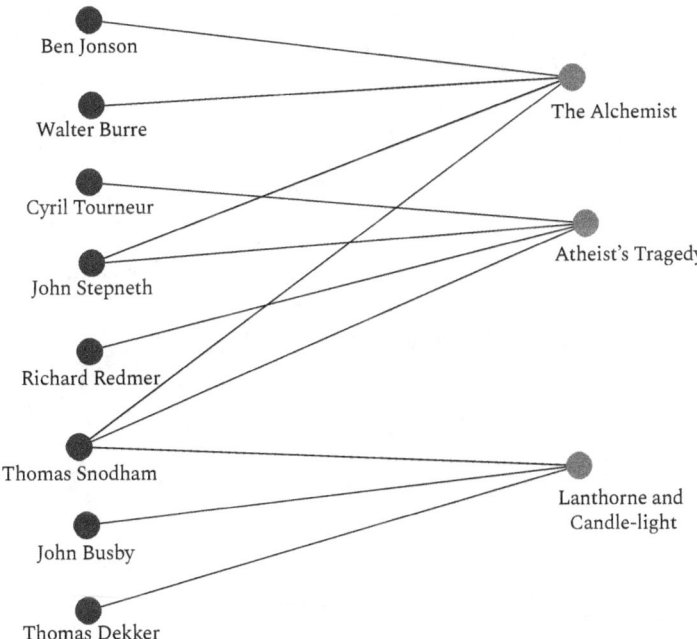

**Figure 1.6** The matrix from Figure 1.5 visualized as a bipartite network of people connected to three publications in 1612.

nodes that are most closely connected. In this book, and in network analysis more generally, we typically project bipartite graphs onto their left or right vertices. This makes analysis more tractable and visualization clearer—ensuring that we are comparing like things to like when asking questions about which nodes are most connected or most central. If we project the network in Figure 1.6 onto its left vertex, we have a network in which the nodes are people, with an edge for every shared publication connecting them. If we project it onto the right vertex, we have a network in which the nodes are publications, with edges for every person connecting them. Each kind of projection offers different analytical possibilities.

Figure 1.7 shows a left projection, in which nodes are sized by their "degree," or the number of connections they have to others. With 8 nodes (N) and 14 edges (E), the average degree of the network is 3.5 ($k = \frac{2E}{N}$). In the visualization, we scale the nodes by their degree, making it clear that Snodham is the highest-degree node, with direct connections to seven

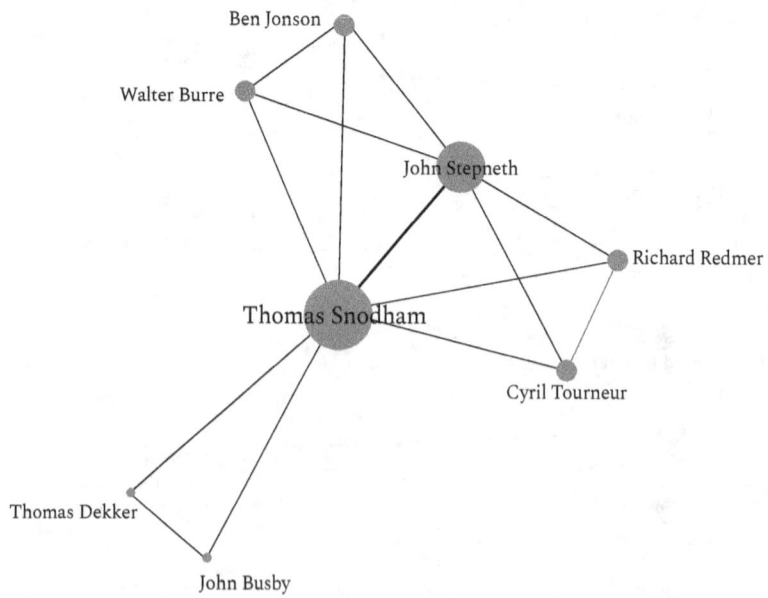

**Figure 1.7** The network from Figure 1.6 projected onto its left vertex, so that people from the 1612 publications are the nodes, and co-publications are the edges (links) between them.

other people (degree seven). In this network, Snodham also has the highest *betweenness centrality*, meaning that when we try to connect any two points in the network, the shortest path usually runs through him. As discussed in Chapter 4, however, the node with the highest degree is often not the node with the highest betweenness.

Figure 1.8 shows a right projection, and this graph of publications, with far fewer nodes, initially looks a little less promising—all three of the publications are connected to exactly one other, and all share the same degree of two. But if we look closely, we'll see the edge between the *Atheist's Tragedy* and *The Alchemist* is twice as thick as the others. These are "weighted" edges, and this one has twice the weight because these two publications share not one, but two collaborators: Snodham *and* Stepneth.

In the examples in Figures 1.7 and 1.8, it is simple to calculate average degree simply by counting, and we can find high-degree nodes, most central nodes, or most heavily weighted edges at a glance. Does a

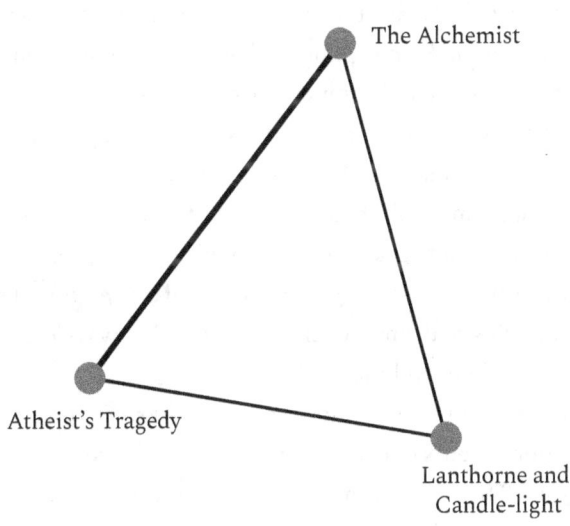

**Figure 1.8** The network from Figure 1.6 projected onto its right vertex, so that the 1612 publications are the nodes, and people are the edges (links) between them.

thicker edge mean they are really "closer" in any meaningful way? Not necessarily. But when performed on hundreds or thousands of texts, such calculations allow us to group texts based on their networks of production in ways that can be both meaningful and surprising. Figure 1.9, for example, is a projection of the connections between publications from 1600, when Jonson first appeared in print, and 1616, when the first folio of his works was published. Communities have been detected and painted using the Louvain method, an iterative process that groups nodes based on the density of the edges between them.[51] The large orange cluster in the center contains Jonson's *The Alchemist,* along with Cyril Tourneur's *Atheist's Tragedy,* Thomas Campion's *Description of a Maske,* John Marston's *Insatiate Countesse,* and many other dramatic texts. Jonson's folio, however, is grouped with the blue cluster just below it and to the right, along with works including John Donne's *Anatomy of the World,* Thomas Shelton's translation of *Don Quixote,* Robert Greene's *Pandosto,* Francis Davison's verse compilation *A Poetical Rapsodie,* and Ariosto's *Satires.* Both clusters might be considered broadly "literary" (they both also contain sermons). But the orange is decidedly "dramatic," while the blue is decidedly not—besides Jonson's *Workes,* the only other "dramatic" texts are the folio *Works of Lucius Annaeus Seneca,* published by William Stansby in 1614, and a description of a royal entertainment given during the queen's progress to Bath in 1613. When Jonson gathered his poems and plays into a single weighty book, he was making clear his desire to be taken seriously as an author rather than a mere playmaker, and this clustering shows that doing so involved a distinct network of printers, publishers, and booksellers who had their own motivations for producing this kind of literature. These texts are prestigious, classical, and generally "literary" in ways that put some distance between them and the public stage.

Other clusters on the map show how networks of production might offer useful supplements or challenges to our typical grouping of texts by genre or author. The dark green cluster (left center) is almost exclusively religious literature, such as John Dod's *Treatise or Exposition upon the Ten Commandments,* Samuel Hieron's *Christian's Journal,* and Arthur Dent's catechism *A Pastime for Parents.* The burgundy cluster (bottom right) is

METHODS AND DATA    41

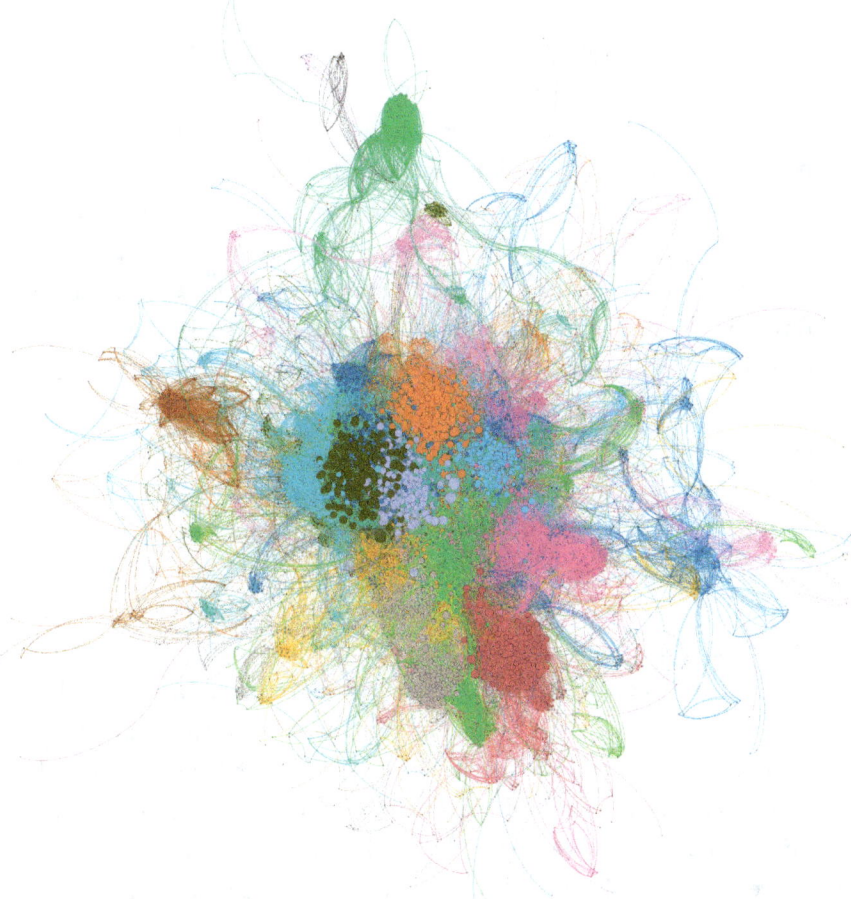

**Figure 1.9**  Publications from 1600 to 1616, shaded by Louvain community detection method, an iterative process that groups nodes based on the density of the edges between them.

almost exclusively legal textbooks and practical treatises including *Littleton's Tenures in English*, Sir Edward Coke's *Reports*, Thomas Ridley's *View of the Civil and Ecclesiastical Law*, and John Manwood's *Treatise of the Lawes of the Forest*. Just as interesting as the books that clearly fit these patterns are the ones that don't. In the midst of the legal treatises, for example, we find Thomas Beard's *Theatre of God's Judgments*, in which he famously cites Christopher Marlowe's death as an act of divine vengeance. Rather than understanding this book as an "antitheatrical polemic," as it is commonly described, should we take seriously Beard's assertion that his book was meant to explicate the divine commandments of "our souveraigne and perfect lawgiver"?[52] Its publication network would certainly imply the book was produced and sold not primarily as an antitheatrical polemic, as it is often described, but as a legal resource illustrating the conjunction between "divine and humane law," as it promises on the title page.

For networks at such a scale, however, counting by hand becomes futile, and we arguably reach the limits of useful visualization (I tried to generate an illustration where the titles of these texts were clear, but there are simply too many). There are 4,023 nodes in this graph and 89,539 edges between them. It takes millions of calculations to find the highest-centrality nodes or to partition nodes into communities. The most powerful and versatile tool for such calculations, and the one used throughout this book, is the open source Python package, NetworkX.[53] It is powerful enough for use on large networks with millions of nodes and hundreds of millions of edges. And it includes a large library of algorithms to calculate basic properties such as degree and betweenness, as well as community detection, link prediction, and more. Brian Hie, who was my undergraduate research assistant when he was studying computer science and English at Stanford University, wrote the code to perform many fundamental calculations—ranking nodes by degree, ranking them by betweenness, ranking the highest-centrality edges, and determining the overall connectivity of the graph. Since then, he has moved to MIT to pursue his doctorate at the Computer Science and Artificial Intelligence Lab, and we have continued to correspond as I have modified the source code to implement additional algorithms used in this book, such as community detection and link prediction. The basic script is available on Github, and I have footnoted to the additional NetworkX functions I used in this book in the relevant discussions.[54]

While NetworkX is a powerful tool for network analysis, its visualization capabilities are not as sophisticated. I have used them for some basic line plots, but for network diagrams—including all the ones in this chapter—I have exported graphs as .gexf files that can be imported to Gephi, an open source visualization platform. The bipartite graph data for 1474–1799 is available in Gephi formats on Github for researchers who would like to download it, and Gephi's graphical interface may make it appealing for users who would like to explore the data without delving into Python and working from the command line. For users interested in exploring the data without installing and configuring anything, we have also included basic visualization and analysis features on the Shakeosphere website, using the .d3 JavaScript library. JavaScript includes a port of NetworkX, called JSNetworkX, and we have used it to allow users to compare the degree of any two people in the network over time, to compare their centrality, and to explore larger structural questions, like the percentage of nodes in the largest connected component over time. However, JSNetworkX is still under development and has a limited number of functions available. Like it, the *Shakeosphere* website and project is a work in progress, and we continue to update it as we link to new datasets and include new features. In the chapters that follow, I hope to show that this process has already yielded important insights into the networks of early English print.

We have been able to evaluate influence in new ways, to identify overlooked figures of real structural importance to the English print network, and to use such discoveries as a starting point for research into how and why they became hubs or bridges within that network. These are questions not only of literary and book history, but also of human agency. And one of the most fulfilling aspects of the project has been the chance to learn how the pursuit of these questions can be facilitated by processes of data collection, cleaning, and structure that we do not always associate with such fundamentally humanistic inquiry. But this, finally, is the reason I've lingered on the collection and transformation of the data, from the beginning of the ESTC project in the 1970s to the present. The goal is not merely to make the analysis transparent and replicable, although that is important, but to reveal the labor and collaboration that makes it possible.

## CHAPTER 2   A SMALL NEW WORLD

Fire, Infection, and Sudden Change
in the English Print Network

**MOST OF US HAVE PLAYED SOME VERSION** of the "small world" game in which we meet a stranger, far from home, and discover through a series of questions and answers that we have some friend in common. While writing this chapter, it happened to me when a doctor in California asked where I lived (Iowa City) and what I did for a living (English professor), which was all it took for us to discover that one of my former colleagues had been his childhood friend. Such small-world conversations are possible in any large, interconnected network, where far-flung individuals have multiple ties outside their own local group of friends or family, and network scientists have suggested that we can link any two individuals on today's hyperconnected planet with fewer than six degrees of separation. Small-world networks make it possible for information or infection to spread rapidly across vast populations. And they behave in ways that will be important to the rest of this book: They emerge suddenly, not gradually; they are dominated by a few hubs that are vastly more connected than everyone else; and they highlight the strength of weak ties in bridging distant communities.

In early sixteenth-century England, small-world conversations would have been rare. The arrival of strangers in a village was still unusual enough to be greeted with excitement and some suspicion, with travel outside one's local area conducted only under the authority of the church or with a "passport" issued by the privy council or a patron. A statute of 1388 required such passports or "letters testimonial" for pilgrims, wandering beggars, university students, or servants traveling without their masters, and this stayed in effect through the sixteenth century. Roads were "fundamentally local resources," with travel "by local people along local roads for the purposes of localized economic exchange."[1] Along these localized roads, postal conditions and routes were "un-systematized, idiosyncratic," and "peripheral to well-established, universal, and affordable European postal structures."[2]

This would change profoundly over the course of the sixteenth and seventeenth centuries, as London became a global city, with ships sailing from English ports to destinations around the world. Despite repeated government efforts to regulate and restrict free travel, a shifting economy (and the magnetic attraction of London at its center) made it increasingly difficult to keep ambitious or restless citizens wedded to agricultural and local village life.[3] There was a "marked expansion of postal routes between the 1560s and the first decade of James I's reign."[4] Strangers gradually became a little less strange, and distant communications became a little more routine. But nowhere was the change in networked sociality more dramatic than in the world of print, where a revolutionary shift reshaped communications in ways that we have been unable to appreciate until now, because we lacked the tools to see it.

In the heady days of the 1960s and 70s, scholars including Marshall McLuhan and Walter J. Ong enthusiastically claimed that a Renaissance print "revolution" had reshaped human consciousness as we know it. And Elizabeth L. Eisenstein's two-volume tome, *The Printing Press as an Agent of Change*, lent such claims scholarly backing for at least another decade. But over the last twenty years, historians of print and the book have moderated her more sweeping claims about the way the print "revolution" gave rise to other dramatic transformations, including the Reformation, the scientific revolution, and the Renaissance itself (all of which, not coincidentally, have themselves come to be understood in less dramatic and more nuanced terms). In place of a sudden and complete print revolution, scholars including Arthur Marotti and Harold Love showed the persistence and vitality of manuscript circulation and publication long after the advent of print.[5] As late as the 1670s—two centuries after William Caxton set up England's first printing press—rival scriptoria in London churned out handwritten newsletters for hundreds of clients, while poets like Rochester and Marvell became (in)famous for their manuscript verse. The transition from manuscript to print also worked in reverse, with individual readers, secretaries, and scholars copying printed sources back into manuscript for their preservation and transmission.[6] "Old technologies," as David Scott Kastan puts it, often "prove far more vigorous than we might have thought."[7] And so Adrian Johns suggests that Eisenstein was misguided to talk about "print culture" at all, rather than the "complex social processes by which books came to be made and used by their society."[8] Indeed, few would now contest David McKitterick's suggestion that "while we speak today, using radical and dramatic vocabulary, of a printing revolution ... innovations in printing were gradual."[9] The debate between Eisenstein and her critics has mostly been resolved in favor of evolution rather than revolution.[10]

This chapter, however, will show that new digital methods make it possible and necessary to speak once again of a print revolution. Indeed, I hope to show that a networked approach can incorporate the strongest observations of both camps—Eisenstein's evidence that early modern people understood that they were living through a communications revolution and Johns's insistence that any developments in "print culture" were driven less by technological shifts than by communities of artisans and intellectuals building upon one another's knowledge and practice. As we explore the newly complex network that emerged during this period, we will also identify some of the people who were at its center, shaping and being shaped by this sudden shift—writers like Robert Greene, the era's first literary celebrity; Sir Philip Sidney, its most illustrious courtly writer; Edmund Spenser, its most ambitious print poet; and William Shakespeare, its most enduring author. It is no exaggeration to say that their work still remains at the heart of the English literary tradition, in part, because the small new world they were discovering is our own.

## I. Tipping Points: Burrows, Books, and Bacon

The continuities in book production are belied by a sudden and radical shift in the print network itself—what network scientists call a *phase transition*. Phase transitions, or "tipping points," happen all the time, reshaping networks as diverse as societies, ecosystems, and neurons. Diseases, for example, become epidemics not gradually but with explosive speed when certain thresholds of virulence and population density, or connectivity, are met. Researchers studying the plague have observed this phenomenon in populations of *Rhombomys opimus* (great gerbils), which become susceptible to plague outbreaks when more than 33% of their burrows become occupied. These complex burrow systems are built over many generations, covering vast swaths of central Asia, and transmission of the plague depends on the movement of infected fleas between them. Below the 33% threshold, plague may decimate a few families but will quickly die out before spreading through the network.[11] Above the threshold, plague jumps from host family to host family, infecting the entire network for miles around. A graph of the relationship between borough occupancy and infectiousness, as in Figure 2.1, shows that this epidemic is a classic phase transition.

Similar examples abound. We know that measles emerged around 6,000 years ago because it requires a population greater than 500,000 to continue perpetuating itself without burning out.[12] And when we analyze trees in a forest as a network, as in Figure 2.2, we find a similar tipping point for the spread of forest fire: At a certain, critical density threshold, flames leap from tree to tree and consume the entire forest.[13]

Each of these phase transitions looks strikingly similar to this seismic shift in the English print network during the 1580s and the early 1600s, pictured in Figure 2.3 with data generated from the ESTC and Shakeosphere. This is the shape of an information revolution. The graph shows the fraction of individuals in the English print network that are linked to

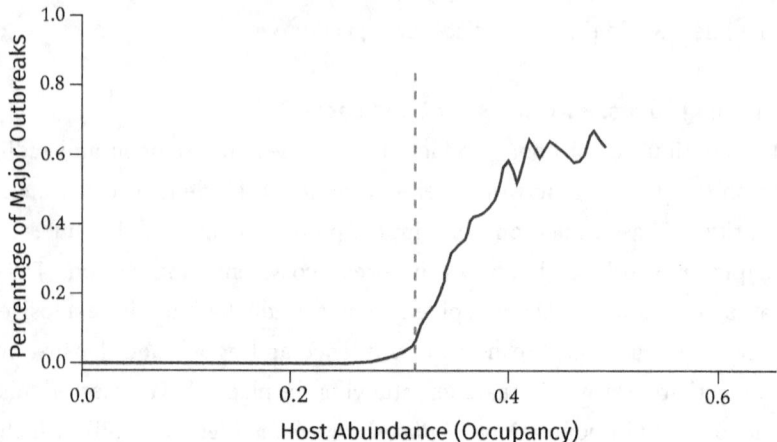

**Figure 2.1** Plague outbreaks and burrow occupancy in great gerbils. When burrow occupancy rises to about 33%, connecting the nodes of the great gerbil population, the plague spreads throughout the entire network.

SOURCE: Adapted from Stephen Davis et al., "The Abundance Threshold for Plague as a Critical Percolation Phenomenon," Nature 454 (2008): 636.

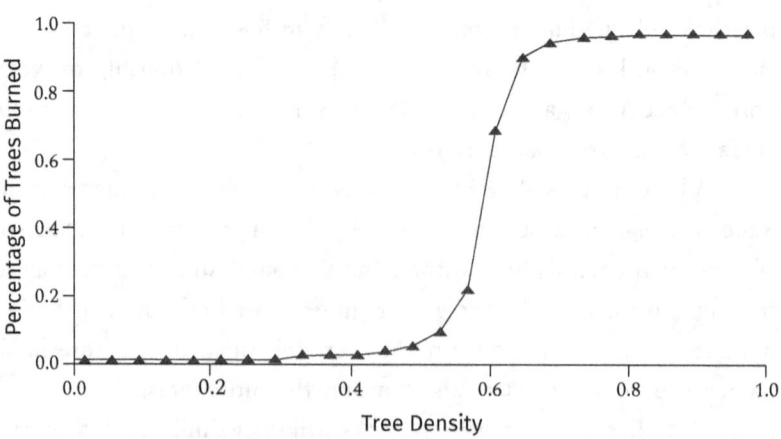

**Figure 2.2** Tree density plotted against the spread of fire.

SOURCE: Adapted from Ricard V. Solé, Phase Transitions (Princeton: Princeton University Press, 2011), 55.

the largest "connected component" (CC) between about 1500 and 1800. To help make sense of it, I should explain that a connected component (often colloquially called a "network map") looks like Figure 2.4, which shows the network from 1590 to 1600. In such a graph, any two nodes can be connected, even if the path between them is long. From the origins of English print until about 1590, most people in the network are not part of such a large connected component. Their print activities generate only a few connections or leave them completely isolated, with the fraction of nodes that are part of the largest connected component hovering between 5–15%. This is true even after 1557, when the Stationers' Company received its royal charter, nominally exerting a new level of control over English print and the ability to hold the number of presses and printers at a constant.

This is the period, as Peter Blayney has shown, when the Stationers' Company became "the dominant presence in the English printing trade," thanks in part to the Marian purge of non-company and foreign printers.[14] That is, the company became more tightly knit and controlled than during the reigns of either Henry VIII or Edward—but the network itself remained dispersed and disconnected for decades after incorporation. Then, between 1580 and the early 1600s, as the company gradually grew, roles diversified and output expanded, and the network's connectivity dramatically changed: Almost everyone became linked to everyone else. It was a larger network but a smaller world.

To put this shift from 5% connectivity to 85% connectivity in perspective, during a similar 20-year period between 1995 and 2014, the percentage of US residents connected to one another online jumped from 14% to 87%.[15] Changes in print technology and the output of books may have been gradual, in other words, just as the growth of a forest may take years to fill in the gaps in the canopy. But beneath the seeming calm, the print network was like dry tinder, ready to ignite, and Shakespeare's generation was born just as the match was lit.

Although the complex network effects emerged all at once, this was a slow rolling revolution of an institution that was established along explicitly conservative and Counter-Reformation lines. Blayney's history of

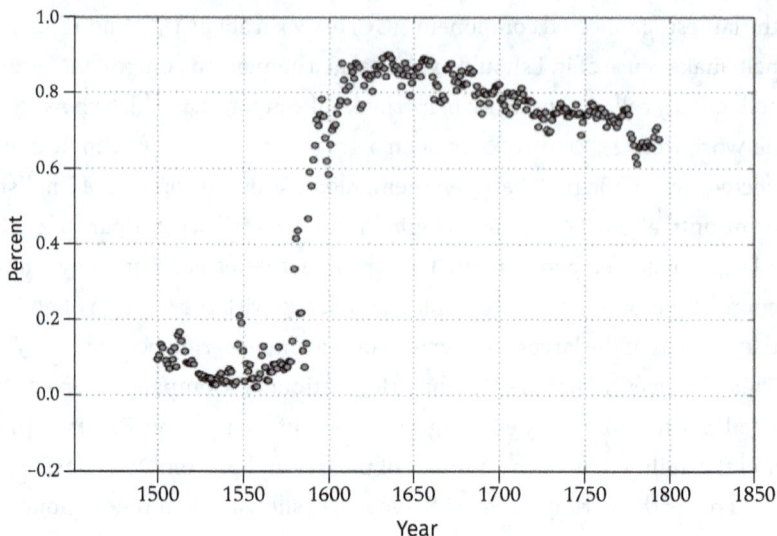

**Figure 2.3** The fraction of individuals in the English print network linked to the largest connected component, 1474–1800. Each point represents one year, and data are not cumulative.

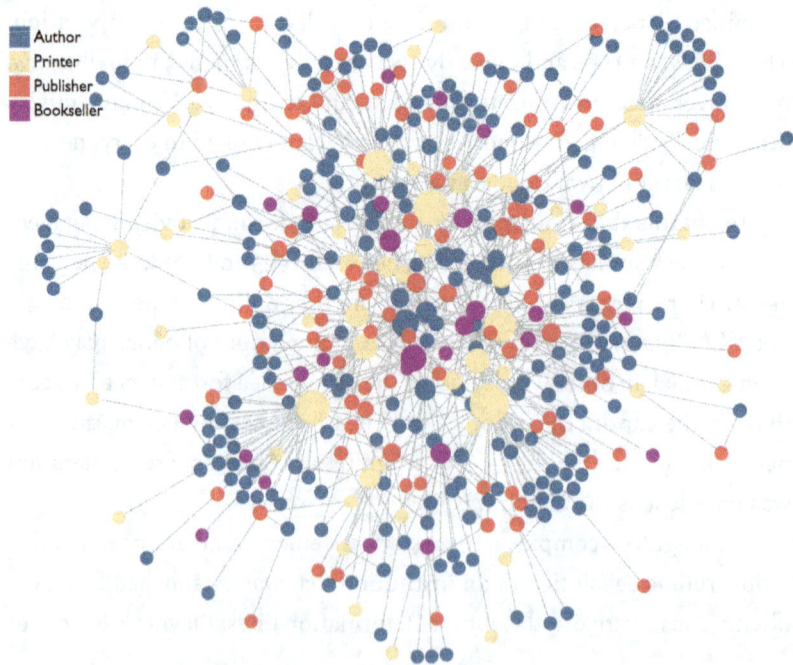

**Figure 2.4** English print network map, 1590–1600.

the Stationers' Company chronicles in granular detail the transformation of the company from a craft association representing text writers, limners (illuminators), and bookbinders, at the beginning of the fifteenth century, to its incorporation as the body in control of printing and all other elements of book production in 1557. Before this date, printers tended to have served their apprenticeships with a wide variety of guilds other than the Stationers' Company, and the book trade was less controlled than it would later become. The 1557 "charter was unquestionably a Marian grant," made possible by a "purge" that targeted "the *Protestant book trade*" and left "the remaining trade in Catholic hands."[16] And while Mary's reign would soon end, the monopoly model established to make book production in England "easier to police and control" did not.[17]

The great surprise then, when we consider Figure 2.3, is that the network's structure changed so completely and so late. From the outset, the Stationers' Company was a relatively small organization, with 97 members in the original charter. And if we think in terms of traditional historiography of communities, families, and groups, rather than in terms of network development, we might expect that the basic structure established in 1557 would persist over the next hundred years, as the company slowly and gradually doubled in membership. Instead, this process of slow growth, link by link, collaboration by collaboration, yielded a very different kind of network all at once.

Suddenly, nearly every author, bookseller, and printer could be traced in a few short steps to any other person in the network, no matter how apparently distant their ideological, political, or familial position might seem. To illustrate the shift, we can play a game. The "Six Degrees of Kevin Bacon" game—in which contestants rise to the (surprisingly easy) challenge of connecting any person in the history of film to Kevin Bacon—would be several hundred years in coming. But in this newly connected world of English print, we can play a version with the English author and polymath Francis Bacon: "Six Degrees of Francis Bacon."[18] In the database of early English books created for this project, Bacon is connected to Shakespeare with only two degrees of separation through the printer Richard Field; to Ben Jonson with two degrees of separation through the printer George Eld; to the astronomer Giordano Bruno with four degrees of separation, through a chain of printers and authors that includes Nicholas Okes, who will be discussed in Chapter 3, and Robert Greene, who will be discussed further below. As with Kevin, there's really nothing special about Francis Bacon. We could do the same exercise with William Shakespeare, Christopher Marlowe, Thomas Kyd, or Thomas Dekker. The point is that in a large, interconnected network, we can *always* find a path between any two people, but in the world of English print this condition does not arise until the late sixteenth century.

As discussed in Chapter 1, the graphs above are generated by analyzing nearly 500,000 publications in the ESTC and creating a connection, or edge, every time two names appear on the same title page. In 1474, for example, William Caxton collaborates with the Flemish scribe Colard Mansion to print a popular work explaining the rules of chess (*De ludo scachorum*). We store this relationship in a database binding Caxton and Mansion in a small network, and every time Caxton collaborates with someone else, the database includes another link. The program registers another set of relationships when the German printer Theodoric Rood sets up his press at Oxford a few years later and produces a school textbook by the English grammarian John Anwykyll. Many small networks continue to form for the next hundred years of English print, but they mostly remain fragmented from one another. Only when the network makes its great leap in the 1590s does it become possible to establish short paths between any two people within it. The small-world phenomenon, in other words, emerges suddenly in this moment, but only after a much longer and more gradual period of growth and change in the print network.

The fact that they are not connected in the sort of small-world network that would later emerge does not mean that Caxton never met Rood or Anwykyll—it is entirely probable that he did, and that they or any number of others had traditional face-to-face relationships that weren't documented in their books. Indeed, as A. E. B. Coldiron has shown, the earliest English printers were in many ways deeply connected to continental print networks that were more advanced and that would have experienced their own phase transitions significantly earlier. "Practically speaking," she writes, "early English print culture was something like a francophone subculture."[19] But our ability to document and measure an emerging, and far more extensive, English print network has serious implications for the way texts were produced and disseminated in the English context. In the real world, the proliferating edges in our network visualizations take various forms: books by competing printers jostling for attention in the same shop, booksellers working with multiple publishers to procure a stock of popular authors, authors looking for teams of publishers and printers who can turn a profit or exercise discretion when handling risqué material. Although our graphs abstract and flatten such moments, they also make it possible to recognize statistically significant shifts like the one documented above. A highly networked book might be available from multiple booksellers or require the joint efforts (and capital) of several different publishers working together to secure rights, commission engravings, and contract with authors.

However abstracted, our map of the early modern print network makes good intuitive sense when compared to what traditional scholarship tells us about the historical development of English print. William Caxton was not exactly a one-man show—after learning the trade in Cologne and producing several books abroad, he imported both a press and men to run it to England. But compared to later printers, his operation was tremendously centralized and did not rely on negotiating the same extended chains of relationships as some of the later printers I will be discussing. Three-quarters of Caxton's publications were translations, mostly from French into English, and he did most of the translation himself. A merchant whose dealings in France and the Low Countries had made him a man of the world, Caxton sought out texts that were fashionable at the court of Burgundy, where he was in regular attendance.[20] Procuring the texts, translating them, writing dedications and prefaces, and selling them in his own shop, Caxton and other early printers took on many roles that would later become specialized professions. In that way, early networks of books and readers still resemble the pre-print world that Neil Rhodes and Jonathan Sawday have described, where "rather than texts circulating amongst communities of readers, it was the task of readers to circulate themselves around those centers where books were known to exist"—a network model of localization, centralization, and hierarchy, rather than diffusion and complexity.[21] By the time Shakespeare's sonnets were published in 1609, by comparison, the title page informs readers that the book is printed by George Eld, published by Thomas Thorpe, and sold in the shops of William Aspley and John Wright. That's a network of five individuals, each of whom have dozens or even hundreds of other connections, linked on a single title page that is itself circulating in multiple shops. As the number of people involved in making and marketing books grew, it only took a few links between such publications, at the critical moment, to create a giant network that was also a very small world.

This sudden shift also seems entirely plausible based on the what we know about the evolution of other historical print networks. For example, Matthew Lincoln's study of artistic print production in northern Europe, drawing on the metadata from the British Museum's collection of 14,821 Dutch and Flemish prints and the Rijksmuseum's collection of 19,980 prints, found that "gradual changes seen in the network population . . . appear to mask more dynamic upheavals in actual network concentration."[22] Although art historians are "unaccustomed to thinking of our subject matter in terms of unpredictable systems," Lincoln concludes, "such rapid structural changes in networks involving hundreds of artists, printmakers, and publishers" indicate typical "'phase change' behavior" familiar from other social networks.[23] These effects were reproducible by running the same analysis on a random network of the same size—a test I also replicated using the ESTC print network data.[24] This seems to imply that the changes result more from a network density effect than from particular historical factors, such as new regulations or decisions made by groups or individuals. As we shall see in subsequent chapters, however, once such a complex network emerges, some individuals would be better equipped than others to take advantage of its new possibilities. The rich would very quickly get richer, with a handful of printers, publishers, and booksellers forging a vast number of connections thanks to their existing resources or to the innovative practices they introduced and embraced.

## II. Writing the Revolution: Robert Greene, Philip Sidney, Edmund Spenser, and William Shakespeare

The next chapter will focus on the handful of printers and booksellers who became major hubs or superspreaders in the network during the 1600s. But during the initial tipping point, many key figures, who unified otherwise disparate parts of the network, are authors who are more familiar to students of literature. To discover who they are, we can examine the first years when the majority of nodes became connected and identify some central authors. What can they tell us about the discursive field at this moment of profound change in the communications network? Were they just in the right place at the right time, or do other qualities of their ambition or authorship help establish them in this position?

The first significant person whose appearance in the graph connects up large parts of the network, in 1588-89, is Robert Greene, and his tempestuous career would seem to imply that more than luck was involved. By all accounts, he was a magnetic if scandalous personality, and his position at the center of Figure 2.5 was mirrored by his position at the center of a wild but exciting literary scene developing in London. The son of poor parents from the provinces, Greene earned scholarships to Cambridge and Oxford, married well, squandered his wife's dowry, and abandoned her for London. There he established himself as a sort of lord of literary misrule, surrounded by a talented coterie of young, Oxbridge-educated writers that included George Peele, Thomas Nashe, Christopher Marlowe, and Thomas Lodge. "At some moment in the late 1580s," Stephen Greenblatt writes, "Shakespeare walked into a room—most likely, an inn in Shoreditch, Southwark, or the Bankside," and found Greene holding court as "the central figure" among this illustrious but dissolute circle.[25]

In Greenblatt's telling, Greene was a Falstaffian presence who would actually become Shakespeare's model for his fat knight. This is colorful speculation, rather than cold fact. But it is exactly the kind of thing that Greene invited through his own writing, where he fictionalized his life and adventures in the London underground so successfully that "Greene" continued to churn out books long after the historical Robert Greene had died. In one of these books, supposedly written on his deathbed (but probably

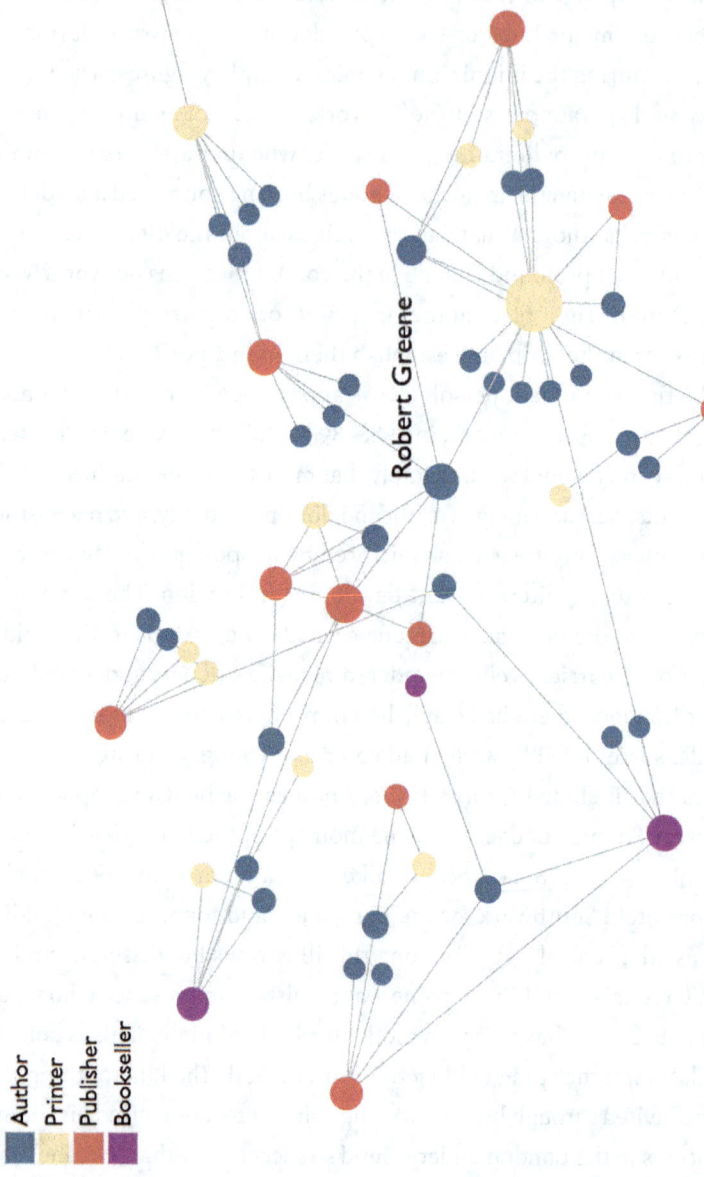

**Figure 2.5** English print network, 1588–1589. Robert Greene plays a central role in the emergence of a large connected component.

authored in part or in whole by Thomas Nashe or Henry Chettle), Greene claims that his "immeasurable drinking had made him the perfect Image of the dropsie."[26] With this comically distended belly and a long list of seductions and scandals to his name, he famously, if perhaps apocryphally, died penniless but penitent after overindulging on a "fatal banquet of Rhenish wine and pickled herring."[27] Whatever the truth of the Greene legend, he was certainly as riotous with his writing as with his drinking, and before his death at age 34 he composed at least five plays and published more than three dozen prose works. This alone is part of the reason that he takes a central position at the moment the network emerges as one large, interconnected web—between 1588 and 1589, Greene published six titles with at least a dozen different printers, publishers, and booksellers. The sheer variety of his collaborations with members of the Stationers' Company suggests to scholars either "that his work was initially a risky venture or possibly that Greene was a writer who was unafraid to look for the best possible price for his copy."[28]

The frequent republishing of his works makes the latter seem most likely, but either way it is clear that Greene represented something new in the annals of popular print. His works were not merely prolific, but exciting and hugely popular, and he made the printing process itself part of the lurid drama of the work. For example, Greene frames his 1588 romance, *Perimedes the Blacke-smith*, as a found story, a series of conversations "overheard" by "chance" between an Egyptian blacksmith and his wife Delia, and at the end of the story, Greene appends four sonnets purporting to have been found in Delia's "chest."[29] A prefatory letter by "William Bubb Gentleman, to his friend the author" claims that these poems were re-discovered and added to the manuscript at the very last minute, when the rest of the manuscript had already been printed: "the last sheete hanging in the Presse, coming into your study, I found in your desk certain sonnets."[30] Such apparently rushed elements, which are everywhere in Greene's work, caused an early biographer to warn that "desiring nothing beyond the immediate sale, Greene took no thought to finishing his work to a degree of perfection, or for removing from it the flaws that might easily have been removed."[31] But these "flaws"—like the marginalia in *Perimedes* that suddenly disappears after only a few pages, as if the author didn't have time to finish—also gave the reader the sense that the book she held in her hands contained secrets rushed into print with barely enough time for the ink to dry.

Readers were hooked. More to the point, a new type of reader was born. Thomas Overbury's satirical collection of character types includes the "Chamber maid," who "reads *Greenes* works over and over."[32] She's so completely enraptured by Greene's fantastic fictions that she neglects her more mundane workaday duties and obligations, daydreaming instead about a world of romance and adventure. The stereotype of the female, lower-class reader of cheap popular print begins here, along with Greene's embrace of his position as "England's first writer-by-trade."[33] In the brief moment in which he established himself at the center of this newly complex network, Greene published one work that anticipates the epistolary novel, one ripped-from-the-headlines piece of nationalist propaganda, and four popular romances—including one that would become the model for Shakespeare's *Winter's Tale*. He simultaneously traded on his status as an educated man of letters, a slum-dwelling degenerate, and a Christian penitent whose excesses should serve as a cautionary tale. As Lori Humphrey Newcomb suggests, in this way he seems to embody the development of popular print itself: "Greene was shaped by the particularity of his career, from his early scholarly training, through his authorial success, to his growing identification with cheap print as his 'ordinary' means of expression, a biographical trajectory that itself charts the spread of the book."[34]

No other author in these early years of massive network connectivity played so distinctive a role as Robert Greene. But it is worth pausing for a moment on a few others who appear in this newly complex network to help convey a sense of the new literature being disseminated by it. If we move from 1588–89 to 1589–90, for example, new names in the increasingly expansive network visualized in Figure 2.6 include Edmund Spenser and Sir Philip Sidney. If Greene was a proto-bohemian hack, Sidney was the ultimate Renaissance man: an aristocrat, poet, scholar, and courtier who died young enough to leave a beautiful corpse. He appears in the graph during this period because it saw the publication of his most extensive

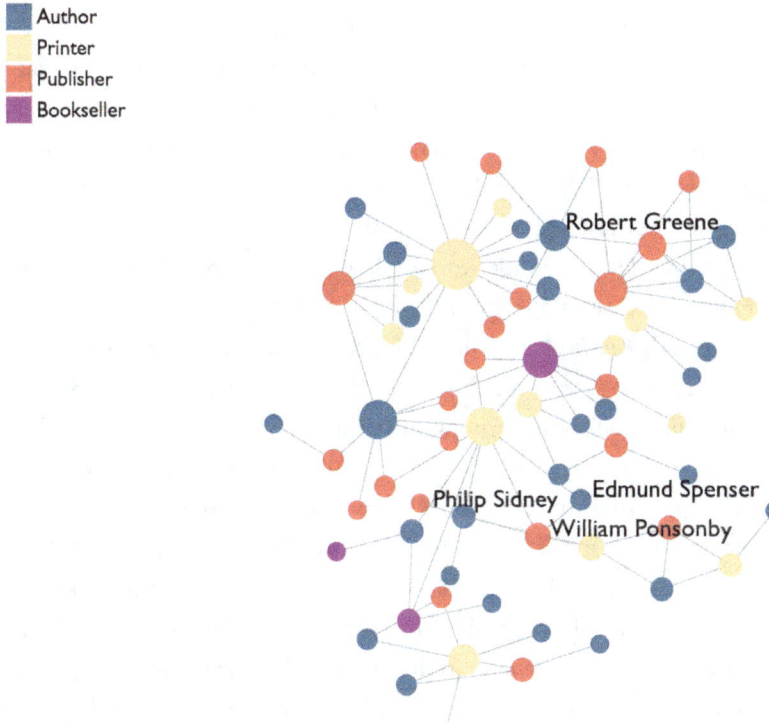

**Figure 2.6** English print network, 1589–1590. Edmund Spenser and Philip Sidney both appear in the graph, connected by William Ponsonby.

work, *The Countess of Pembroke's Arcadia*. This is significant at least in part because Sidney emblematizes a characteristic aristocratic aversion to print authorship or at least preference for manuscript circulation among a select coterie, which avoided any hint of commerce and limited exposure to the common view.[35] But Sidney's death "had stunned the whole nation and quickly aroused the commercial instincts of some members of the Stationers company."[36] The question of how to protect his legacy was accordingly a delicate one for his family, and the stationer William Ponsonby was able to use this to his advantage.

Ponsonby was "remarkable to modern eyes on account of his ability to blend his commercial instincts with genuine literary discrimination," limiting his publications to texts "which could almost always be connected with influential court circles."[37] Astutely, he sent the family news that a rival stationer was about to produce a unauthorized version of the *Arcadia* and made it clear that he would be a better steward of the Protestant hero's literary remains. Their publishing relationship persisted over multiple issues and editions, as Ponsonby built a reputation for quality literary publications, largely on the work of Sidney and the other poet to appear in Figure 2.6, Edmund Spenser.[38]

Spenser's *Faerie Queene* links him to Ponsonby, and through him to Sidney, and it is safe to say this is exactly the sort of association Spenser was hoping to cultivate through the printing of his poem. It was one of the most ambitious works of English verse ever composed, and certainly the most ambitious one conceived explicitly as a print work. In terms of sheer size and scope, it was quite simply "the largest work of English poetry ever seen through the press by a living author."[39] But more than this, it was Spenser's boldest gambit to establish himself as the nation's laureate poet, and his involvement in the printing process included stop-press interventions to secure and advertise his patronage by Walter Raleigh and Queen Elizabeth herself.

Spenser had lost his most prominent early patronage connections, with Sidney and the Earl of Leicester dead and the Lord Deputy of Ireland, Arthur Grey, recalled to England in disgrace.[40] The 1590 edition of *The Faerie Queene* was accordingly a "landmark example of a poet experimenting with print patronage conventions in an innovatory and ambitious way" to repair and transcend these losses.[41] There is good evidence, for example, that Spenser stopped the press to add its dedication to Elizabeth on the verso of the title page, once he secured her patronage.[42] Moreover, Spenser appears to have been "intimately involved" with the production process in those sections of the book that spoke directly or alluded to her and his other patrons.[43] And he procured an orgy of paratextual material to court such patronage, including ten dedicatory sonnets to other aristocratic benefactors; seven commendatory poems by authors including Gabriel Harvey, Walter Raleigh, and others; and a letter from Spenser to Raleigh "expounding his whole intention in the course of this worke."[44] In short, the appearance of Spenser and Sidney in the print network during this moment represents a real shift in the system of cultural production and consumption. Print did not supplant manuscript, but it was becoming an essential tool for making and maintaining connections.

With Ponsonby, Spenser succeeded in situating his epic alongside Sidney's as a central text in the English literary tradition, even if he did not reap the material rewards of this newfound canonicity during his lifetime. That was not the case for the final writer I will mention here, William Shakespeare, although his accumulation of modest wealth owed more to his investment in property and the theatre than to his engagement with print. This, however, does not mean that he had no interest in print authorship, as has sometimes been asserted.[45] Instead, it probably reflects the initially low value—both culturally and materially—of printed plays in the sixteenth century.[46] So, ironically, the author best known to us as England's preeminent playwright first entered print as a patronage-seeking poet, in the mold of Spenser, only to have his reputation reshaped in the years after his death by stationers who promoted his plays. This authorial reconstruction began with Shakespeare's first folio, which unlike Ben Jonson's folio *Works*, did not contain poems. And Adam Hooks has shown that the remaking of Shakespeare as a playwright gathered momentum in the mid-seventeenth century with a series of stationers including Humphrey Moseley, William Leake, Andrew Crooke, and especially Francis Kirkman, who elevated his position as England's preeminent dramatist during the interregnum, when the theatres were closed, and the Restoration, when they were being enthusiastically rediscovered.[47]

But as Lukas Erne has shown, "Shakespeare's arrival in the book trade was sudden and massive," and "the view that Shakespeare was not discovered by the book trade until after his death and that the rise of his reputation was gradual and posthumous is thus precisely wrong."[48] That arrival is marked in Figure 2.7, with Shakespeare connected to the printers Richard Field and John Danter and the booksellers John Harrison, Edward White, and Thomas Millington. The first of these connections was to Field, who grew up in the small market village of Stratford at the same time as Shakespeare and likely attended school with him. Shakespeare's

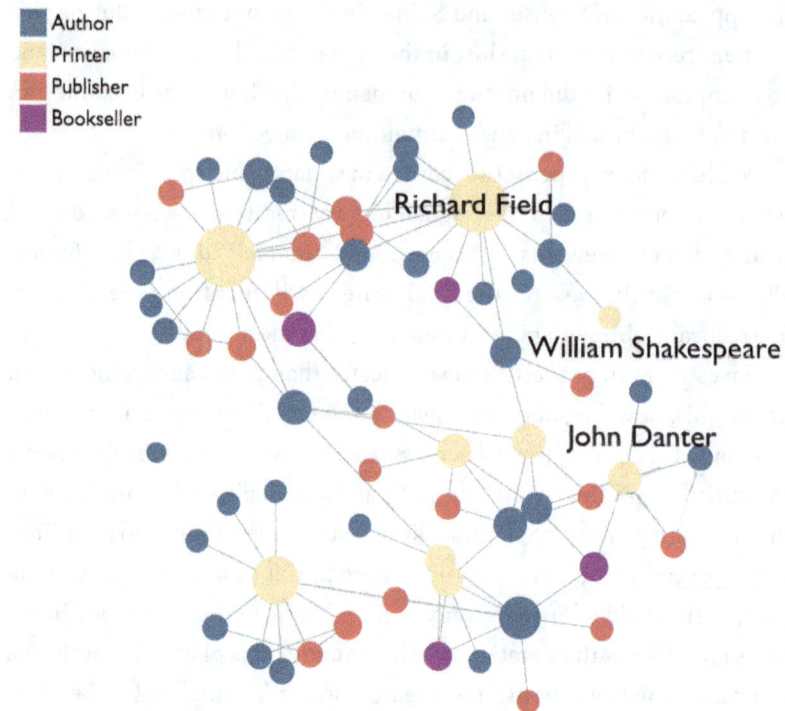

**Figure 2.7** English print network, 1593–1594. William Shakespeare's first published works make an immediate mark on the print network.

"old friend," as Katherine Duncan-Jones has described him, then became his first printer and publisher, producing *Venus and Adonis* in 1593 and *The Rape of Lucrece* in 1594.[49] This made him the first to invest in and present Shakespeare to the public as a print author.[50]

I will discuss Field further in the next chapter, because one of his apprentices, Nicholas Okes, became the era's most connected printer by throwing out much of what he learned in Field's shop. But for now suffice it to say that this was an important early contact. In part, this is because Field printed some of Shakespeare's most important sources, such as *Sir Thomas* North's 1,200-page translation of Plutarch's *Lives*, Ovid's *Metamorphoses*, Sir John Harrington's massive folio translation of *Orlando Furioso*, and Richard Crompton's *Mansion of Magnanimitie*. Some of these texts would have been quite expensive; at 2–3 pounds, the Plutarch would have easily cost a month's salary for a player in one of the leading theatrical companies. And this has suggested to Duncan-Jones that the young Shakespeare may have used Field's shop as "a working library" where he would have had "unlimited access to the historical sources he needed."[51] This may or may not be true, but one thing is indisputable: Field invested in quality, and this is the other reason he was an important connection. His early editions of Shakespeare's works began positioning him as a significant literary figure, rather than as an "upstart crow, beautified with our feathers," as Robert Greene had supposedly called him—a mere actor or maker of plays who did not belong in the same literary company as the Oxbridge men.[52] Field's positioning subsequently influenced the way those plays were marketed and received—and obviously outlasted Greene's sneering dismissal.

This is even more striking when we consider the other printer we see connected to Shakespeare in Figure 2.7, John Danter, who produced the quarto of the playwright's blood-drenched revenge tragedy, *Titus Andronicus*. This was a cheap but competently printed text, probably from Shakespeare's own papers. But to call Danter's reputation "mixed" would be generous. Just three years later, in the same year he pirated an edition of *Romeo and Juliet*, his unauthorized printing practices led the Stationers' Company to raid and destroy his premises.[53] Shakespeare's name does not actually appear on the title page of *Titus Andronicus* at all; instead it is presented as an attempt to capture the ephemeral but exciting performances by the three companies of players that had already staged it. Figure 2.7, in short, captures a telling snapshot of the print network and of Shakespeare's own career at a pivotal moment—poised between the high literary connections of Field, the transience of the theatre, and the disrepute and disorder of Danter. As Hooks writes, "Shakespeare, or rather, the various versions of Shakespeare in print, were created and circulated by commercial networks whose motives were independent of any he may have had."[54]

"Independent" might seem a bit strong. Surely each of the figures we've read had some agency in the placement of their own work. In their own ways, Greene, Sidney, Spenser, and Shakespeare were innovators in poetry, drama, and prose. But at the same time they are powerful examples of writers whose authorial identities were shaped by forces not entirely within their control or even within their own lifetimes: Greene, an early and enthusiastic professional print writer whose "ghost" continued to issue books from his grave; Sidney, an aristocrat whose personal brand became a precious and protected resource after his romantic death; Spenser, a rising poet who saw potential for a new print patronage model he would not live to see fulfilled; and Shakespeare, whose early attempts to establish himself as a print poet enjoying aristocratic patronage were outstripped by demand for printed versions of his plays. In this motley array of figures from wildly different backgrounds and with such wildly different contemporary and subsequent reputations, we can also see just how closely everyone in this network was now connected to everyone else.

### III. Information, Infection, and Wildfire

What are the implications of this new, small-world network of English print? As mentioned in the Introduction, scientists have become fascinated by small-world networks because they exhibit many counterintuitive behaviors, such as a radically uneven distribution of connections that creates some enormous hubs and some small but crucial bridges. They also allow us to find very short paths through systems that otherwise seem dauntingly enormous. We can navigate the internet's billions of pages effectively because it is structured as a small-world network, allowing us to hop from a hub like Google or Wikipedia, to an obscure article about gerbils in Kazakhstan, to an even more obscure hyperlinked article about plague epidemiology. Medics are fascinated by small-world networks because they expose our vulnerability to infectious diseases that can hop within days from a remote village in Africa, to an airport hub, to an Alaskan village. In the early modern print network, this structure makes it possible to trace connections between any two people, no matter how different their religious beliefs, social status, or profession. And in these extended chains of authors, printers, and publishers, we see the material pathways along which influence acted and ideas leapt across ideological, religious, or geographical gulfs. In a digital visualization, a vast, interconnected print network looks like a hairball. But this abstraction reflects real-world developments that we will be exploring throughout this book. It means many books were being produced in collaboration to facilitate speed and evade regulations; it means a handful of bookshops were acting as a hubs, linking an increasingly diverse set of authors, printers, and publishers; it means that any given reader browsing such a shop experienced an expanding world of information, the collision of ideas and cultures, and the proliferation of choice.

The "increased volume of information" now readily available in the early modern period, Rhodes and Sawday observe, made it necessary to develop new systems of navigating and categorizing texts, and "print technology was harnessed to create vast collections of adages, aphorisms, examples, figures of speech, proverbs and similitudes."[55] As Ann Blair notes, the experience of "information overload" was hardly new to the Renaissance, but she argues that the period's readers sought to seek and stockpile information with new intensity, and "the increased scale of compilation and range of sources in turn inspired new methods of working and new kinds of finding devices": an abundance of books about books, encyclopedic texts, and entirely new genres such as printed guides to forming a personal library.[56] In other words, although scholars have become less willing to speak of a print "revolution," we do know that print had major consequences for texts and the experience of reading them. And when we understand that certain changes to the print network really did emerge abruptly and explosively, we can begin to understand why so many early modern people describe those consequences in ways that sound revolutionary rather than evolutionary.

In particular, they clearly had the sensation that dangerous ideas were suddenly and surprisingly able to outpace the efforts of church and state to extinguish them. Although they lacked the language of "networks," and although they lived hundreds of years before the advent of modern epidemiology, they sought to describe the way print was changing their world by invoking metaphors of "pestilence" and "fire"—two phenomena now understood as clear illustrations of phase transitions and small-world behavior. On the continent, where developments in print and the book trade were several decades ahead of the English, Pope Adrian VI warned in 1522 that Luther "daily issues new books replete with errors, heresies, insolence, and sedition" that spread "like a pestilence (*pestem*) pervading the length and breadth of Germany and the adjacent countries." Mixing his metaphors, but staying consistent with the examples of explosive network growth we have seen so far, the pope added that the "helping hands [of] every man" were needed "to quench this public fire" (*commune incendium extinguendum*).[57] Sir Thomas More laments the "pestilent books" of "Luther and his fellows" in "Latin, French, and Dutch" being brought into England, and rightly worries that England's printers are becoming part of an unstoppable plague.[58] Luther not only mockingly quoted the pope's warning in subsequent books, but also characterized the church's use of print in similarly infectious terms. In 1534 the English printer William Marshall published a Lutheran primer complaining about the "innumerable pestilent infections of books and learnings with which the Christian people have been perilously seduced and deceived."[59]

In England, the transformation of the print network into a dangerously connected complex happened later but was no less consequential, as Charles I wrote just before his execution, when he blamed the nation's upheavals on "those rude and scandalous Pamphlets (which like fire in great conflagrations, fly up and down to set all places on like flames)."[60] Even some of the figures most involved in lighting that fire, like the aptly named bookseller Michael Sparke, worried the conflagrations they unleashed could not be controlled. "All cry 'Fire, fire fire,'" he writes, and he implores the Parliament to

> [B]ring out the Engine, come and begin this *Reformation* against base poisonous Popish Books, *against* Conjuring, horrid Blasphemous Books. . . . Execute those your *Acts* (upon such horrid *Books,* as hath been Printed) also set out *Licensing* and *Licensers;* Look to *Peddlers, Hawkers, Running Mercurists* and sellers of *Popish Blasphemous Books.*[61]

The irony is that Sparke had helped create the structure that made this fire so difficult to extinguish. Sparke described himself as a "a *Stationer* and a *wholesaleman*," and the latter term is particularly interesting since, as Adrian Johns has noted, Sparke was "among the first" to use it to describe his bookselling activities in something other than a retail capacity.[62] As I will discuss in a later chapter, this helped make him a hub in the network—someone who was unusually connected to other booksellers, printers, and authors—because he had broken so completely with the older model of mostly vending books that he had some hand in producing. Under the aptly fiery pen name "*Scintilla*," he had also printed a tract for free distribution that launched an all-out attack on monopoly and copyright, which he claimed hindered the spread of knowledge. Promising to shine a light "*Into Dark Warehouses*," the younger Sparke's book had "anatomised and laid open" the practice of "forestalling and ingrossing of Books in Patents, and Raising them to excessive prices," taking aim very directly at books that made up the Stationers' Company's lucrative joint publishing venture, the English Stock, and the monopoly in Bible printing.[63] Because many of these are what we would now consider books in the public domain, like Bibles, Sparke considered their publication part of the public interest and argued that their monopolization "robs the Common-wealth" itself.[64] He proposed a radical liberation of this information for the commons, arguing that "if they will not Print such Copies as are there entred to the Company, it may and shall be free for any to imprint or Import them, until such times they Print them here to furnish the Kingdome."[65] This and other efforts against company and church censorship succeeded so well that Archbishop Laud would later claim "a bitterer enemy, to his power, the Church government never had," than Michael Sparke.[66]

But an older, wealthier Michael Sparke—who by this time had a stake in the Stationers' Company—would reap the whirlwind of his earlier efforts to promote the free circulation of knowledge and find himself publishing another book to counter the "bad" ones that he now saw spreading without control. His hope, with his later publication, was to see them "consumed by this second Beacon set on fire."[67] The metaphor draws from the practice of creating firebreaks by pulling down houses or, in the absolute worst cases, blowing up whole streets in a fire's path to create a gap or break the link of transmission.[68] Without the language or metrics of network science, both the practice and the metaphor demonstrate an acute understanding of network behavior, in particular the uncanny resilience of complex networks. Sparke's anxiety was becoming a common sentiment by the 1640s, when the most astute observers of the print landscape had intuited that this was a network with no obvious center. This meant infectious ideas would have to be combatted by fighting fire with fire or inoculating against infection.

These are the terms, for example, in which the clergyman and member of the Westminster Assembly, George Walker, answered a tract by one of Sparke's most visible and controversial authors, William Prynne. When he first encountered Prynne's *Four Serious Questions*, "fleeing abroad in print into every Book-sellers shop in *London*, and ready upon the wing to take flight into all parts of the land," he worried that it would lead to the "infection of the minds of the vulgar" and felt the need for "composing Antidotes against" it.[69] Some authors even embraced the idea that although their texts were potentially dangerous, they were the only way to prevent greater infection. "Surely this book will infect no man," wrote the English translator of Machiavelli's *The Prince*, Edward Dacres, on the eve of the English Civil War, "since even "poisons ... have their medicinal uses.""[70] And when Parliament tried to close the lid on Pandora's Box by reinstituting pre-publication licensing after it lapsed with the abolition of the Star Chamber in 1641, Milton responded in *Areopagitica* with a similar argument. Since books are "soonest catching to the learned, from whom to the common people whatever is heretical or dissolute may quickly be conveyed," we cannot hope to erase the spread of bad ideas—especially when vendors run daily through the streets hawking "wet sheets" of libels, "for all that licensing can do."[71] In this newly decentered world, Milton suggests that the wise man will view even bad books neither as "temptations, nor vanities, but useful drugs and materials wherewith to temper and compose effective and strong medicines" against infection.[72]

The inability to account for or credit the language of print as a raging fire or explosive epidemic is a weakness of gradualist or evolutionary arguments about print. There are good reasons to question the "notion that print provided a radical historical rupture," and perhaps even to insist, as Christina Haas does, that "print's effects are initially not noticeable at all, and later are only gradual."[73] But to import a sentiment from actor-network theory into the realm of network analysis, we must learn to let actors speak in their own terms and "to resist," as Bruno Latour puts it, "the idea that there exists somewhere a dictionary where all the variegated words of the actors can be translated into" a critical vocabulary that we use to expose the false consciousness behind the expression.[74] When we let Renaissance actors speak, we clearly hear them connecting print technology with the infectious "swarms of new books" that Erasmus feared were corrupting reader's minds and distracting them from the classics.[75] "We live in a printing age," wrote the author of the anti-papist tract *Martine Mar-Sixtus*,

> [W]herein there is no man either so vainly, or factiously, or filthily disposed, but there are crept out of all sorts unauthorized authors, to fill and fit his humour, and if a man's devotion serve him not to go to the Church of God, he need but repair to a Stationer's shop and read a sermon of the devil's: I loath to speak it, every red-nosed rimester is an author, every drunken man's dream is a book.[76]

Even the authors of those books, like the prolific and notorious pamphleteer Thomas Nashe, cautioned in 1592 that "one bad pamphlet is enough to raise a damp that may poison a whole Term," warning "Booksellers and Stationers" lest their "shops be infected."[77]

These are the voices of people who lived through revolution, not evolution. Their communication and social networks were reshaped as surely and as vertiginously as our own have been during the leap from typewriters to microcomputers. The language of epidemic and fire does not necessarily testify to a new volume of books, or even necessarily to the newness of their ideas. Much of what was now most controversial, from Lucretian physics, to Copernican astronomy, to Wycliffite iconoclasm, had been proposed decades or centuries earlier. What is new is a sudden sense of the ubiquity of such heretical books, a confused forest of interlocking branches, a shop catering to every taste or connecting every wayward reader with a devilish idea. Even in years where the number of titles published stayed the same—or declined as it appears to have done between 1604-1605, 1607, and 1608—the impact of increasing collaboration, and an increasingly connected network, was more titles available in more shops, combined with more efficient production of timely material.

Perhaps rather than the language of Renaissance that was once used to describe the literary and cultural moment now more typically called early modernity, it would be useful to think in terms of phase transition. The late sixteenth and seventeenth centuries are an "early modern" period, in part, because they ushered in a set of complex, pervasive networks of textual communication with real parallels in our own hyperconnected communications age.[78] As the disgruntled printer and small-time playwright Henry Chettle explained, suddenly "every corner of cities and market towns of the realm" was overrun with "ballads and pamphlets full of ribaldry and all scurrilous vanity, to the prophanation of God's name, especially at fairs, markets, and such public meetings."[79] Although much of this printing originated in London, it was becoming a network with no clear boundaries between center and periphery. Michael Sparke shipped books to Bermuda and Virginia, while provincial booksellers and printers set up shop in Dublin, Edinburgh, Worcester, Norwich, Exeter, and Plymouth, and traveling vendors sold pamphlets and broadsides in every corner of the kingdom.

Chettle sardonically names the ballad singer in his own book "Anthony Now Now," indicating just how insistently this print network depended on spreading news, literally "new things." Like the rest of his contemporaries, Chettle (who printed the tract describing Shakespeare as an "upstart crow," and who later apologized) lacked the vocabulary of the "network" to describe what he was witnessing and helping to perpetuate. Instead, he turned to metaphors of the body, of rivers and their branches, and of the speed and virulence through which infection spread through such systems. "They that intend to infect a river, poison the fountain," Chettle warns. And he notes that just "two or three" printers can push the infection past a tipping point, releasing "a flock of Runagates" that "overspread the face of this land." In the next chapter, we will explore how such infection worked by going to some of the heads of the fountain, or as we would call them now, the hubs of the network.

## CHAPTER 3   HUBS IN THE NETWORK

Nicholas Okes and the Making
of Infectious Information

**IN SMALL-WORLD NETWORKS,** as we have seen, illness, fire, and information can spread quickly because all nodes—whether they are trees, people, or computers—are connected with only a few degrees of separation. We have also seen that when contemporaries sought to describe the way the evolution of printing and selling books was changing their world, they intuited the dynamics of this structural shift, employing metaphors of diseases and fires that emerge suddenly and move quickly and relentlessly. One person who noted the phase transition documented in the previous chapter was Henry Chettle, who straddled the roles of playwright, pamphleteer, and stationer, and whose uniquely "modern" editorial and journalistic practices have been described as an important contribution to the "invention of the commodified literary author."[1] A keen observer of the print network, he complained that suddenly "every corner of cities and market towns of the realm" was overrun with "ballads and pamphlets full of ribaldry and all scurrilous vanity," and he perceptively noted that just "two or three" printers, in this newly connected world, could unleash a pestilence that would "overspread the face of this land."[2] With his sense that just two or three individuals could play a hugely outsized role in a very complex system, Chettle had intuited one of the most fascinating characteristics of network behavior, which this chapter will illuminate. To do so, I will begin with an analysis of the English print network between 1564—when Chettle, Christopher Marlowe, and Shakespeare were born—and 1616 when Shakespeare died and Ben Jonson published his folio *Works*. During this hugely important period in the development of English literature, who were the most highly connected individuals in the book trade? And how did the changes they brought to that network shape the flow of information in the years leading up to the English Civil War? The answers to these questions will force us to reevaluate the legacy of stationers who have mostly been described as bit players in a history in which they were, in fact, surprisingly central.

## I. Hubs and Superconnectors in the English Print Network

Chapter 1 showed that many real-world networks are incredibly robust because their degree distribution is incredibly uneven. If we randomly shut down a US airport, it is statistically much more likely to be one of the 13,000 local or regional ones offering a few flights per day than one of the 30 hubs that handle the vast majority of traffic, so most flights will still get where they are going. Such networks are often described as "scale free" because they contain a handful of outliers with a disproportionally high degree of connections, compared to what we'd expect in a normal distribution of connections in a random network.[3] If connections were distributed randomly, degree distribution would follow a normal, or Gaussian, curve, in which a few nodes were poorly connected, a few were very well connected, but most were somewhere in the middle (Figure 3.1).

But the networks that have been of most interest to network scientists in recent years do not follow this pattern at all. Whether we are exploring the connections between airports, between pages in the World Wide

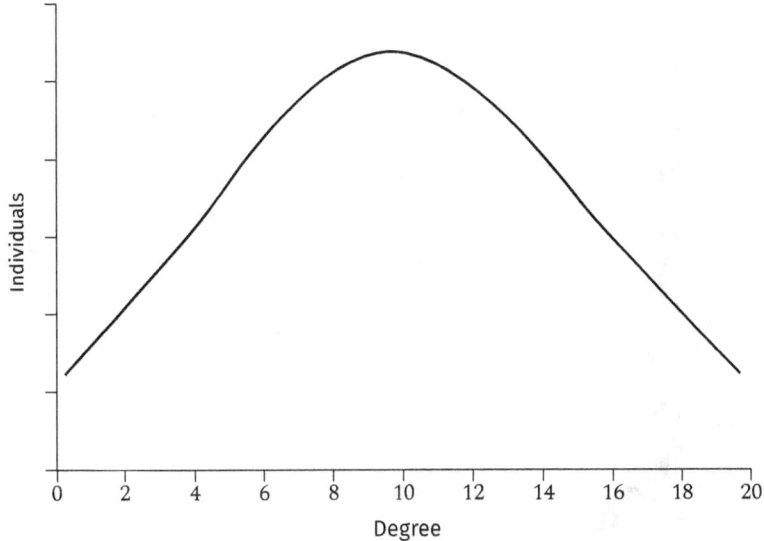

**Figure 3.1** In a random network, the average degree would lie at the peak of the curve, with few extremes on either side.

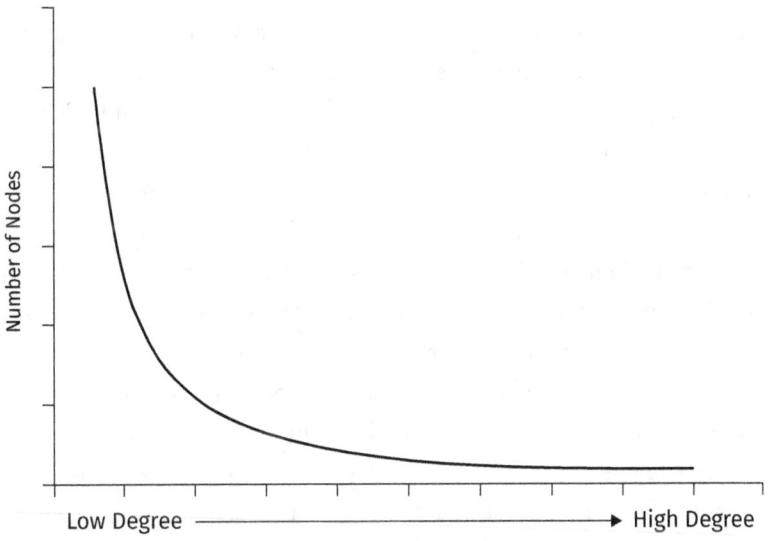

**Figure 3.2** In a scale-free or power-law distribution, most nodes have low degree relative to a long tail of very few nodes with vastly more connections.

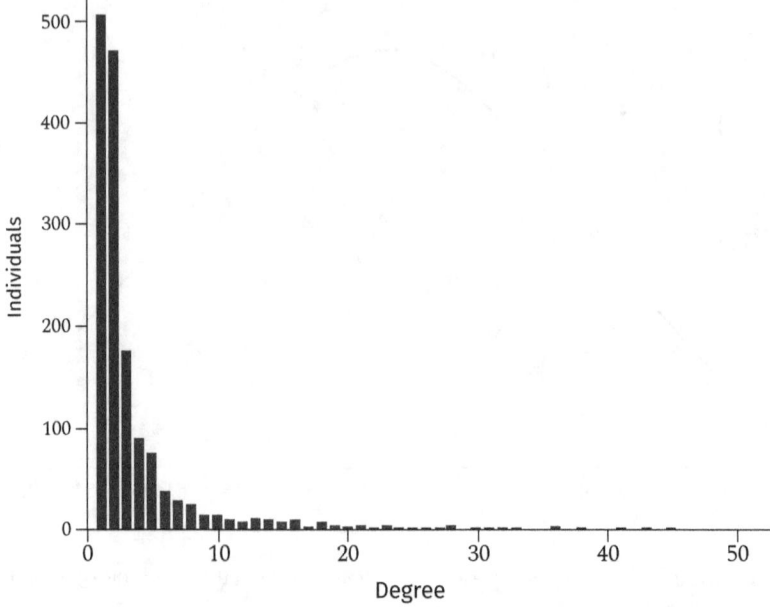

**Figure 3.3** Degree distribution of the English print network, 1564–1616. Cutoff is 50, leaving the highest-degree nodes "off the chart."

Web, or between actors in the IMDb, we find a power law distribution, as in Figure 3.2. In such networks, most nodes have only a few connections while a very few are hyperconnected, as witnessed by the graph's "long tail" (for every website like Wikipedia, linked to by millions of readers, there are scores of lonely blogs lying fallow and unread). The English print network from 1564–1616 shares this type of degree distribution (Figure 3.3). A vanishingly small number of individuals at the far right end of the chart have many dozens or hundreds more connections than the majority of individuals, who have somewhere between 1 and 10.

In fact, the tail is so long that it can't really be represented in this type of chart, which is why such degree distributions are usually represented on a log-log plot, as found in Figure 3.4. Unlike linear scales, where each step along the x or y axis represents a constant value (1, 5, 10, etc.), a log-log plot uses a logarithmic scale, so that each step along the axis is a multiple of the previous value ($10^1$, $10^2$, $10^3$, etc.). Since they are based on orders of magnitude, log-log plots are better at displaying large ranges than standard

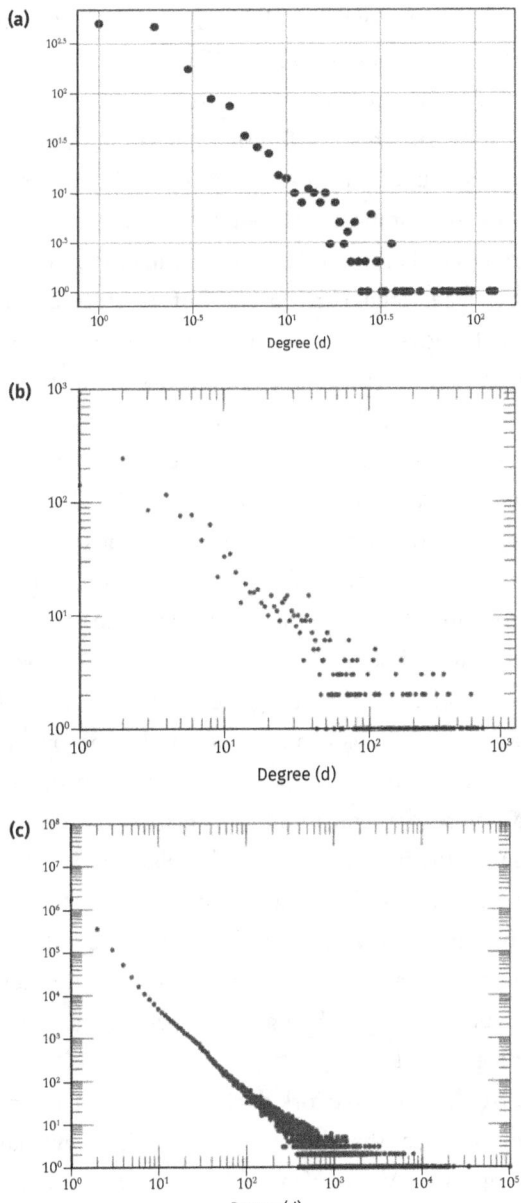

**Figure 3.4** (a) Degree distribution of English print network, 1564–1616; (b) degree distribution of US airports; (c) degree distribution of Wikipedia pages.

SOURCE: Airport and web data adapted from the Koblenz Network Collection: Jérôme Kunegis, "KONECT—The Koblenz Network Collection," in *Proceedings of the 22nd International Conference on the World Wide Web* (New York: ACM, 2013), 1343–1350.

linear scales, and when a given variable changes as a *power* of another, they display a straight line, as in the charts in Figure 3.4.

Such degree distributions are so common in large networks that they are not, in themselves, interesting. But they have important consequences for the way networks function and the way people, in the case of the English print network, function within them. First, scale-free networks demonstrate the principle of preferential attachment, or the rule that the "rich get richer." The rich get richer partly because of structural advantages associated with growth (the first two settlements in a province will need a road between them, and as new villages are established on the frontier, they will typically link back to the established settlements). The most recent node to join the system will always be the poorest, in terms of connections. But the rich also get richer because of preference associated with that growth. In a network such as this, a stationer with many connections is more likely to be chosen by an author seeking to publish her book. After all, it is more likely that one of the author's friends would have published with that stationer or that the author would be familiar with that stationer's work from the books in her own home. All other things being equal, a printer with a high degree and many connections is more likely to be approached by a new bookseller who needs to get a pamphlet or book produced quickly. After all, those many connections mean that this printer is more likely to have worked with one of the bookseller's friends, relatives, or colleagues. And by the same principle, an author with many connections is more likely to find her work in demand by a publisher than an author whose work is an unknown quantity. In networks like this, the fact that the rich get richer has at least as much to do with being in the right place at the right time as it does with merit or skill.[4]

If we visualize the print network during this period as a map, scaling nodes by degree, it is clear that this is a network with a few major hubs, as can be seen in Figure 3.5. Viewed from this perspective, it is also clear that while such networks are resilient against random node loss, they would be vulnerable to targeted attacks on the hubs. Removing only a few can quickly fragment such a network. Chettle realized this too, turning for his metaphor to one of the natural structures that have recently been of interest to network scientists: a river system.[5] "They that intend to infect a river," warned Chettle, "poison the fountain."[6] Chettle was elaborating his point that a few bad actors could spread pestilence throughout the land, but he was also intuiting the logic of targeted attack. This logic can also frame our exploration of the network in this chapter. If someone were to launch an attack on the print network, who would be the high-value targets? If someone wanted to stop the spread of dangerous ideas—the sort of ideas that pitched a newly united British kingdom into civil war in the mid-seventeenth century—who would they need to eliminate?

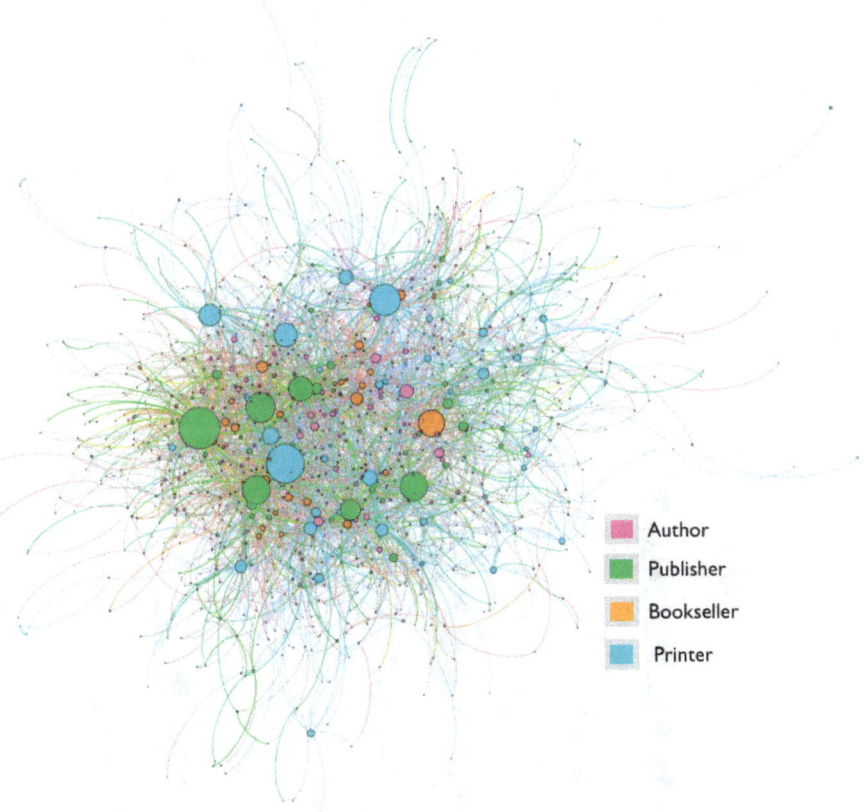

**Figure 3.5** People in the English print network, 1564–1616. Although there are far more authors, the stationers—such as printers and publishers—are the obvious hubs.

Looking at the network map in Figure 3.5, we see that they are stationers—particularly printers and publishers. This is perhaps overly obvious, since a typical printer would clearly be involved with far more books in a given year than an author. But out of all the thousands of stationers involved in the book trade during this period, only a handful really stand out as the true hubs. Who are the 10 most connected? This is much less obvious and much more surprising. Figure 3.6 shows the 10 most connected hubs, and if we compare it to the graph of overall degree distribution in Figure 3.3, we see that all of these names would literally be off the chart. And yet, as Figure 3.6 also shows, over half of them have no entry in the *Oxford Dictionary of National Biography* (ODNB)—a work that has long purported to be "the national record of men and women who have shaped British history and culture."[7] That may not be entirely surprising, since the ODNB has usually included biographies of printers, booksellers, and publishers in this period only if they had sustained contact with a handful of canonical authors, especially Shakespeare. But for precisely that reason, such examples help demonstrate the potential of network analysis to reorient our understanding of cultural history and reconsider the agents and agencies involved in making it.

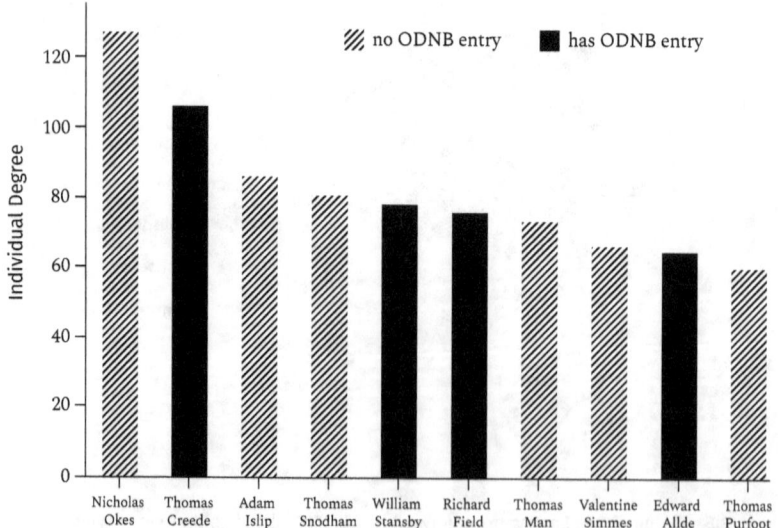

**Figure 3.6** The 10 highest-degree people in the English print network during Shakespeare's lifetime, 1564–1616.

The person at the top of Figure 3.6, Nicholas Okes, is a useful case study. He's an outlier even among printers and booksellers, with twice as many connections as some of the others in the top 10. During his own active time as printer, 1607-1637, the results of a ranking by degree are even more dramatic, with Okes towering above his more famous contemporaries. Although Okes has no entry in the ONDB (as of July 2020), he is known in a small corner of literary studies, almost exclusively because he printed the first quarto versions of Shakespeare's *King Lear* (1608) and *Othello* (1622), works that exist in substantially different versions in the 1623 folio of Shakespeare's works. But although his sometimes-slipshod work on the quartos has made him the subject of some speculation, much derision, and extensive bibliographic work, his larger role in the print network has been misunderstood. For example, the editor of the Arden *Othello*—E. A. J. Honigmann—explicitly contrasts Okes with the "well-connected stationer" Thomas Snodham, who is fourth on the list in Figure 3.6, and who published Ben Jonson, John Donne, Sir Walter Raleigh, and Francis Bacon.[8] While both that list and Figure 3.6 clearly show that Snodham *is* a well-connected part of the print network—and while it is also clear that Honigmann uses "well connected" in a more anecdotal sense to mean something like "respectable"—this also helps illustrate the way critics have brought a level of casual disregard to the career of another stationer who was exceptionally "well connected" in a different sense. Generally, critical appraisals of Okes have not been kind: He was a "notoriously sharp operator" with a penchant "for printing pirated work," or simply an "inferior printer."[9]

Most recently, the Shakespeare scholar Brian Vickers took both the speculation about Okes and the derision of his work to new levels in his book, *The One King Lear,* where he pins the blame on Okes for shattering what he sees as Shakespeare's originally seamless design. *Lear* was the first play Okes printed, and in Vickers's account it was riddled with rookie mistakes: "Okes muddled" the distinctions between verse and prose; "Okes may have been unaware of the theatrical convention of direct address," inadvertently cutting some asides because he did not recognize their relevance; and "the typesetting practiced by Okes and his compositors . . .

can best be described as directionless."¹⁰ But Okes's original sin, according to Vickers, was to underestimate the amount of paper needed to print the play. The "cuts in the 1608 Quarto were made to save space in consequence of Okes's potentially disastrous underestimate of the paper quantity."¹¹ This led to "desperate remedies" to make the text fit on 10½ sheets, including the omission of whole swaths of the play.¹² A total of 102 lines from Shakespeare's original manuscript were cut, according to Vickers, only to be restored with the 1623 folio—which unfortunately introduced cuts of its own—meaning that modern editors must conflate the two editions to return to Shakespeare's original intent. Quoting Adrian Weiss, Vickers reminds us that early printers were, after all, "coarse, uneducated tradesmen who laboured hard and long for their keep," and they lacked the "refined taste" that, presumably, Shakespeare and his modern editors would share.¹³

The problem with this argument is that Vickers's Okes, like the unified text the printer allegedly cut to save space, is almost wholly a product of Vickers's imagination. To be clear, no early manuscript exists of *King Lear* in Shakespeare's hand; we only have the printed editions. And those printed editions simply do not tell the story that Vickers wants them to. The 1608 quarto, for example, includes more than enough paper to contain Vickers's imaginary text without resorting to wholesale cuts. To cite the most obvious example, while most pages contain 38 lines, two pages contain 39: Simply by printing the extra line throughout Okes could have added 77 additional lines. He also did not *need* to include a large "*Finis*" on the final page, or to take up a full third of the first page by reusing the large title page font and an ornament to announce "William Shak-speare / His / Historie, of King Lear." And it is puzzling why, after apparently discovering in the second and third sheets that he could pack more type into less paper by switching from the narrow measure to the large measure and printing verse as prose, he would keep forgetting this lesson and essentially abandon it in the next three sheets, where he would instead continue to make wholesale cuts to the manuscript. Finally, although it was common to do so, Okes also did not need to include a full blank page preceding the title blank to protect the book from stains before binding, nor did he need an entire blank page after the final "*Finis*" for the same reason.¹⁴ In short, on the 10½ sheets of paper that he used, Okes could have easily found room for double the number of lines that Vickers claims he was forced to cut.[15] To put this another way, if he had maintained the rate of compression that he achieved in sheets C and D (via printing verse as prose and condensing short exchanges of dialogue onto the same line), Okes could have printed *Lear* on *nine* sheets. The story of Okes desperately cutting 102 lines from a 3,000-line text, to make it fit into 10½ sheets, is a work of fiction, with Okes cast as the bumbling villain.

Peter Blayney, who wrote the monumental *Texts of King Lear and Their Origins,* knows Okes's career better than anyone, and sums up the case by saying that Okes "was inexperienced, not stupid."[16] Instead, he suggests that Vickers is the one who misunderstands how an early modern printshop worked or what it would mean to save space within one. But if Okes is not of historical interest because he botched the printing of *King Lear* and gave us a fundamentally altered text, is he of interest at all? It is worth noting that without the broader view that network analysis affords, even Okes's chief chronicler and defender is ambivalent about this question. At the end of nearly 300 pages of analysis of Okes's work on *King Lear* and other texts, Blayney sounds downright apologetic about turning our attention to so humble an object in the first place:

> The documentary basis of the character-sketch ... could have been presented as an appendix with minimal commentary, but Okes is of some interest in the wider context of Jacobean play-printing. He was a less respected member of the Stationers' Company than were Jaggard, Kingston, and Purfoot; ran a smaller establishment than did Allde, Beale, and Eld; and seems on the whole to have been a little more law-abiding than Raworth, Stansby, and his own partner, John Norton. But he can in several ways be considered usefully representative of the printers responsible for many of the more important pre-Restoration play-quartos, and deserves a little more than a mere calendar of documents.[17]

The Nicholas Okes revealed through network analysis stands in stark contrast to this modest character, of whom Blayney more pointedly remarks elsewhere that there is "obviously no way in which he can be considered at all exceptional."[18] As we've established, when observed in a context much broader than Jacobean play-printing, his extraordinary connectivity means he is not "representative" at all, and might better be described as a complete anomaly.

It is worth learning why, because the one thing that both Blayney and Vickers agree upon is that a printer's decisions really do matter in the transmission of texts and the shaping of literary history. "Any printer whose presses were not starved of work would have been able to exercise his own preferences (both personal and literary) when choosing between available offers of work," says Blayney. "Price, speed, and workmanship were important factors, but even they cannot be fully dissociated from the master printer's personality."[19] Like most printers, Okes not only exercised agency in what he chose to print, but he also often acted in a publisher-printer role, procuring texts himself. A closer look at Okes's career will help explain what sets him apart and will show that, as a networked theory of viral transmission would predict, his facility for forging connections gave him an important role in defining a field of print authorship and communicating important, dangerous, and disruptive ideas. Alternately painted as a hero and an opportunist by his contemporaries, Okes helped start fires that could not be put out—including one that would consume England's highest church official, Archbishop Laud, during the Civil War. This was only the most spectacular of the many trials to which Okes found himself a witness, in a world he helped turn upside down.

### II. The Early Career of Nicholas Okes: Making Connections

Nicholas was the son of John Okes, a member of London's Company of Horners. Judging from the will that he made in 1614, John had evidently prospered in the trade of making and selling products made of horn, which could be beaten into translucent sheets for use in windows, lanterns, and the small hornbooks with which children learned their alphabet. As the emerging glass industry made inroads on the horner's craft, John wisely invested in London property and destined his son for a career in print.[20] Actually, Nicholas was the second son destined for this career.

His older brother Peter was initially apprenticed to the apparently torpid shop of the stationer William King, who left little trace in the records.²¹ But Peter evidently had a taste for adventure and left both the apprenticeship and the country. Nicholas took his place on 25 March 1596, although he soon transferred his apprenticeship to the thriving shop of Richard Field, who granted Okes his freedom on 5 December 1603. Field himself is sixth on the list of most connected stationers 1564–1616, and one of the best-known members of that list, largely because of his association with William Shakespeare. As mentioned in Chapter 2, Field grew up in Stratford at the same time as Shakespeare and then became his first printer and publisher, producing *Venus and Adonis* in 1583 and *The Rape of Lucrece* in 1584. But just as significantly, Field printed some of Shakespeare's most important sources: expansive, expensive books, such as North's 1,200-page translation of Plutarch's *Lives*, Ovid's *Metamorphoses*, Sir John Harrington's massive folio translation of *Orlando Furioso*, and Richard Crompton's *Mansion of Magnanimitie*. In fact, Shakespeare's poems were something of an anomaly for Field, as "the only original vernacular poetry" he had published—more typical volumes of poetry to issue from his shop were Thomas Campion's Latin *Poemata* and Petruccio Ubaldini's Italian *Rime*.²²

In other words, whether or not Katherine Duncan-Jones is correct that the young Shakespeare may have used Field's shop as "a working library," we can say with more certainty that *Okes* trained in a shop known for producing serious books and quality work, often for upmarket readers.²³ Surviving printer's copies show that the queen's godson, John Harrington, worked closely with Field on the book design for both his lavish *Orlando Furioso* and his notorious *Ajax* pamphlets, which were produced during Okes's apprenticeship.²⁴ This seems to have been a special case rather than an indication that Field was running a courtly salon, but Okes was clearly not being trained to become the "coarse, uneducated tradesman" of Vickers's imagination. Between 1596, when Okes was apprenticed, and 1603, when he was freed, Field's shop printed the first complete edition of Spenser's *Faerie Queene*, Plutarch's *Lives*, Cicero's *De Offici* and *Sententiae*, as well as John Calvin's *Institutes of the Christian Religion*, Martin Luther's

*Commentary on the Epistle of Paul to the Galatians*, King James's *Basilikon Doron*, and many more serious literary and theological works. In their own ways, all of these books demanded skill and care.

Okes's career after his apprenticeship, however, would bear little resemblance to his master's. A young man in a hurry, he applied for a license to marry Elizabeth Beswick within three days of gaining his freedom. She soon gave birth to a son, while he quickly moved to set up his own shop. Paul Mulholland has speculated that the Stationers' Company "appears to have been reluctant" to give full control of a printing shop, and the status of Master Printer, to the 27-year-old Okes, who had only three years of experience beyond his apprenticeship.[25] But if this was the case, Okes circumvented them by taking control, in stages, of the rather sleepy operation run by two brothers, George and Lionel Snowdon. On 29 January 1607, Okes bought Lionel's junior share in the shop. On 13 April, he took control of George's remaining share, and he immediately transformed the shop into a very different sort of operation.[26]

On the day Okes became George Snowdon's partner, the shop was printing a very lengthy book with 35½ sheets.[27] The shop's average book size was 20½ sheets, which was substantial, although a bit smaller than the average of 29 sheets per book in Richard Field's shop during the last year of Okes's apprenticeship. After Oakes became a partner in the Snowdon shop, no book for the rest of the year would exceed 13 sheets, and the year's average was 7½ sheets per book. A printshop was mechanically constrained in the absolute number of sheets it could produce; an "hour" of printing was equal to 250 impressions, and while a shop with a single press could theoretically set and produce books with 300 edition-sheets of type per year, the actual number was usually under 200.[28] Okes's key decision was to divide those sheets in a new way. How dramatic was the change? In the year in which he took over the shop, Okes printed as many titles as the Snowdons had during their entire careers. This radical operational shift set the pace for the rest of Okes's long working life, during which he would rarely print books that required more than 20 sheets. These books were not the most poorly printed in London, but they also lack the attention to detail found in books produced by a printer like Field.

Incomplete inking, battered type, and other signs of slapdash production abound in Okes's books. We could observe only that quality suffered, but considering his training and the fact of his long and busy career, it seems more appropriate to say that Okes sacrificed quality on the altar of speed.

When he did work on larger books, Okes was far more likely to share that work with other printers than either his master or his former partner. Sharing was standard practice—a bookseller who wanted a timely book printed quickly could divide it among multiple printers, and works belonging to the Stationers' Company were often distributed in a way that kept needy printers occupied. But tracing co-occurrence in the ESTC metadata, we see that Okes was more than twice as likely to be involved in shared work than most of his contemporaries. A comparison with Field is especially useful not only because Okes trained under him, but also because they both enjoyed long and overlapping careers. Okes printed his first book in 1607 and his last in 1637, a period of 30 years in which he shared work with 27 other printers; Field printed his first book in 1588, and his last appeared (posthumously) in 1625—a period of 37 years during which he shared work with 11 other printers, including his former apprentice.[29] Okes clearly believed that publishers would pay a premium for speed, or at least that the promise of meeting early deadlines would help him procure and retain their custom, and he reconfigured his shop to meet this demand.

Along with this shift in format and method, Okes's books marked a decided shift in tone and content from the Snowdon printing house. In the two years preceding Okes's partnership and takeover of the business, a representative sample of the Snowdons' work included Philemon Holland's massive folio translation of Suetonius's *De Vita Caesarum*, William Bucanus's monumental *Institutions of Christian Religion*, a substantial Latin New Testament, and various other sermons, moral treatises, and instructional guides. Okes, by contrast, would make his career printing fare like *A True Relation of a Barbarous and Most Cruel Murder, Committed by One Enoch ap Evan, Who Cut Off His Own Natural Mother's Head, and His Brother's*, which sported both a pious epigraph from Ovid's *Fasti* and a ghoulish woodcut of the smirking decapitator.[30] Showing little inclination to produce expansive systematic theologies or necessarily meticulous sacred texts, Okes could instead churn out timely sermons, plays, satires, works of controversy, and humor. Almost overnight, his shop became a destination for publishers of small and sensational books that would make a quick profit, often by responding to very contemporary events.

Soon after taking complete control of the shop, for example, he printed the explosive *Lord Coke His Speech and Charge*. This was the first of many works Okes would produce for the rising publisher Nathaniel Butter, and the eight sheets were divided for speed (and perhaps for discretion) between Okes and his fellow printer Robert Raworth. The pamphlet was the opening volley in a prolonged campaign that "elevated [Sir Edward] Coke to the status of an idealized, independent, judicial figure who could be used as a figure of opposition to the growing arbitrariness of the crown."[31] It recounted a speech given by Coke at the Norwich Assizes on 4 August 1606, in which he detailed Catholic plots from 1569 to the present and marked them, along with corruption in the judiciary itself, as existential threats to James's Protestant rule. Coke's charge was for the assize judges to do their duty in rooting out corruption from the realm, which would seem inoffensive enough, except that Coke framed the charge in terms that directly challenged the doctrine of absolute monarchy that James was working to promote: "[T]he *King's* Majesty at his Coronation is sworn to do Justice unto all his Subjects, which in his own Person it is impossible to perform. And therefore his Highness is constrained by his *Ministers, Deputies, Justices,* and *Judges,* to administer Justice unto all his people."[32] Shortly after publication, Coke disavowed the text, maintaining that it had actually been written, or so badly misreported that it might as well have been written, by the anti-Catholic pamphleteer Robert Pricket. The controversy and subsequent efforts to suppress the text do not seem to have hurt its popularity and probably fueled it.[33] It quickly went through two issues and exists in several different states, testifying that both shops were working speedily to keep production moving even as circumstances shifted.

Although Coke (or "Coke") declaims in his speech against monopolists, alchemists, and "the abuse of stage players," his speech in fact borrows liberally from John of Gaunt's description of "this sceptered isle" in Shakespeare's *Richard II*, demonstrating, as Paul Raffield has noted, that "law and literature of the early modern period ... inhabited a common rhetorical schema."[34] They also inhabited, and appealed to, a common print market, with Okes and Butter producing both Coke's speech and *Lear*, where the mad king promises to "arraign" his daughters before the "most learned Justice" Tom-of-Bedlam in a travestied courtroom scene.[35] For a printer and publisher catering to this market, the kinds of generic boundaries we might tend to draw between a play quarto and a speech by a chief justice mattered less than shared demand for short, timely works that could be consumed in one or two sittings. Timeliness is the most common thread of the works produced by Okes, and this seems to be by design. An edition of Plutarch's *Lives* or a new translation of the Bible might be a major publication event with a ready audience, but the sales of such extensive (and expensive) works did not depend on a moment of contemporary controversy or the production of an especially popular play. By contrast, the works that Okes printed were especially likely to be connected to such events or to take advantage of methods that we would now describe as "cross-media marketing"—methods that Tiffany Stern has suggested were also used to cross-promote plays and the cheap, popular ballads that were based on or connected to them.[36]

Again, comparison with Field is useful. While it was not the runaway success of *Venus and Adonis*, Shakespeare's *Lucrece* had been reliably reprinted for several years after Field produced the first edition for John Harrison, in 1594, to be sold in his shop at the sign of the White Greyhound.[37] But demand seems to have flagged after the fourth quarto of 1600, and no further edition appeared until after Thomas Heywood's play, *Rape of Lucrece*, brought the story to the stage of the Red Bull in or around 1607. Heywood's bizarre play alternately treats Lucrece's rape and suicide as the stuff of tragedy and of broad, bawdy comedy—and has presented something of a problem to critics who have found its prurient moments problematic or simply distasteful. But it was "clearly one of Heywood's most successful plays."[38] In an apparent effort to capture part of this newly invigorated market, John Harrison had Okes produce the fifth quarto of Shakespeare's poem in the summer of 1607.[39] Unlike Field, who did not print plays, Okes then went on to print Heywood's version too, in 1608, to be sold by Nathaniel Butter. This kind of cross-pollination is everywhere in the work of Okes's first year. To cite one more example: In 1605, Francis Faulkner entered a book in the Stationers' Register called *The Jests of George Peele*; Thomas Middleton apparently gained access to the manuscript shortly thereafter and used it to write *The Puritan*, which introduced the scholarly trickster Peele to the stage in 1606; George Eld printed Middleton's play in 1607 (with an attribution to "W.S." surely intended to boost sales), while Okes simultaneously printed a prose collection of *The Merrie Conceited Jests of George Peele, Gentleman* for Faulkner in that same year, providing a much more extensive account of the "lecherous animal" and grifter who had now officially transformed from a historical personage to a contemporary legend and stage event.[40]

Okes concluded his first year as master of a printing house working on texts that included *Belman of London* and *King Lear*, neither of which would appear until 1608, but both of which would include title page announcements of their up-to-the-minute relevance (the former for "bringing to light the most notorious villainies that are now practiced in the Kingdome" and the latter "as it was played before the King's Majesty at Whitehall upon S. Stephan's Night in Christmas Holidays"). Some of the publishers that Okes was working with during this time have been the subject of recent critical reevaluations that might also help put the activities of Okes's first year in perspective. Butter, for example, has often been described as one of "the sort of people who were clapped in jail for piratical printing" and who "stigmatized the print with their own vulgarity."[41] But Zachary Lesser suggests that it is better to understand him not as someone who brought stigma to print, but as a "specialist" who was astutely aware of readers' demands and adept at finding texts to meet those demands.[42]

Butter entered *King Lear* in the Stationers' Register with John Busby, who would also be the publisher of Heywood's *Rape of Lucrece* and who has likewise been called a "notorious pirate" precisely because his attachment to texts often seems to have been brief and mysterious, as it was with *Lear*.[43] But as Gerald D. Johnson has argued, Busby never actually infringed a copyright, and as Lukas Erne has added, a "sharp generic and chronological division in Busby's activities suggests that he took a conscious decision in or around 1599 to change his publishing profile" in a way that allowed him to focus on purchasing the copyrights to playbooks and then sharing the risks and costs of publication, or selling them for a profit.[44] In the work of his first year, Okes looks less like an outlaw or an incompetent than a fellow innovator: He came from a fairly well-to-do family, he was well capitalized enough to gain control of his own shop at a very young age, and he determined to change that shop's profile completely. Such a dramatic change to his printshop—and one that registers so clearly on the larger print network—was not a simple matter of chance, but a motivated response to a market demand that was either not being met or that Okes thought he could meet better than his fellow printers. His strategy was successful enough to keep him doing steady business for the next 30 years and allow him to set up his son in his own profession. Along the way, as Paul Mulholland has noted, he brought to press "an unmatched range and quantity of works of literary and theatrical distinction," as well as a number of documents that the authorities tried, and failed, to keep from spreading like wildfire throughout the land.[45]

Although none of these works would be considered especially fine examples of early modern printing, it would also be a mistake to imply that in configuring his shop for speed and low costs Okes routinely mutilated texts or produced works or unacceptably low quality. The fact that so many publishers and authors brought him their work for so long implies otherwise, and Heywood even made a point of comparing Okes's work favorably with William Jaggard's in an open letter "to my approved good Friend, Mr. Nicholas Okes," attached to the 1612 edition of *Apology for Actors*. Heywood writes the letter in part to settle scores with Jaggard, so his praise for Okes's "honest endeavors" may be exaggerated, but the letter warrants an extended quotation to capture a contemporary glimpse of two printshops at work:

> [I]nfinite faults escaped in my book of *Britain's Troy*, by the negligence of the Printer, as the misquotations, mistaking of sillables, misplacing half lines, coining of strange and never heard of words. These being without number, when I would have taken a particular account of the *Errata*, the Printer answered me, he would not publish

his own disworkemanship, but rather let his own fault lie upon the neck of the Author: and being fearful that others of his quality, had been of the same nature, and condition, and finding you on the contrary, so careful, and industrious, so serious and laborious to do the Author all the rights of the press, I could not choose but gratulate your honest endeavors with this short remembrance. Here likewise, I must necessarily insert a manifest injury done me in that work, by taking the two epistles of *Paris* to *Helen,* and *Helen* to *Paris,* and printing them in a less volume, under the name of another, which may put the world in opinion I might steal them from him [Shakespeare]; and he to do himself right, hath since published them in his own name: but as I must acknowledge my lines not worthy his patronage, under whom he [Jaggard] hath published them, so the Author I know much offended with M. Jaggard (that altogether unknown to him) presumed to make so bold with his name. These, and the like dishonesties I know you to be clear of; and I could wish but to be the happy Author of so worthy a work as I could willingly commit to your care and workmanship.[46]

The letter has been quoted often for its depiction of a Shakespeare who chafed at the way Jaggard had "made bold" with Shakespeare's increasingly vendible name in *The Passionate Pilgrim,* in part by padding the volume with works he knew to be by Heywood and others.[47] More broadly, it is a reminder that the outsized role of printers in this network was not merely an indication of their mechanical role as reproducers of text. Here we see them actively selecting texts, correcting them, working with writers, and sometimes pirating them, as they shape authorship into a vendible commodity.[48] Okes's decisions to configure his shop to print a particular kind of work—which was smaller, a little cheaper, and sometimes a little more rushed—both served this market and shaped it. And far from associating these efforts with some stigma of print, the university-educated poet and playwright Heywood—who produced works for the public stage but who also nursed more elite aspirations—spoke warmly of Okes's "care and workmanship."

## III. Controversy, Censorship, and Revolution

Okes's career as a nimble superconnector often placed him in gray areas where he navigated between the Stationers' Company, state authorities, and the scofflaws who scraped out a living by skirting those authorities. As Blayney notes, "one of the notable features of Okes's record is how much he managed to get away with, and for how long."[49] At least once, according to the records of the Court of the Stationers' Company, he was "warned not to print any book hereafter without license upon pain to have his press taken down" and made inoperable, and he was fined on many occasions for disorderly printing practices, including using apprentices who were not properly bound, employing workmen who were not members of the company, and printing copyrights that he did not hold.[50] But as Cyndia Susan Clegg has argued, "while licensing is most often viewed as the means by which the 'state' assured its hegemony, this can only be the case when the King and the clergy were of a single mind, which was not the case in Jacobean England."[51] Rather than Okes, or any other printer or author, evading some hegemonic censor, "multiple agencies sought and employed censorship in Jacobean England," and "censorship operated at different times, in different ways, and for different reasons."[52] Okes got away with so much for so long because he navigated these competing interests with skill. In doing so, he helped build a print network that fueled, and profited from, governmental and religious controversies in the years immediately preceding the Civil War.

To see how, it will be useful to turn to a later stage of Okes's career and examine his printing of two authors on completely opposite sides of the religio-political spectrum: the staunchly Protestant poet, satirist, and journalist George Wither, and the Catholic evangelist Francis de Sales. In this later phase of his career, we will see how Okes cultivated connections that will be of interest as subsequent chapters explore the oppositional print network that emerged in the years leading up to the English Civil War. This will also offer an opportunity to observe a final property of superconnectors like Okes: Whether we are discussing networks of airports, cities, or books, hubs are not only where disparate nodes meet, but also where they collide. In Okes's case, those collisions would land him in courtrooms large and small, including an appearance in the witness chair at one of the century's most spectacular trials, in which England's highest church official was convicted of treason.

Okes first printed Wither's *Preparation to the Psalter* in 1619, marking the beginning of a relationship between Wither and London's stationers that was as close as it was contentious. The *Preparation to the Psalter* was an unusually large book for Okes—a folio in 41 sheets—and it announced a project that would have been hugely lucrative for both men. The book was an elaborate introduction to a new translation of the psalms, which Wither said he would release in "decads," or installments of 10, ultimately providing an alternative and an update to the Sternhold and Hopkins psalter that had monopolized the English book market since 1562. Such a project was a deliberate affront to the Stationers' Company, which in 1603 had paid the huge sum of 9,000 pounds for the royal patent giving them the exclusive right to print "Primers Psalters and Psalms in meter or prose with musical notes or without notes both in great volumes and small in the English tongue."[53] This was an especially lucrative part of the English Stock, since a psalter was used in every church in England in addition to being in homes and schools. The printing would be doled out to one or more printers each year to keep them in steady work, and the profits would be distributed among all the shareholders, providing a reliable supply of income. The company had rejected Okes's attempt to buy a share in the English Stock just two years earlier, and he was surely aware that Wither's ambitious project would challenge the company's rights, so he did not register the book. Unsurprisingly, he was promptly called before the Court of Wardens and fined 20 shillings; surprisingly, considering his track record, he actually complied with their demand to desist. More curiously, in the following month, he was offered and purchased a share in the English Stock. It would seem that the threat of a rogue psalter helped convince the company to bring Okes in from the cold, and he found it more profitable to work with the company than to flout its authority.

Although Okes's new status as a sharer in the English Stock had eliminated any incentive for him to print Wither's psalter, he continued to thrive on Wither's ability to generate controversy and his own aptitude for working at the soft margins of legality. As David Norbrook writes, Wither "believed it to be a Protestant poet's duty to speak out in times of political crisis," and this landed him in prison for several months in 1613 when his satire, *Abuses Stript and Whipt* offended the powerful Earl of Northampton with its attacks on Catholicism and Spain (Northampton, who was both Catholic and a Spanish pensioner, was doubly invested in maintaining peace).[54] But Wither's ensuing notoriety was a vendible commodity, and *Abuses Stript and Whipt* went through five editions in its first year. No wonder then that printers, including Okes, rushed in 1621 to print and pirate his return to satire in *Wither's Motto*, even though it explicitly reignited the quarrel over his psalter as it decried those "who invent / New Monopolies."[55] Wither's satire was just in time for a new Parliament, where a bill to curb monopolies would be hotly contested, and it was an instant sensation, going through at least seven editions in its first year and, according to Wither, selling 30,000 copies.[56] Even though monopolists, including stationers, were his targets, they were doing a brisk business peddling Wither's indignation.

As Norbrook says, with Wither's "eye for a growing market," he was turning "prophecy into a commodity" and in the process inventing "something new, the tone that was much later to become familiar in popular journalism."[57] Specifically, Wither reacted with expected Protestant hostility to the proposed Spanish Match of Prince Charles to the Infanta of Spain. That same issue brought matters between James and his Parliament to a head in December, leading the king to dissolve the legislature and step up his campaign against the regime's critics.[58] Wither's poem landed in the middle of it all, entered by Edmund Weaver in the Stationers' Register on 14 May 1621, but with publication explicitly forbidden "until he bring in further authority."[59] Almost immediately, though, the rogue printer Augustine Mathewes, who we'll encounter again in Chapter 5, printed an edition of 1,500 copies without a publisher's name, and by June 4 at least three editions and over 3,000 copies were in circulation, "in Contempt of the orders of the company."[60] After being reentered as "corrected" on June 16, the poem was reprinted with a defiant postscript in which Wither boasts that "Quite through this *Iland* hath my *Motto* rung" and issues a challenge to those who "spite it" to do their worst.[61] Wither seems to have been expecting that their worst would be a barrage of verse libels, but instead he was called before the House of Lords on June 27 and immediately committed to Marshalsea Prison for contravening the ban on political speech.[62] He was not released until 1622, well after the second session of Parliament had been dissolved.[63]

In the middle of the building quarrel between Wither, the Stationers' Company, and the crown was Okes. The Stationers' Company fined four men for printing the book without proper authority: the publisher John Marriot and the bookseller John Grismond received fines of 5 pounds and 1 pound, while the printers Augustine Mathewes and Okes were fined 4 pounds each. Subsequent testimony, however, made it clear that Okes was something of an odd man out in this group: Marriot had properly registered his copy with the Stationers' and then, before securing the necessary additional authority, had improperly taken it to Mathewes to print and Grismond to sell. Okes, on the other hand, had simply and flagrantly pirated the book—except on closer examination, there was nothing simple about it, since his piracy was facilitated by some of the very authorities who later levied the fines against all four men. Those same authorities apparently offered to shield Okes from trouble, and it is notable that he is the only person involved who seems to have escaped all jail time and paid only a token amount of his fine.

This story emerged in pieces after Okes and the others were hauled before the authorities at the Court of High Commission. There, a series of witnesses testified that while the other printers and booksellers had acted in ignorance, "notwithstanding he knew of the said fine and imprisonment," Okes "printed first 3,000 of the Books and afterward 3,000 more."[64] Another witness, Thomas Trussell, clarified that Okes's bold move was less reckless than it appeared, since it had the tacit approval of friends in high places. Trussell was a messenger and a soldier who had written the militant *Soldier Pleading His Own Cause*, printed by Okes for Thomas Walkley in 1619. A note under his signature in the court records relates a conversation with Okes:

> Mr. Okes the Printer told me that he had done nothing about Wither his book but by the consent of the Company of Stationers, and that

the master of the Company bade him send word how it went with him, and if he were committed, they would get him disregarded, also he said that the master of the Company had sent to the Clerk of the company to go along with him.[65]

The master of the company was Humphrey Lownes, whose brother and partner was the bookseller Matthew Lownes. Other witnesses eventually made it clear not only that Lownes was levying fines on the printers of the illegal books and confiscating them from the unauthorized booksellers, but also that he was then selling them and asking Okes to supply more.[66]

Okes was coy when he faced the court, but his answers imply that the other witnesses were not fabricating their accounts. He claimed he had printed his edition from an existing printed copy "which was licensed *for ought he knoweth*" and was not the first "by two several Impressions."[67] He was then asked why he had used Marriot's name, instead of his own, on his title page, without the other printer's knowledge:

> He sayeth he bought the Title ready printed, and so fixed it to the Book to make it perfect. . . . He sayeth that the Impression was done before it was questioned in the Stationers Hall, or elsewhere *for ought he knew*. . . . Being demanded whether Lownes, late Warden of the Company, did not sell some of the Books after they were prohibited, He sayeth that he this Examinant never sold any one Book to Lownes, *nor knoweth that he sold any after the prohibition*: but *he thinketh* some were sold here and there, but cannot accuse any one man.[68]

He can't remember—he can't recall—for all he knows. Such non-denial denials might be called the Frank Pentangeli strategy, after the character in the *Godfather* films who suffers a sudden bout of amnesia when on the witness stand. Apparently Okes had struck a deal with the printer Mathewes, or some other intermediary, to buy title pages that had already been printed for the earlier edition, although it is difficult to believe that these pages would have been available had not some moves to prohibit the book already been afoot. The scheme hinges on Okes's ability to act as a middleman between the more powerful and "respectable" Lownes family and the more shadowy Mathewes, who as we will see in Chapter

5, spent his career just on the other side of legality, often operating in dire financial circumstances and at great legal peril.

When he was released from prison, Wither would vent at length in the (illegally printed) *Schollars Purgatorie* about the monopolies of the Stationers' Company and the booksellers in particular, whom he described as "needless excrements, or rather vermin" who sucked the blood of authors. But he also praised other parts of the trade, especially the "printers mystery," which is "ingenious, painful, and profitable."[69] It is difficult to know whether Wither's dealings with Okes would have bequeathed him the title of ingenious artisan or worthless vermin, but it is clear that he profoundly amplified Wither's voice as he facilitated the production of thousands of copies of his *Motto*. It was in reference to this incident, and as part of an attack on Wither's growing infamy, that Ben Jonson lashed out at Okes as a "Printer in disguise," who "keeps / His Presse in a hollow tree" (a pun on "Oak" and on a printer's mark he used bearing the image of a tree).[70] Jonson was troubled by the new commodification of news and information, and he saw Okes as one of its emblematic figures. The thriving market for novel and sensational information that Okes was helping create threatened to upset traditional power structures and "have the giddy world turned the heels upward."[71]

This disruptive potential was not, however, strictly ideological, as became clear in Okes's dealings with a book on the other end of the religious spectrum—*An Introduction to a Devout Life*, by the Catholic Bishop Francis de Sales. If Wither's book had spread "Quite through this Island," the 1637 printing of Sales's *Introduction* demonstrates the rapid chain reactions that could be initiated by such viral spread. Okes printed an uncensored version of the Catholic text that shocked public opinion with its "gross popery," as one contemporary petition put it.[72] Sales's book then came into the hands of the puritanical William Prynne, who was confined to the Tower with Henry Burton and John Bastwick for sedition, and who used it to file a counterclaim that Archbishop William Laud was conspiring to restore Catholicism to England.[73] In traditional accounts of this event, Okes is merely a bit player or an afterthought—a printer who was not very scrupulous, or very bright, and so found himself caught up in a larger drama. But when we think of him as a networked hub, who had rebuilt his shop precisely to feed such a market for controversy, it may make more sense to emphasize his capacity for promiscuous connections than his lack of scruples.

Okes's precise allegiances are mysteriously hard to pin down, but in this case Jonson's premonitions of a world turned upside down by scandalous and sensational publishing proved prescient. Laud would ultimately lose his head after a trial for treason in which Okes, his book, and the books sold and promoted by his sometimes partner Michael Sparke would play an outsized role. In Chapter 2, I discussed Sparke's pioneering role in book wholesaling and his premonition that books could spread like an uncontrollable fire in the new system he helped to create. His innovations in book marketing and selling strategies also helped make him a hub; as measured by degree, he was easily the most connected bookseller during his most active period in the two decades leading up to the Civil War. As such, he was well positioned to help shape the events surrounding Laud's trial, which he did by producing and selling books that framed Laud's crimes in terms of corrupt attempts to control and influence the press. Indeed, Sparke himself is one of the few named individuals to appear in Wenceslaus Hollar's famous engraving of the trial (Figure 3.7): Mustachioed, he stands in profile—one eye cast upon the reader, the other upon Laud. Sparke commissioned the engraving to adorn the books in which Okes would appear as a victim of Laud's crimes.[74] Two hubs in the network, Sparke and Okes were very much at the center of this historical moment, although their role has rarely been observed.

Okes testified at Laud's trial on 27 June 1644 that he had printed a "purged" version of Sales's text in 1616, but that in 1637 "a Priest" brought a copy of the book to Laud's chaplain, William Heywood, who "did license it with the passages of Popery in it. And I wished my son that printed it to go & acquaint ~~the Archbishop~~ Dr. Heywood with it, & he bid him go on in the printing of it & he would justify ... everything as was in it, because he did license it."[75] These notes from the trial, compiled by John Browne, are consistent with a letter written by J. V. (probably the polemicist John Vicars) several years earlier, in 1639. The letter, which was introduced at

**Figure 3.7** Engraving of the trial of William Laud, Archbishop of Canterbury, by Wenceslaus Hollar. Michael Sparke is highlighted, lower right ("S").

SOURCE: Thomas Fisher Rare Book Library, University of Toronto. Reprinted with permission.

trial, explained that "when old Oakes his father saw his son Oakes about to print that book he should say unto him; Son, take heed what you do for about 20 years pas[t] my self printed this book but was shrewdly pinched by it and paid soundly for it. Wherupon young Oakes was startled and went presently to Heywood that licensed it."[76] The priest would seem to be Christopher Barrows, who was born a Protestant but who had converted to Catholicism and been ordained at Douai in 1621, returning to England in 1623.[77] The 1637 edition contains a preface "To the Christian Reader" signed "C. B.," which employs provocatively Catholic language and is likely by Barrows.[78]

Okes's testimony was supported by his son's widow, Mary, whose deposition cast the blame on Heywood and Laud while adding that her husband had been imprisoned for three weeks over the affair.[79] Later, in the more overtly propagandistic account of Laud's fall, *Canterburie's Doom*, Prynne and Sparke would edit out the younger Okes's role and cast his father Nicholas directly as a God-fearing citizen ruined by corrupt church officials. They did this with some warrant, however: The Privy Council order of 19 April 1637, demanding that all books should be seized from the bookseller William Brooks and burned at Smithfield, also names only Nicholas; and when Laud's deputy, Sir John Lambe, drew up a list of 20 officially authorized printers that would be recognized in the Star Chamber decree to regulate printing, he deleted Nicholas Okes's name with a large cross and inserted the note "He printed [th]e book lately burnt: he petitioneth [tha]t his son John Okes may be in his stead."[80] In Prynne's account, Nicholas noticed many "Popish Passages," including one specifically "touching the Pope's supremacy," but when Okes told Heywood he could not print it, the doctor "bid him go on and say nothing ... adding, that he himself would preach as much as that."[81] At the trial, Prynne testified that Laud and the king ordered the books to be called in and burned only *after* Prynne and Okes had exposed them, and that in retaliation the "poor printer *Oakes* was imprisoned divers Monthes almost to his utter undoing."[82] The prosecution, in short, presented Okes as a conscientious printer, or at least one who had learned from his mistakes and who had been unduly wronged by a Laudian establishment that had turned him into a scapegoat after their popish activities had been exposed.

In the afternoon session of his trial, Laud's account sharply differed, claiming the whole affair was an elaborate trick to discredit him. John Browne records Laud tersely responding that "Mr. Okes speaks but hearsay, his son is dead" and protesting that "I never heard of this book before the business came into the Star chamber . . . Let Dr. Heywood answer for it, if any thing be amiss."[83] A month later, he was still contesting the charges, arguing that "Dr. Heywood put out all the unsound passages in Sales book, but the printer did put them in again."[84] Laud also wrote his own account of the trial, which remained in manuscript until 1693 and which adds some detail to his defense. The whole episode, Laud insists, was a "notable piece of Villany" practiced against him; he even claims the "Jesuited Recusant" who brought the text to be licensed in the first place was "Lodged, for that Time of Printing, in Oakes his House" and that "young Oakes was in all likelihood well payed for his pains."[85]

Laud does seem to be correct in some points. Thanks to his prompt orders, "Eleven or Twelve Hundred Copies were Seized and Burnt" *before* Prynne filed his countersuit charging Laud with promoting popery—so Prynne's conspiracy theory cannot be completely correct. Indeed, because two or three hundred copies had already been sold, the Privy Council issued additional proclamations demanding the confiscation and destruction of all the books in private hands, and Laud diligently wrote the vice-chancellor of Oxford asking for his assistance in implementing this order.[86] And although he insisted that his censor Heywood had acted properly, Laud also removed him of his duties.[87] Nigel W. Bawcutt has scrutinized the complete case and its supporting documents and concluded that the true story was probably neither Prynne's (that the book was part of a Laudian attempt to promote popery) nor Laud's (that the book was part of a "trick intended to discredit Heywood in the first place and ultimately himself").[88] Instead, he concludes that Barrows and Brooks, the priest and popish bookseller, were probably responsible for inserting passages after Heywood's initial censorship.

Setting culpability aside, the most remarkable aspect of the episode is that a fairly decisive response by Laud didn't matter. It was truly a case of viral spread of information, facilitated by superconnected hubs in the print network. On 28 April 1637, George Garrard wrote to the Earl of Stafford describing vigorous efforts to suppress the book, which was nevertheless "on Every Post, and on Every Stall to be sold."[89] The same month, a scandalized Devonshire justice and MP, Walter Yonge, noted the episode in his diary, while the Earl of Leicester's secretary wrote to him in Paris detailing Laud's ongoing attempts to "beat down" the furor over popery provoked by the book.[90] In June, the vice-chancellor of Cambridge personally interrogated the town's booksellers and found multiple copies still afloat both among the scholars and people of the town.[91] Heywood's own parishioners at St. Giles in the Fields would list Sales's book as their first grievance in their (successful) petition to Parliament for his removal.[92]

One thing that both Prynne and Laud could agree on is that Okes had produced a poison pill. Not only that, he had helped construct a machine that ensured both the book's controversy and its viral spread, triggering a cascade of events that, without exaggeration, can be said to have helped shake the foundations of church and state—at least it seemed that way to contemporaries and to the generation that followed them. Around 1641, a satirical engraving circulated showing Laud vomiting a stream of books while Henry Burton darkly predicts that his illness will last "till Head from body part."[93] The "popish" books Laud supposedly promoted have become the most damning evidence against him, a cause and cure of the sickness infecting the English church. And although Okes's own role would soon fade from the story, his work would live on in notoriety: Thirty years later, as Andrew Marvell contemplated the role of print in fostering debate and fomenting revolution, he quipped in the first part of *The Rehearsal Transpros'd* that with print, "two or three brawny Fellows in a Corner, with mere Ink and Elbow-grease, do more harm than a *hundred Systematical Divines* with their *sweaty preaching.*"[94] He later specifically recalls this bit of "harm," in which Sales's "book was thought fit to be Licensed ... although afterwards it was called in, and burnt by Proclamation."[95]

I began this chapter by noting the outsized role that hubs play in scale-free networks and suggesting that we could gain insight into the spread of dangerous ideas in the English print network by identifying and studying these hubs. The career of Nicholas Okes makes for a surprisingly rich case study. Although he is often dismissed as incompetent or as a crook at worst, or an average workman of little interest at best, his status as the most highly connected printer in his lifetime is neither accidental nor inconsequential. It is the result of decisions taken early in his career that allowed him to produce work cheaply and quickly when time was of the essence. Without clearly discernible loyalties, he would print Puritan sermons, withering Protestant satire, tawdry plays, or Catholic propaganda—and he knew how to play one side against the other. But in serving the market for timely, controversial works, he helped reshape the network that produced them. And just as critics of print had long warned, he helped start fires that could not easily be put out.

## CHAPTER 4  RADICAL BETWEENNESS

Eleanor Davies and Mary Cary

THE PROTOTYPICAL "HIDDEN HISTORIES" have often been women's. This remained the case even after Marxist scholars of the 1960s and 1970s turned their attention away from the great men of the English Civil War to chronicle the revolutionary ideas of the merchants, laborers, and soldiers who populate books like Christopher Hill's *World Turned Upside Down*. Capacious as it was, Hill's "worm's eye view" still tended to see women as marginal players in radical movements, and he followed more traditional historians in discussing them largely in terms of relaxed sexual mores and Ranter orgies (borrowing a phrase from Abiezer Coppe, Hill titled his chapter on women "Base Impudent Kisses").[1] Later scholars including Elaine Hobby, Hilary Hinds, Nigel Smith, and Phyllis Mack have allowed us to see that women were much more involved in leading sects such as the Fifth Monarchists, Diggers, and Ranters than earlier bottom-up histories had suggested.[2] And projects like Cait Coker and Kate Ozment's Women in Book History database are collecting resources that highlight the role that some of these women took in producing their own writing.[3]

But questions of female prophets' influence and audience have remained difficult to answer. Even champions of radical women's writing who have excavated their stories have typically described them in terms of thwarted voice and lost opportunity, cut off both from the mainstream of contemporary thought and the later development of Restoration feminism that, in Elaine Hobby's words, would represent "a retreat, a loss of visionary potential of the revolutionary years."[4] As Sharon Achinstein has described this moment, the Civil War years may "be seen as a pivotal moment in which women's place in the political life of the nation was being considered," but their "vivid participation in the public sphere" also prompted the subsequent "attempt to exclude women" more completely from this sphere.[5] This is the triumphant "conjuring trick" of enlightenment liberalism described by Carole Pateman, in which a supposedly universal social contract became embodied in an implicitly male "civil fraternity."[6] From this angle, the female prophets of the tumultuous 1640s and 1650s seem more like a brief aberration than part of a continuous feminist or political tradition, and questions of their influence are understandably foreclosed.

This chapter uses network analytics to open up those questions in an exploration of two especially remarkable female prophets: Eleanor Davies[7] and Mary Cary.[8] Both have largely been erased from histories of the period.[9] Both seem especially suited to an understanding of interregnum prophecy as a dead end, and to its prophets as lost cases who were ultimately cut off from the main currents of intellectual life. Stevie Davies, for example, writes movingly of Mary Cary as a "prodigy" who proposed far-reaching reforms of church and state before lamenting that "few," if any, were "listening to Mary."[10] In an even more profoundly disheartening anticlimax, Esther Cope's extensive biography addresses the critical neglect of Eleanor Davies, who published more than 60 works and landed herself in prison for her outspoken protests against the Laudian church, but Cope's book concludes by admitting that Davies "had relatively little impact upon her contemporaries."[11] I want to suggest that studying these writers' place in the English print network offers some exciting new insights into their influence, the modes of authorship they develop, and the kinds of radical agency they express.

## I. Degree Versus Betweenness

How do we address questions of agency and influence in complex networks? Previous chapters have used connectivity as a rubric, and so have focused on degree, which measures the number of a node's connections. But degree is only one way of assessing a node's structural importance. Another is *betweenness centrality*, which measures not the number of a node's connections but its role in connecting others. The simplest definition of betweenness is that it measures the number of shortest paths between any two points on the network that run through a given node. The importance of betweenness becomes obvious in a simple graph such as Figure 4.1. Here nodes A and F have the highest degree, with four connections each; node E has half as many connections, but to trace a path between the graph's two distinct communities, you must go through E, which acts as a bridge. Remove it and the network falls apart.

It is easy to identify high-betweenness nodes visually in a small graph like this, but in a graph with tens of thousands of nodes it becomes impossible without computational analysis, which must calculate the shortest route between every node in the graph and every other node. For a graph

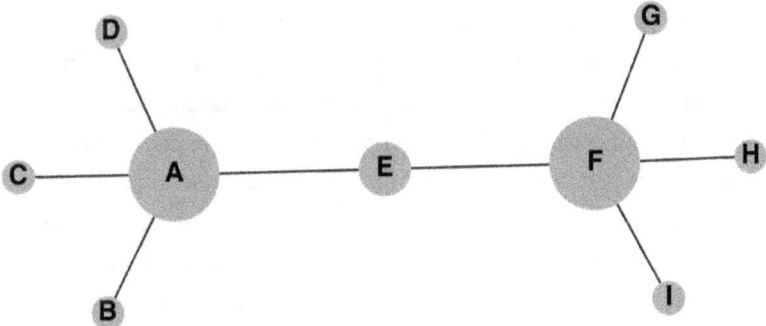

**Figure 4.1** Betweenness centrality. Node E has low degree (few connections) but high betweenness, because many paths between other nodes run through it.

of the English print network, this means millions of calculations. But the results can shift our understanding of the way information and influence operate in a network, as this chapter shows, by demonstrating the way an analysis of betweenness yields insights into the works of authors that have been overlooked by the traditional methods of literary analysis and historiography.

Hubs often have high betweenness, since they connect many otherwise unrelated people, and therefore it is not surprising that stationers such as Michael Sparke and Nicholas Okes, who were examined as hyperconnected figures in previous chapters, are also highly ranked for their betweenness centrality. Likewise, when Ruth Ahnert and Sebastian Ahnert calculated the top 20 nodes for degree and betweenness in their study of Protestant letter networks, they found much overlap between the two lists. Prominent martyrs such as John Bradford, John Careless, John Hooper, and John Philpot—who feature prominently in John Foxe's "Book of Martyrs" and in English Protestant history—were obvious hubs, because they wrote so many letters. And because those letters established links to many correspondents who were otherwise not in the network, these hubs also had high betweenness centrality. But Ahnert and Ahnert also discovered that some individuals with high betweenness centrality were far more obscure and unexpected. These were not hubs but relatively low-degree bridges who performed an important mediating role in the network, often as couriers or caregivers, funneling goods and materials to and from communities of prisoners and martyrs. They were "infrastructural figures; individuals whose role may have been given minimal coverage in Foxe's 'Book of Martyrs,' or edited out altogether," but who played an essential role in maintaining network connectivity.[12] Most significantly, in terms of reorienting traditional histories of the period, women were especially well represented in these bridging roles. By focusing on betweenness, Ahnert and Ahnert's work allows us to understand the impact of these women in a new way, situating them as important agents within histories in which they have mostly remained invisible.

Other studies have also suggested that network analysis, and especially the betweenness metric, may be well suited to identifying the hidden histories of women and other structurally significant but understudied people. Similar patterns have emerged in communities as diverse as the nineteenth-century socialist Fabian Society and an international group of twenty-first century researchers publishing in the field of quantitative science studies.[13] Much closer to my own subject in this book, Evan Bourke has shown that while the intellectual community known as the Hartlib Circle has often been depicted as "entirely male in its membership," network analysis reveals several women "at the very centre."[14] Hartlib, a German expatriate "projector" and "intelligencer,"[15] was described by his friend and frequent correspondent John Dury "as a conduit pipe of things communicable."[16] But the women with the most impressive betweenness centrality scores in his network, Dorothy Moore Dury and the Viscountess Ranelagh, collected and distributed information as well as playing key roles in organizing and structuring the circle's social and intellectual life. Hartlib, for example, sometimes received letters at Ranelagh's house, which was a center of activity for London's growing community of projectors, experimenters, and intellectuals (her brother was Robert Boyle, and she actively shared his interest in chemistry). Ranelagh was also involved with the group of literary and intellectual personalities known as the Great Tew Circle and may have linked Hartlib to its various members, as well as to writers like Andrew Marvell, who wrote her daughter's epitaph, and Milton, with whom she was close and whom she made the tutor of both her nephew and her son.[17] For her part, Dorothy Moore Dury was a multilingual intelligencer, Hebraist, and advocate for women's education. Her brother was Edward King, the subject of Milton's "Lycidas"; the volume in which Milton's poem first appeared also included a poem praising his unusually learned sister, who is described as "no other / But your sex transformed brother."[18] Structurally, she was central to the Hartlib network not only as a key correspondent but also as a fundraiser. When we analyze the English print network, 1641–1660, we find a strikingly similar pattern of structurally significant individuals, including women, with high betweenness and relatively low degree.

Using English print network data, we have several options for considering which ideas or texts were most highly connected at the core of debate during this volatile and explosive period. One strategy, for example, might be to consider the highest degree or most connected authors. Such an analysis yields a list of fairly familiar names, as in Figure 4.2. This list obviously leaves much room for debate: Was the publishing career of Richard Baxter, who has been described by one historian as "the most influential Puritan of his time," really more consequential than that of John Cotton, who has been called by another "the most influential" person among a group of American colonial ministers that had "a profound influence on the development of American history"?[19] But although the results of this network analysis do not give much insight into such fine-grained questions, the approach seems to have identified a set of authors of almost undeniable importance, who are well documented in histories of the period and who would have been known to just about any customer frequenting London bookshops at this time. Likewise, this kind of analysis may not yield much insight if we are interested in questions of influence within more rarefied publishing areas such as poetry, but it helps illustrate the extent to which works of theology and religious controversy dominated the publishing field during these years.

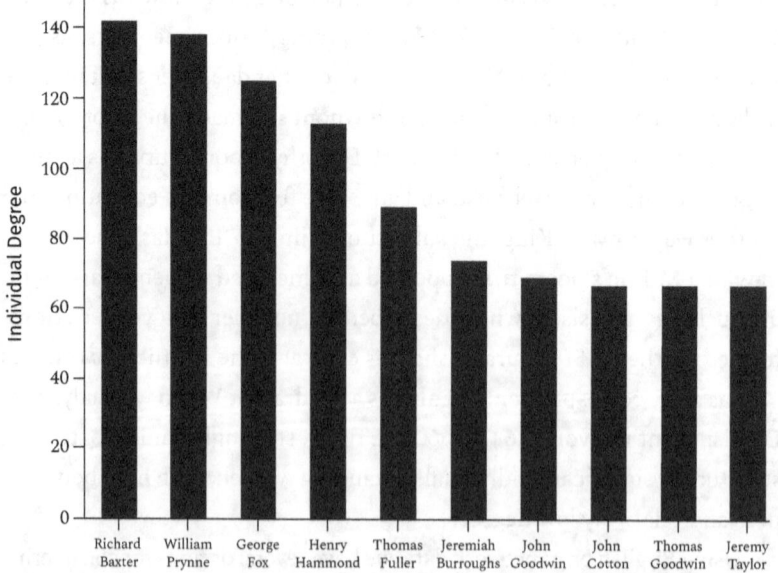

**Figure 4.2** The list of highest-degree authors during the Civil War years, 1641-1660, is dominated by well-known theological writers.

A betweenness centrality ranking of authors shifts the results and adds a few additional names, but still leaves us with authors whose influence is fairly obvious and well documented, as seen in Figure 4.3. Five names appear on both lists (Taylor, Burroughs, Prynne, Fuller, Cotton), which is expected since people with many connections also tend to have high centrality. Baxter drops from the list. Compared to a writer like Cotton, he actually published more during this period, and so is almost guaranteed a higher degree, but his booksellers are specialists in Puritan and religious literature. Cotton's books, on the other hand, are sold by a wider variety of booksellers. They include Robert Ibbiston, who specialized in news; John Stafford and Thomas Banks, who carried many works of theology; Charles Greene, who sold a wide array of plays and romances; and Andrew Crooke, whose literary offerings included Ben Jonson's works and Thomas Browne's *Religio Medici*.

Others on the centrality list may be less connected and slightly less discussed than authors such as Cotton, but they are not exactly obscure. All held prominent positions in the church or state, or are otherwise well

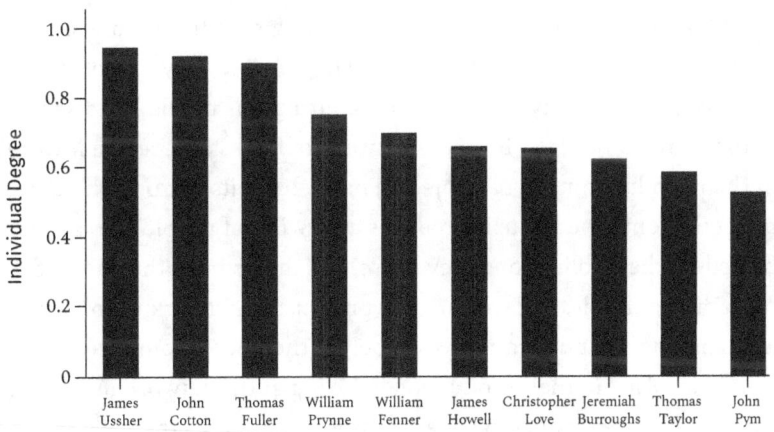

**Figure 4.3** The top 10 betweenness centrality authors, 1641–1660. Normalized betweenness centrality gives us the relative rather than absolute values of betweenness between zero and one, since our concern is not the absolute number of shortest paths that cross through a node but how this compares with other nodes.

known for their writing, but in comparison with the degree ranking, the betweenness metric tends to reward authors of structural importance who appealed to clearly divergent ideological and religious communities. James Ussher, for example, is the rare high church official who successfully navigated both his loyalty to the crown and his Calvinistic, anti-Laudian tendencies. According to his biographer, "his intellectual stature, his wide circle of friends, the ease with which he moved in both parliamentary and royal circles, mean that it is difficult, indeed inappropriate, to 'place' Ussher politically," a "Janus-like quality" that made him "ideally positioned to mediate between the opposing sides."[20] This is almost a textbook definition of the profile we'd expect from a high-betweenness "bridge." Likewise, James Howell positioned himself during the Civil War as the ultimate moderate and mediator, urging "reciprocal concessions" between king and Parliament in a series of works in which he attempted to master the art of not taking sides.[21] Others who appear on this list of high- centrality writers, but not the list of highest-degree ones, moved similarly between extremes, as in the case of Christopher Love, an early supporter of Parliament who was later executed for backing a plot to restore Charles II, and who used his execution to stage a "politically effective" act of resistance that positioned himself at the center of interregnum factions that were quickly cleaving apart.[22]

While these results point to the intriguing possibilities of using the betweenness metric to explore structural importance, they are not the only way to study centrality and connection during this period. As discussed in the Introduction, the bipartite network of books and people involved in their production can be projected onto either its left or right axis. A projection onto the left axis produces a network of people who are connected by the publications they share, which has been the basis of the preceding analysis. But we can also project the network onto its right axis, making the publications themselves the nodes, connected by the people involved in their production. Looking at the network in this way, a high-degree text would be one that was produced by the most prolific printers, since such printers would form edges between each of the books they printed. It would likely be sold by booksellers carrying the largest inventory, for the same reason. To stand out as a hub, it would need to be printed, published, and sold by many people who in turn print, publish, and sell many other works. A list of high-degree texts, in other words, is going to point toward high-volume production, particularly works that involve much collaboration in their printing, are sold in multiple bookshops, or are repeatedly reprinted. By contrast, a high-betweenness text will not necessarily be found in multiple bookshops or be published and printed by the most prolific people. But a high-betweenness text likely *will* be found in the bookstores where the inventory is exceptionally diverse or eclectic, and it is likely to be produced by people who are most disparate in their affiliations, making it a potential bridge between communities. For example, a high-betweenness text might be that rare pamphlet stocked by both ultra-royalist booksellers and radical regicides, sharing shelf space with Digger manifestos and royal proclamations. Since betweenness at the scale of the entire print network operates by analyzing millions of pathways, such a text will also likely involve authors and printers who engage with multiple, diverse communities. In a time of upheaval, it will be positioned at the center of the storm.

Figure 4.4 includes a ranking of the top 10 texts, by degree, between 1641 and 1660. With the exception of *Scot's Discovery of Witchcraft*, these

---

1) *Scot's Discovery of Witchcraft* (1651)

2) *Two Letters from William Basil Esq; Attorney General of Ireland* (1649)

3) *27 Junii, An Act for Borrowing* (1649)

4) *Die Jovis, 8 Novembr, Two Orders of Parliament Against Highway Robbery* (1649)

5) *An Act Against Unlicensed and Scandalous Books and Pamphlets* (1649)

6) *An Act for a Day of Publique Thanksgiving* (1649)

7) *Die Martis, 6 Augusti, The Parliament Doth Declare ... Powers ... for the Militias* (1650)

8) *Resolutions of Parliament, Touching Delinquents* (1648)

9) *A Letter from the Lord Lieutenant of Ireland to ... Speaker of the Parliament* (1650)

10) *A Letter from the Right Honorable, the Lord Lieutenant of Ireland, to the ... Speaker* (1649)

---

**Figure 4.4**   The top 10 highest-degree texts, 1641–1660.

are all "official" publications and proclamations, printed and produced by the "printer to the Parliament of England" (usually Edward Husband and/or John Field) and distributed broadly. The lone anomaly, Reginald Scot's *Discovery*, was a perennial favorite printed in this instance by Richard Cotes, who did a brisk business during the period as the printer for the City of London, and sold by Giles Calvert, a radical and prolific bookseller to whom we will return. In other words, as expected, the texts with the highest degree are widely distributed by many individuals, often in an official capacity.

As with the author rankings, there is some overlap between the highest-degree texts and a list of texts with the highest betweenness centrality. The *Discovery of Witchcraft* remains on the list, and at least four other titles, highlighted in bold in Figure 4.5, might be described as "official" publications with a broad expected reach. But even these official texts clearly represent a greater ideological diversity than the ones on the high-degree list, which were all issued by printers to Parliament. Here, only the second ranked text is officially printed by order of Parliament (although the tenth—*Of the Foure Last and Greatest Things*—might be considered semi-official, as it is dedicated to Parliament by William Sheppard, who was appointed by those same lawmakers to translate the laws

---

1) ***His Majesties Declaration to the Ministers, Freeholders, Farmers . . . of Yorke* (1642)**

2) ***Two letters from . . . Robert Earl of Essex . . . Printed by Order of Parliament* (1643)**

3) *Scot's Discovery of Witchcraft* (1651)

4) *Twelve Humble Proposals to the Supreme Governours of the Three Nations* (1653)

5) ***A Letter from the Earl of Essex to His Highnesse Prince Rupert* (1645)**

6) *Strange and Wonderfull Prophesies by the Lady Eleanor Audeley* (1649)

7) *La Stratonica; or the Unfortunate Queen* (1651)

8) *The Marrow of Modern Divinity* (1646)

9) ***A Caveat for Covenant-Contemners and Covenant-Breakers* (1647)**

10) *Of the Foure Last and Greatest Things: Death, Judgement, Heaven and Hell* (1649)

---

**Figure 4.5** The top 10 texts ranked by betweenness centrality, 1641–1660, with "official" publications in bold.

into English). But the work with the highest betweenness centrality, *His Majesties Declaration*, comes from the king rather than Parliament and was printed at York by Stephen Bulkley, who had fled London with his printing equipment after being called before Parliament to answer for his royalist political tracts. The king too had sought refuge from Whitehall in York, and Bulkley and his press would follow the royal army, working under the imprint of the King's Printer, Robert Barker, who was in prison for debt.[23] The fifth ranked text, *A Letter from the Earl of Essex to His Highnesse Prince Rupert*, was thus issued from Bristol by the King's Printer. As the title suggests, the publication includes a letter from the parliamentary commander Robert Devereaux protesting Rupert's execution of his prisoners, but its real purpose was to disseminate Rupert's withering response, which explained that his actions had been justified by the massacre of Irish and other troops who had been "barbarously murthered, in cold blood" after their surrender to parliamentary forces.[24] The ninth-ranking text, *A Caveat for Covenant-Contemners and Covenant-Breakers* (1647), reproduced the agreement— known as the Solemn League and Covenant—between English parliamentarians and Scottish Presbyterians.

Broadening our understanding of what might count as an official or at least as a prestige publication, we also find Luca Assarino's romance, *La Stratonica*, which has fallen into obscurity but which was one of the most popular seventeenth-century novels, reaching nearly 40 reprints during the period. This edition was produced by the influential literary publisher Humphrey Moseley. Edward Fisher's *The Marrow of Modern Divinity*, a dialogue that attempts to find a middle ground between the leading theological factions of the day, might also in some ways count as a prestige publication, as it includes laudatory epistles by a veritable who's who of leading Independent divines, including Jeremiah Burroughs, William Strong, and Joseph Caryl, who were all members of the Westminster Assembly, and Joshua Sprigge, who served as General Fairfax's chaplain.

With these last texts, though, we are probably stretching to its breaking point anything that resembles the official status shared by the texts in the high-degree table. No matter how influential their writers, the letters in the *Marrow of Modern Divinity*, according to David R. Como, also serve as "a powerful testimony to the ties of ideological and personal association that constituted London's antinomian underground, both before and after 1641."[25] Perhaps rather than viewing them as official documents, we should simply say that even when these texts do not have an abundance of connections (because, for example, they have not been reprinted by dozens of printers and sold by dozens of booksellers), they are well situated. They are well-connected texts not only or primarily because they are produced often, but because they are produced by well-connected people and distributed broadly across communities that share few other texts in common. And with that shift in mind, we can perhaps make more sense of the two texts on this list that, by any conventional measure, would be unlikely to appear in a group of the most influential or important publications of the period: Mary Cary's *Twelve Humble Proposals* (fourth on the list) and Eleanor Davies's *Strange and Wonderfull Prophesies* (sixth on list).

At first glance, it may not seem surprising to see these two texts in a list that is, by any measure, eclectic. But as with the findings of Ahnert and Ahnert, this is an outsized representation of female authors among the thousands of texts that appeared from 1641–1660 and the 9,386 of those texts with non-zero betweenness. It is also one of the most pronounced differences between the list of high-degree texts (which are all male-authored and produced by male institutions such as Parliament) and the high-betweenness texts. Moreover, these women were distinctive prophetic authors, often operating under severe financial constraints and in the face of harsh opposition. What put them at the center of the print network, and how can we understand their prominence as bridges between disparate communities?

Scholars have long observed that early modern female prophets were viewed as mediators, channeling messages from God to men. Indeed, women's "identification as 'weak vessels' particularly prone to irrational, hysterical acts, provided the framework" that allowed their words to "be interpreted, by themselves and others, as issuing from God."[26] As we shall see in the rest of the chapter, Eleanor Davies and Mary Cary employed this framework in ways that were anything but irrational and were, in fact, carefully embedded in contemporary debates over political and religious reform. Ultimately, I would like to suggest that these women's rhetorical positioning as mediators between God and man—their navigation between what Phyllis Mack has called "the Scylla of their audience's praise of them as mindless vessels and the Charybdis of their critics' attacks on them as aggressive or self serving"—is reflected in the place they established for their texts in the print network.[27] Betweenness was not merely a rhetorical stance, in other words, but part of a broader strategy of communication that included the print production of their works.

## II. Eleanor Davies and the Labor of Print Prophecy

Although her biographer downplays her "impact upon her contemporaries," Eleanor Davies—or Lady Eleanor, as she would be known most commonly throughout her long career of widowhood and remarriage—made her presence felt in international English society from the moment she married the poet Sir John Davies in 1609 until her death in 1652.[28] In those years she was jailed on five occasions, committed to Bedlam, fined, and forced to watch her books publicly burned. She also established a remarkable web of connections to the key literary, political, and religious leaders of her age—from Queen Henrietta Maria to Samuel Hartlib and the Digger firebrand Gerrard Winstanley—and inserted herself into the very center of the controversies that defined the era of revolution.

John Davies was not perhaps the most conventionally appealing catch: Contemporaries described him as grotesquely obese, ugly, and ill tempered. But he was a subtle poet, whose *Nosce teipsum*, printed by Richard Field, was widely admired in courtly circles. King James also recognized John Davies's considerable legal acumen, making him the solicitor general for Ireland and setting him on the path to his appointment by Charles I as Chief Justice of the King's Bench in 1626. Davies felt he had been delayed in that journey by the increasingly notorious behavior of his wife, who quickly became embroiled in libelous Jacobean court culture. Outspoken and fractious, one of her disputes, with Lady Mary Jacob, was serious enough to be referred to the court of Star Chamber for resolution, and we get some insight into the figure Lady Davies cut in Jacobean

London thanks to a letter to her by Lady Jacob's husband, Christopher "Kit" Brooke, which was introduced into evidence. Brooke was friends with Ben Jonson and compared Eleanor Davies to "my Lady Would Be in the Play" *Volpone,* painting an elaborate picture of her "fastidious punctualities" and claiming she "hast no fig leaves to cover thy shame but the titles of thy house."[29]

Brooke repeatedly returns to this line of attack: Eleanor Davies, whom he terms "Lady Tryfle," was insufferably proud and used her name and family to escape censure for transgressive speech and behavior.[30] "If thy husband did not cover thee," he writes, all would be revealed as "coxcomicall braveries." Brooke was a member of the "Sireniacs," an Inns of Court Club that famously met at the Mermaid Tavern and included John Donne, Ben Jonson, and Robert Cotton, and his letter is both highly literary and made for coterie circulation and public consumption.[31] In it, he quotes from Juvenal's eighth satire, suggesting that Davies ask her husband to "expound" it for her, before (loosely) translating it himself: "Better Thersites were thy father far, so thou wert virtuous wife & debonair, then that Achilles had thee (monster) made, as thou now art, a sorry & lying jade."[32] The literary allusions continue: Eleanor Davies is a Spenserian "blatant beast," a "Hecate, Medusa, Legion, cloven footed Gorgon," and Brooke, sounding a bit like one of Jonson's characters himself, histrionically threatens her with physical violence that involves making a "minced pie for a dog from thy ill kept, filthy, dunghill arse."[33]

It is unclear how exactly Eleanor Davies provoked this heated response, although Brooke accused her of "abusing" his wife and child. The two women had known one another for some time: Mary Jacob had been married to Robert Jacob, who had worked until his death under John Davies in Ireland and who seems to have been a family friend.[34] Brooke's letter implies that Eleanor may have thought ill of Mary's subsequent marriage and sexually slandered her, perhaps by pointing out that their son was born just before their marriage and so might be accused of bastardy. What is clear is that this was not merely a private dispute. As Michelle O'Callaghan writes, "Brooke was part of a network, which included John Hoskins and Richard Martin, which was known for its composition of burlesque poetry and verse libels, including 'The Censure of the Parliament Fart,'" and this letter was written at least in part to entertain such a group of wits.[35] Mary Jacob was a bit of a libeler herself, with at least one bawdy poem in her husband's circle attributed to her. In short, even before Eleanor Davies began to print her works, she was becoming a public personality, and one whose works were embedded in an important courtly network.

Rather than shying away from this notoriety, as her husband wished her to do, she used it to amplify her voice, publishing her opinions for increasingly broad audiences. In the months after Charles succeeded his father to the throne in March of 1625, Davies had become increasingly pessimistic about his reign, his marriage to a Catholic queen, the continuing influence of Buckingham, and the direction of the English Church. In July, at her country home at Englefield, she experienced what she considered a prophetic revelation, as a voice from heaven awoke her and proclaimed "there is Ninteen years and a half to the day of Judgement and you as the meek Virgin."[36] She understood this as the voice of the biblical Daniel, and it prompted an intense period of writing in which Davies produced *A Warning to the Dragon and All His Angels*, a tract explicating the book of Daniel in terms that pointed ominously toward corruption in the court, church, and state. Published under an anagram of her name ("A Snare O Devil"), the tract ended with her bold proclamation:

> The whole world is numbered and those that work abomination therein, and the delights thereof, weighed in the balances, are found lighter than vanity itself. There is nineteen years and a half to the day of judgement. . . . And I think that I have also the Spirit of God.[37]

This prophecy—many iterations and careful publishing decisions later—would reappear in the text that served as such an unlikely bridge between royalist, radical, and other divided communities of the 1650s.

Although she was never a member of the group that would later become known as the Fifth Monarchists, Davies believed, like them, that the destruction of the anti-Christian fourth monarchy prophesized in the book of Daniel was at hand, and that this called for the present establishment of Christ's kingdom on earth. She called her explication of this prophecy

"A Warning," but it would have been difficult to see it as anything but a threat. This was especially apparent when she delivered a copy of the work, in front of "no few witnesses," to Archbishop of Canterbury George Abbot, who was attending Parliament at Oxford.[38] He must have wondered especially at her text's proclamation that "Thy Bishoppricke shall be void" and "become a habitation for devils."[39] Eleanor Davies, "A Snare O Devil," did not obey a chain of command. In her view, God's inspiration infinitely outweighed considerations of sex or status, and it demanded action. As she said in the introduction to her tract, "no age so weake, nor sex excusing; when the Lord shall send and will put his words in their Mouth."[40]

John Davies did not relish his wife's increasingly high profile, which he feared might inhibit his own rise, so he responded to the Oxford spectacle by seizing and burning copies of her book. This prompted her to prophesy his death within three years, which he dutifully fulfilled, ironically bolstering his wife's claims to divine inspiration. If John Davies meant to shut her up, in short, his plan backfired horribly. Instead, it launched her onto a path of increasingly public confrontations with authority. In coming years she became a savvy print publisher who smuggled texts between Amsterdam and England, a saboteur and iconoclast who mobilized a group of women to vandalize Lichfield Cathedral, and a patron of the radical Gerrard Winstanley, fitfully supporting his egalitarian movement even as she insisted on her own unique aristocratic and prophetic status.

She wrote about her husband's attempted censorship in *The Lady Eleanor Her Appeal*, which she had printed 20 years later, in 1646, although by then the story was well known. The text details her entire prophetic career after 1625, "beginning at home first, where this Book of mine was sacrificed by my first Husband's hand, thrown into the fire, whose Doom I gave him in letters of his own Name (*John Daves*, Joves Hand) within three years to expect the mortal blow."[41] Having announced that he would die within three years, she put on her "mourning garment from that time."[42] This unsettling sight became even more eerie "when about three days before his sudden decease, before all his Servants and Friends at the Table, [I] gave him passe to take his long sleep."[43] Davies's phrasing may require some glossing: According to her own and contemporary accounts, John

Davies was at dinner with friends when his wife entered the room in her mourning attire and began to weep about his imminent death. At the time, John brushed her behavior aside with a grim joke, but both her theatrical display and his sudden death three days later, just before he was to take up his long-awaited post as chief justice, shocked London society. John Donne preached the funeral, and Eleanor's reputation as a prophetess grew.[44]

In network terms, she had already begun to look like a bridge, maintaining her connections to multiple communities even as she became distanced from the close friendships that helped to define courtly society. People began to keep her at arm's length, but they continued to seek out her prognostications and remained wary of alienating her completely. According to Davies, even Queen Henrietta Maria was not above asking the prophetess if she would have a child. Davies cryptically answered in the affirmative, with the caveat that Maria would be happy "for a time," and when she was pressed to specify, she said the queen would remain happy for 16 years, or until 1643.[45] King Charles himself "interrupted" this conversation to comment, with some disapproval, on Davies's macabre predictive powers.[46] And it is clear that he was not alone among his court in fearing her special line in predicting death. When the queen became pregnant, Davies rightly foretold that the baby "should go to a Christning and Burying in a day," and most famously, she predicted that the Duke of Buckingham would not outlive August 1628—a prognostication that was known and chronicled by the politician Sir Edward Dering and the intelligencer Joseph Mead, who maintained an extensive network of correspondents informed about gossip, news, and current events.[47]

If Eleanor Davies was becoming a notorious news item, this did not prevent her quick remarriage to the Scottish soldier and courtier Sir Archibald Douglas, who had been knighted and offered a 10,000-pound pension by King James. But their relationship also soured, as he attempted to thwart her prophetic career by "burning my book, another Manuscript."[48] She wryly notes that "he escaped not scottfree" for this offense—a pun on Douglas's nationality that gives some indication both of her dark wit and of her willingness to use her husband's subsequent affliction to advance her career as a print author and a public person.[49] After he had burned her manuscript, Davies reports that she signed a document, in the presence of "Lady Berkshire and Lady Carlisle," avowing that if within three months "some such wonderful judgement from God came not upon him, then in a Sheet I would walk to [St.] Paul's [Cathedral] barefoot."[50] Once again, she was turning her prophecy into a very public ceremony, attended by individuals of some importance in the court (Lucy Percy-Hay, the Countess of Carlisle, was a figure of high betweenness herself, celebrated by cavalier poets like Sir John Suckling and acting as a spy, and mistress, to major players on both sides of the Civil War).[51] And once again she was able to claim victory over the doubters: As Douglas, her second husband, was taking communion three months later, he "was strooken bereft of his senses, instead of speech made a noise like a Brute creature."[52] Davies relishes the sensational details of this sudden affliction, adding that "doubtless his heart changed too, for so would put his head into a dish of Broth, of Lettuce, or Herbs, and drink Oil and Vinegar, and sometimes Beer all together, insatiable that way."[53] Silenced for attempting to suppress God's prophet, Douglas was, in his wife's telling, transformed inwardly and outwardly into the pig that he was.

In addition to publicizing his affliction as a testament to her power, Davies employed her husband's voicelessness even more directly to amplify her own voice and extend the reach of her publication network. Recalling her strategy in *The Everlasting Gospell* (1649), she explains that she used her husband's illness as a ruse, traveling to Holland under the pretense of a visit to the spa when she really intended to skirt England's printing restrictions:

> That it might be fulfilled *out of the Low Countries, &c.* as the Virgin when undertook her voyage, she fleeing for the Babe's preservation thither; also constrained for printing the same, to go into *Holland*, those plain swathing bands for wrapping it in, pretending in her husband's behalf the *Spa*, obtained a License, since none for printing to be had here.[54]

Here "the babe" is Davies's own work, delivered to her in a new immaculate conception, word made flesh via the printing press. Like Mary, who fled into Egypt to protect her child, Davies is blessed among women. Upon her return to England in 1633, she took the works she'd printed in Amsterdam directly to Archbishop Laud, but she was "no sooner arrived then apprehended, of her childe ravished," and hauled before the Court of High Commission.[55] As her language implies, she saw this not only as a crime against an author but also as a sin. Elsewhere, she calls "their taking away of my Books printed at *Amsterdam*" both "blasphemous" and "accursed," and in the alternative history of the Civil War she would eventually tell, it was instrumental in the downfall of Charles's regime.[56] She appeared before the High Commission on the 23rd of October, and would keep a running list of disastrous events that later occurred on that day, including the 1641 Irish Massacre, which helped start the Civil War, and the 1642 Battle of Edgehill, which marked its first battle.[57] Davies recalls that Laud had mocked her as he burned her book "with his own hand," joking about her prediction that a great judgment would come to the country in 1644–45 by "saying, *She hath taken good long time, till 44, for Dooms-day then; My Lords, I hope I have made you a smother of it.*"[58] And with relish, she reminds readers that the mocker met "his own fatal hour" exactly when she'd warned.[59]

Unlike the later high-betweenness text that first called our attention to her—*Strange and Wonderfull Prophesies by the Lady Eleanor*—Davies's daring and deliberately provocative self-publishing actually makes most of her works decided outliers in the early modern print network. Figure 4.6 depicts all the books in the English print network between 1641–1660, connected by the authors, printers, publishers, and booksellers who produced them. The main cluster of Davies's works, indicated by the red arrow, are set apart because they include only her own name. Some of these works may have been produced in London by printers who remained anonymous (Figure 4.7), but by her own account at least some of them were the result of her travels into Amsterdam. Although they were outliers in the broader print network, her use of them to stage provocative encounters with authorities made them an important part of her growing notoriety.

Whether they knew her as a witch, an iconoclast, or a madwoman, people both inside and outside the court were paying attention to Eleanor Davies. The High Commission ordered her imprisonment in the Gatehouse

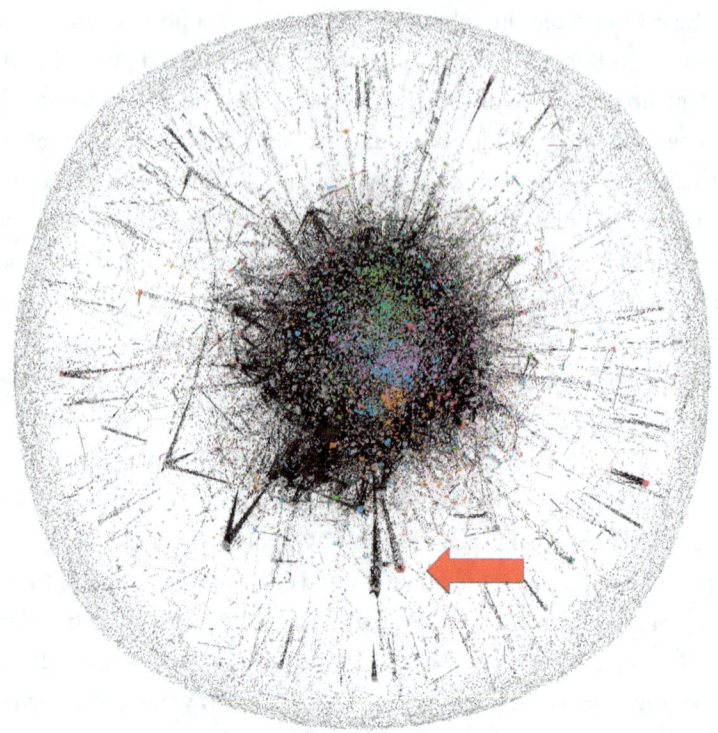

**Figure 4.6** The English print network, 1641–1660. Books are nodes, people are edges. The cluster indicated by the red arrow is works by Eleanor Davies.

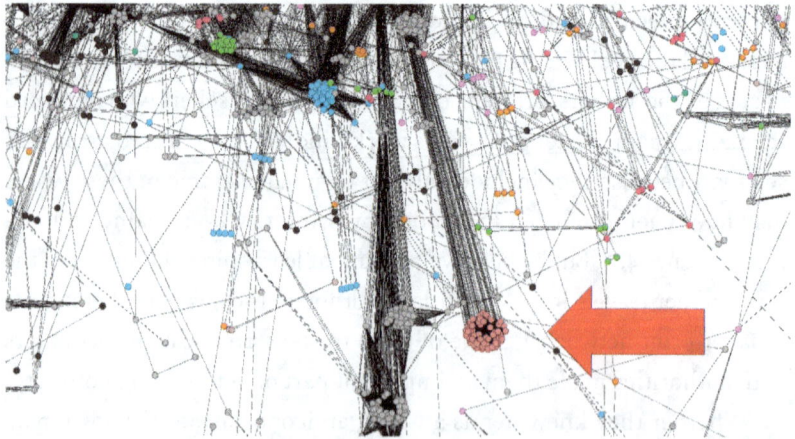

**Figure 4.7** Detail of Figure 4.6, showing a cluster of self-published works by Eleanor Davies or works with anonymous printers, publishers, and booksellers.

at Westminster, where she remained until 1635. It was during this time that her brother, Mervyn Touchet, Earl of Castlehaven, became embroiled in the era's most sensational sex scandal, and she once again leaned into an apparent catastrophe in a way that injected her works into the center of contemporary debates. In the same year that Davies called down God's punishment on her second husband, Touchet was accused of committing shocking sexual abuses against his wife and stepdaughter. Condemned to death for buggery and rape, he was beheaded on Tower Hill on 14 May 1631.

Perhaps it would be going too far to suggest that a young John Milton had a Circean Lady Davies on his mind in 1634, as he composed *A Maske*, commonly known as *Comus*, in which Circe's son transforms victims into bestial creatures who "roll with pleasure in the sensual sty," just as Davies's husband had found himself eating from a bowl like a "brute creature."[60] But Touchet's wife Anne was the daughter of the Countess Dowager of Derby, for whom Milton wrote an earlier masque, and her sister Frances was married to Sir John Egerton, the patron of *Comus*. The girl victim at the center of the Castlehaven trial, who had been raped by Touchet and one of his servants, was the cousin of Alice Egerton, whose ironclad chastity was the subject of that masque, and many critics have argued that its performance functioned as an attempt to disavow Davies's brother and purify the family name from the taint of association with him.[61] At the very least it seems a huge oversight that Eleanor Davies has never seriously been considered part of the story, because if Milton's masque mounted a defense of the family in the wake of Touchet's conviction and public execution, Davies mounted the loudest defense of her brother, using print and manuscript to depict his plight as part of a broader campaign against her family and her own visionary mission.[62]

Her account is a mirror image of one familiar in Milton studies, in which the earl's perversions led to his downfall. In a broadside of 1633, which she had printed in Amsterdam under the cover of her husband's illness, Davies produced the Stanley coat of arms with the names of Elizabeth and Anne Stanley (sisters to Frances and daughters to the Countess Dowager of Derby). She then turned their names into anagrams for "That Jezebel Slain" and "A Lye Satann," before describing a trial in which "children of Belial, and the men of Belial" witnessed against her brother.[63] Elsewhere she wrote that "The Earle of Castle-Haven was accused by his wife *(such a wicked woman),*" but *"he was as innocent as the child new born."*[64] Davies continued to argue as late as 1649 *that* her brother "unmercifully was sentenced to death" and "his house utterly ruined chiefly, because [he] had declined popery," and she would ultimately suggest that the fates met by Charles and Laud were a direct result of their crimes against her and her brother.[65] In other words, if there was a reason the scandal was still very much alive as Alice Egerton took the stage to perform Milton's lines in 1634, it was at least in part because Eleanor Davies had used a series of spectacular performances and her husband's illness to turn herself into one of England's most notorious authors.

**Figure 4.8** All the texts connected to Eleanor Davies's *Strange and Wonderfull Prophesies* with fewer than two degrees of separation. Davies's text is highlighted in the red circle and enlarged for visibility, and communities have been shaded using the Fruchterman-Reingold algorithm.

It is less important to show that Davies was a direct influence on Milton, however, than to emphasize that she, like Milton, was at the center of a cultural field that was becoming increasingly polarized, and that the high betweenness of her texts reflects her ability to maintain and establish ties between people and groups on every part of the spectrum. We can see this in Figure 4.8, which testifies to Davies's profound betweenness and the broader connectivity of the print network during this era. It is a visualization of all the texts connected with two or fewer degrees of separation to her highest-ranking work for betweenness centrality, *Strange and Wonderfull Prophesies* (this node is just below center and has been shaded red and vastly enlarged for visibility). Nodes are colored via a community detection algorithm, and the communities vary widely from the blue, mostly royalist one that includes King Charles's *Eikon Basilike*, to the mustard-green, mostly parliamentarian one that includes Milton's *Eikonoklastes*. The orangey-red cluster, connected to Davies's text and to the left, mostly contains works sold by Giles Calvert, including radical Digger texts by Gerrard Winstanley; the teal cluster in the upper right contains works of rigorous Presbyterianism, many published by Michael Sparke and written by William Prynne. I've argued elsewhere that Milton's *Comus* finds him at a juncture between his earlier orthodoxy—marked by his affiliation with courtly clients such as Henry Lawes and the Earl of Bridgewater—and a radicalism that would emerge only in the following years, as he watched the Laudian church exert increasingly strict control over difference and dissent.[66] Davies's emerging identity, as author and prophet, bridged even more stark extremes. Her "entire body of work," as Katharine Gillespie has noted, "may be understood as a meditation upon the nature of political power and, as importantly, the culture of excess to which it inevitably gives rise."[67]

An aristocrat chafing against a strict licensing regime, a one-time courtier who saw corruption at the heart of the court but wanted to preserve her family's place within it, Davies would be hauled before a judge again, soon after her release from prison, for taking direct iconoclastic action against the Laudian church at Lichfield Cathedral. The episode once again illustrates her tendency to engage with many ideological camps, but to be at home in none of them, and it shows once again the role her texts played in this process. The details of why Davies ended up in Lichfield are murky—perhaps to be near her daughter and grandchildren, with whom she maintained correspondence throughout her time in prison—but the court records make it clear that she maintained something of a radical salon there "from about Midsummer 1636 till near Michaelmas following."[68] During that time, several local women "resorted to the said lady daily and had continual private conference with her, and took her to the cathedral," where they evidently took great offense at the new Laudian embellishments.[69]

It was during this time that Davies wrote *The Appeal to the Throne*, which she sent to the Bishop of Lichfield but which does not survive. What does survive is the record of her subsequent behavior, in which she led her group of women to the cathedral, where she "went into the bishop's throne and sat there, and said she was primate and metropolitan. She also with a pot of water, tar, and other filthy things, most profanely defiled the hangings at the altar."[70] The performance landed her back in custody, this time in Bedlam and the Tower, where she remained until 1640. Although court records make careful note of Davies's co-conspirators, Esther Cope observes that Davies herself tends to elide them from the story of her time in Lichfield. "The distinctiveness that she claimed because she was a prophet and the noble birth of which she was so conscious separated her from the townswomen," Cope notes, and Davies tended to see "others as audience or instruments," whether they were the courtly ladies before whom she had performed her earlier prophecies or the townswomen of Lichfield.[71] From the perspective of network analysis, we could say that Davies's prophetic vocation was based on the cultivation of weak rather than strong ties, a strategy of radical betweenness.

To see just how far afield this drove her from the Caroline court culture of her youth, it is worth concluding this section by considering her remarkable relationship with Gerrard Winstanley, leader of England's Digger moment. After the violent suppression and collapse of his communistic society at Cobham Hill, Surrey, in 1650, Winstanley and his followers sought respite and support working on Davies's estate in

Hertfordshire. Although Winstanley may have originally felt that Davies was a kindred spirit, relations between them quickly deteriorated and ended in mutual accusations. Winstanley's only extant personal letter is to Davies, and although he addresses her "one who hath loved you with true friendly Love," he goes on to defend his own stewardship of her estate against her accusations that he had cheated her.[72] More vehemently, he says he "must speak whether you will hear or no" about the deeper sense in which she was becoming corrupted by pride over her birth and prophetic mission, "for you are no more to me than any other branch of mankind."[73] Winstanley's letter seems to show that she shared her prophecies with him, and he developed a close enough relationship with her to speak boldly. As usual, though, she held herself apart from his group even as she interacted with it, maintaining that her status as prophet and daughter of Lord Touchet required a degree of deference from Winstanley and his followers. She seems to have thought of herself as a patron—not a member of this radical group, but a bridge between it and the world of power and place.

But for Winstanley, her acts of mediation looked more like plays for power than acts of charity, patronage, or fellowship. He recognized that in fashioning herself as a mere vessel of the lord, even as she was maintaining her legal grip on her estates and their profits, she was actually setting herself up in an important position:

> You said in Purton Barne, that you were the prophetess Melchisedecke, which is a high assumption. You might as well call yourself The Christ, for you set yourself in the chair of the Almighty God. . . . Therefore let not secret pride and selfwill, which you are full of, blind your heart any longer. Look into the scripture, and you shall find that the true prophets delayed not to keep covenant and promise. They were no taxmasters over their brethren.[74]

He goes on at length to accuse Davies of abusing her reason and compromising her legacy. But he also notes her ability to "moderate your words before others," implying that if she is mad, there is a method to it. Rather than breaking with her, he vows to continue in her "property business."

For her part, Davies endorses the letter with the dry observation that "He is mistaken" and with her own, surprisingly dispassionate, account of what Winstanley owes her.[75]

It has long been easy to dismiss Eleanor Davies by noting there was "Never Soe Mad a Ladie," the anagram of her own name that Sir John Lambe supposedly presented to her.[76] But her daughter, Lucy Countess of Huntington, provided an epitaph for her grave that called her "learned above her sex," "for a long time breathing of God, and aspiring above, of her own and the Commonwealth's fate divining beforehand."[77] As Nigel Smith has argued, her techniques were "part of a long Reformation tradition of prediction."[78] Mad or ecstatic as she might have appeared to some of her contemporaries, Davies cannily positioned herself as a mediator, even referring to herself simply as a "Writer or Secretary" for messages that were not her own.[79] This is surely why the printer and publisher Robert Ibbitson agreed to put his name on the text at the center of this chapter and the print network of her day. Ibbitson had been printing documents for Parliament and parliamentary factions since 1647, including the newsbook *Perfect Occurrences*, and has been described as a "specialist in the printing of army newsletters."[80] But his connections were vast, and the bookshops that carried his works crossed the ideological spectrum.[81] Davies had established herself as exactly the sort of author capable of speaking to all these audiences simultaneously; betweenness was both a rhetorical posture and a network effect of her print and publication strategy, which made her a sensation and a scandal from the court to Cobham Hill.

### III. Mary Cary and the Reformation of Female Authorship

If Eleanor Davies's version of prophecy included elements of ecstatic performance that we sometimes associate with the term, Mary Cary's writings almost seem to demand an entirely different label. As Katharine Gillespie argues, "while Mary Cary's works have been cited as a penultimate example of the manic rhetoric that allegedly defines" female sectarian prophecy, "they should, in fact, be read alongside such 'Grand Instauration' writers as Samuel Hartlib and Henry Jessey."[82] Gillespie draws this comparison chiefly because of Cary's arguments for "a free market in ministerial labor that promised to provide the lasting material conditions necessary for allowing all men and women to preach," but we shall see that Cary actually is connected to Hartlib through a shared publication network and a shared reformist agenda that goes well beyond efforts to expand the ministerial franchise.[83] Cary's rationalistic, even Baconian, style sounds very unlike Davies; but Cary resembles her fellow female prophet in her canny use of print, bookselling, and patronage networks. Acting as her own publisher, Cary placed her books with the era's best-connected radical booksellers, cultivated a network of powerful women who were married to key revolutionary leaders, and gained endorsements from the era's leading sectarian ministers. Like Davies, her authorship of one of the highest-ranking texts for betweenness during the Civil War era is not accidental but is at least in part the product of this shrewd strategy. The work that earns that distinction, *Twelve Humble Proposals,* was a collaborative production of Cary with Giles Calvert and Henry Hills. Calvert was easily the most prolific radical bookseller and publisher of the period, and Hills was a printer to the Council of State under Cromwell who was flexible enough to survive and thrive as an official government printer after the Restoration. Although the two of them were tremendously well connected, they were ideologically distant and rarely worked together, with only a handful of other joint productions that were all official publications for Parliament.[84]

The result can be seen in Figure 4.9, which shows all the works within two degrees of separation from Cary's *Twelve Humble Proposals,* the large white node at the center. This textual network, which is colored here by a community detection algorithm that groups texts with the most links in common, is a far more political one than Davies's: It includes works ranging from Hobbes's *Leviathan* to Milton's *Tenure of Kings and Magistrates* and *Eikonoklastes,* to King Charles's *Eikon Basilike.* The large burgundy cluster just below Cary's work includes mostly works sold by Calvert; the pink cluster below it is mostly work by George Fox and other Quakers. The dark green and bright teal neighborhoods are mostly texts for and about the law and Parliament. The two worlds, Calvert's and Hills's, cleave on either side of Cary's *Twelve Humble Proposals*—a neat visual reminder of this text's status as the fourth most central, ranked by betweenness centrality,

**Figure 4.9** All the texts connected to Mary Cary's *Twelve Humble Proposals* with fewer than two degrees of separation. Cary's text is the large, central node in white.

from 1641–1660. Why is this text, by this now obscure woman, the exception that brought their publishing worlds together? How did Cary—who described herself as a "weak and unworthy instrument" and whose early works show little promise of major impact outside a small community of fellow travelers—establish an authorial identity and publishing profile that was appealing to both Calvert and Hills?[85]

Unlike Anna Trapnel, a fellow Fifth Monarchist with whom she is sometimes compared, Cary avoided spectacular public performances and focused instead on positioning herself as a print author. Perhaps this is why, as David Loewenstein has recently noted, Cary has "received little attention from literary scholars working on the English Revolution," even as prophets like Trapnel have garnered increased critical attention.[86] I hope to begin addressing that critical neglect here by seeking to understand how Cary crafted texts that served as bridges between disparate communities in the print network.

Cary's ideas are consciously revolutionary, calling for a complete reshaping of society that will empower all ranks of individuals in the church, state, and economy. Her first, anonymous works of 1645 and 1647—*The Glorious Excellencie of the Spirit of Adoption* and *The Resurrection of the Witnesses*—pick up very much where tracts like Milton's *Reason of Church Government* and *Areopagitica* left off in 1642 and 1644, illuminating some of the central ideas that animate her entire canon. In the *Reason of Church Government*, Milton argues against the suppression of sectarian and dissenting preaching as he develops his core belief that "the reforming of a Church ... is never brought to effect without the fierce encounter of truth and falsehood together."[87] In *Areopagitica* he warns that pre-publication censorship threatens to turn the "streaming fountain" of God's truth "into a muddy pool of conformity and tradition."[88] Cary similarly believes that truth emerges from a contest with error, invoking a Miltonic image of God's church being built from diverse materials, such as "wood, hay, & stubble"; and she argues for the free circulation of ideas by warning that "if you do prohibit any from Preaching Jesus Christ, you do quench the spirit, and oppose the freeness of the spirit, who is a free Agent. And as the wind bloweth where it listeth, though we see it not, so doth the spirit."[89]

This idea that God's spirit is freely given and universally distributed lies at the center of all her other arguments about church, state, and society. But she goes considerably beyond Milton as she combines this idea with the social egalitarianism that characterized advocates of lay preaching.[90] As robustly as Milton argues for freedom of conscience and the priesthood of all believers, he also clearly imagines the voice of truth emanating from a learned elite, like the "learned Minister" he contrasts with the "Dunce prelate" in *Reason of Church Government* or the ingenious men (and they are all men) "sitting by their studious lamps, musing, searching, revolving new notions" in *Areopagitica*.[91] By contrast, Cary insists that God has not "tied up the spirit" among "such and such degrees of humane learning," and "for you to silence any that do preach Jesus Christ, of what rank soever, it is an endeavoring to quench the spirit."[92] The violently productive encounter of truth and falsehood only results in total reformation if it is totally inclusive. "Let it be far from you to hinder any, because every talent which the Lord Jesus hath given, he requires an improvement of it to his use; and it ought not to lie hid in a napkin."[93] Referring to Christ's parable, which was so important to Milton's understanding of his special vocational calling, she reiterates that "All ought to improve their talents," and only this will lead to a truly universal reformation in which truth emerges from an unrestrained field of discussion and debate.[94]

In subsequent works Cary makes it clear that this reformation is not confined to church discipline, but that it also entails the kind of pansophic program associated with Samuel Hartlib and his circle, often articulated in strikingly similar terms. Her best-known "prophetic" text, published in a single edition with two title pages as *Little Horn's Doom* and *A New and More Exact Mappe* in 1651, describes the coming reformation and "Kingdom of Christ" not through mystical anagrams, but through the language of cartography, offering a "description or map of this new world, from the first entrance of it, to the utmost borders of it, as far as I have yet discovered, (or rather hath been discovered to me from the scripture,) in my weak travels, inquiries, searches into it."[95] In a move familiar from other prophetic texts of the time, she positions herself as a simple mediator, communicating messages from a higher power: "I am a very weak, and unworthy instrument, and have not done this work by any strength of my own, but have been often made sensible, that I could do no more herein, (wherein any light, or truth could appear) of my self, then a pencil, or pen can do, when no hand guides it."[96] But her technique is scholarly rather than ecstatic. She carefully sets down biblical evidence to demonstrate that the revolutionary events of 1645 mark the overthrow of "the beast" and the beginning of Christ's return and thousand-year reign with his saints. She then maps out the contours of the coming social and religious reformation with clear headings, footnotes, and numbered lists that can make her work read more like a policy paper than a visionary text. (The question of whether the saints can use the "material sword" to punish malefactors and advance God's work is "resolved in the Affirmative."[97])

The equal spiritual authority of all members of society is explained in granular detail: "[N]ot only men, but women shall prophesy, not only aged men, but young men; not only superiors, but inferiors; not only those that have University learning but those that have it not; even servants and handmaids."[98] This will, however, require the kind of linguistic reform envisioned by pansophists like Hartlib and Jan Amos Comenius, so that the saints "shall all speak a pure language, a spiritual language, having a pure, heavenly style" that can be easily comprehended by all.[99] Like Milton, who proposed that educational reform could "repair the ruins of our first parents" in a tract he dedicated to Hartlib, Cary suggests her reformist program will constitute an Edenic return, although in her case this comes complete with improvements in child mortality rates and an end to the enmity between men and beasts ("for what put an enmity between some of these creatures and Man, but Man's corruption?)."[100] Cary imagines a total social transformation, and she's rarely willing to propose utopian ideas without considering both their practical implementation and their scriptural justification.

Hilary Hinds has argued that Cary's "apparently characteristic self-effacing" description of herself as a simple pencil or pen for God to write with "begins to seem more double-edged and ambiguous" when we consider the ways in which it "both shifts the focus from the unworthy 'instrument' herself on to God, the wielder of the instrument, and at the same time it draws attention to the authority of her words and the power of the figure in the position of the author."[101] Indeed, to claim such a direct line from God is not just ambiguous, it is downright audacious, especially when the author's message involves a complete reshaping of society. Which is why Cary seemed to understand that she could not take even such a "modest" claim to authorship for granted. Instead, it was part of a larger, longer strategy for situating herself within the publication network and establishing her authority as a print author. Although *Little*

*Horn's Doom* is now her best-known work, in network terms it is also a bridge to nowhere; unlike *Twelve Modest Proposals*, it was published by Cary herself, with only her name on the title page, and it is not among the 9,386 publications of the era with non-zero betweenness.

The volume containing *Little Horn's Doom* and *A New and More Exact Mappe* is the first in which Cary clearly acts as the publisher, with the title page announcing that the book is "printed for the Author," although she has arranged for it "to be sold at the Black Spread-Eagle, at the West end of Pauls." This is the shop of Giles Calvert, who had acted as the publisher and bookseller of Cary's two previous books. Calvert was tremendously important: In a basic network analysis of all people in the English print network, 1641–1660, he is easily the one with the highest overall degree *and* betweenness centrality. Like Nicholas Okes in a previous generation, he's an outlier, with nearly twice as many connections as the second- or third-ranked individuals, a hub in a network that seems to orbit around him. Like Okes, he took risks by publishing hundreds of new titles, and in particular, as John Barnard has noted, he "dominated" the publishing of radical works by Quakers, Ranters, Levellers, and Independents.[102] In 1651, when Cary sold her text through his shop, Calvert was also becoming one of the booksellers most involved with distributing Samuel Hartlib's works, including Hartlib's own foray into prophetical literature, *Clavis Apocalyptica*. As D. F. McKenzie wrote, Calvert's bookshop was "the *one* point in London where nearly all radical writers went to seek a sympathetic trade response to, and efficient dissemination of, their new ideas."[103] It was also "well known as a meeting place for radicals or sectaries in London."[104]

Figure 4.10 shows all the people connected to Calvert with two or less degrees of separation. The sheer ideological range, from the cavalier poet John Suckling to the Quaker visionary James Naylor, is impressive. But Cary's name is the only one on the title page of *Little Horn's Doom*, and although she'd trusted Calvert with the efficient dissemination of her ideas, a wealth of additional paratextual information makes it clear she was exercising new control over her authorial self-presentation and that she was interested in finding and speaking directly to new readerships. For example, not only is this the first text in which she uses her full name,

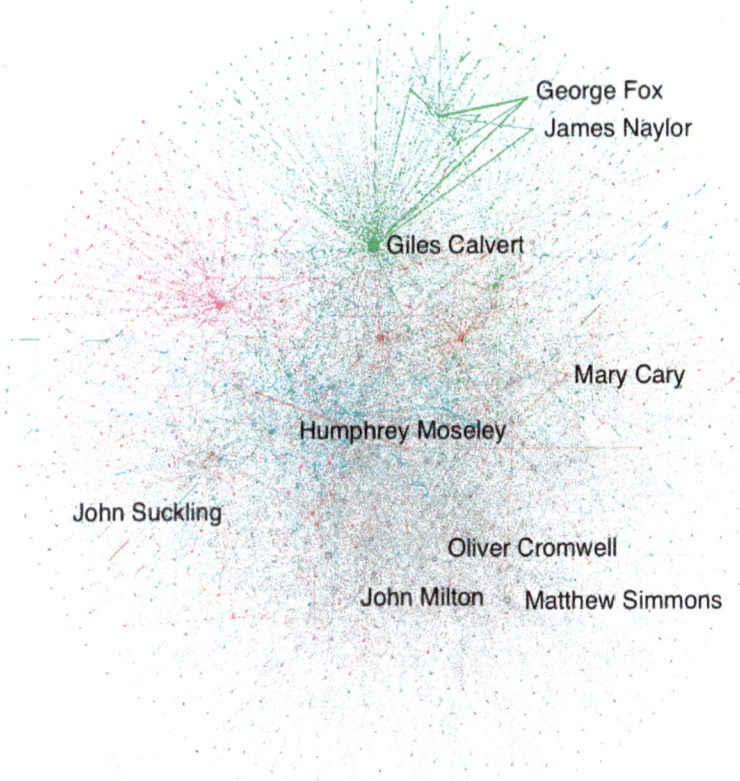

**Figure 4.10** Giles Calvert's egocentric network, 1641–1660, limited to two degrees of separation. Calvert was the highest-degree figure in the English print network during this period.

but in a note to the reader she also explains that, thanks to a recent marriage, it had changed:

> [I]n my former book ... I subscribed my name *Cary*, for that was then my name; for which reason I have thought good, to subscribe the same name in the title page of this Book also, that the reader may not be put into any doubt, by finding different names in the Titles; (since I have so often in this book referred the reader to that,) but let the reader know, That (having since changed my name) I am now known by the name of *Mary Rande*.[105]

Who exactly Cary had married remains unclear, although Christopher Hill suggested that likely candidates include Eleanor Davies's agent John Rand, or since her works were "known in chemical circles," William Rand, a chemist and correspondent of Hartlib.[106] Either way, she was likely the person John Beale, an early fellow of the Royal Society, had in mind when he wrote to Hartlib that "Mary Rante hath prophesied . . . of amplifying the dominion of good men over Gods works, & of turning curses into blessings."[107] According to another letter by the German natural philosopher Henry Oldenburg, Hartlib was seeking information about "Mary Rante" and "her prophecy, among those booksellers in Westm[inster] Hall."[108] The curious might seek out Anna Trapnel in the pulpit at Somerset House in the Strand; they sought Cary/Rande among the booksellers.

This, Cary explains, is precisely the reason she retains her maiden name on the title page: She wants this book to be read alongside her earlier works as part of a continuing project, and she wants her works to be easy to find without confusion. Indeed, elsewhere in the preface to the reader she explains that she had long planned to produce a cohesive body of work but needed to wait until the right time to release it.

> I had written the first of these Treatises, titled *The Little Horn's Doom and Downfall*, about seven years since, but have been with-held from publishing of it until now . . . because that men would then generally have been more uncapable of receiving of such things, than now they are, because now these things are fulfilled; and prophesies are then best understood, when they are fulfilled. But now, am I so pressed to publish both this first Treatise, and this other which I have but lately written, upon this 27 verse of this seventh of *Daniel*, as that I cannot, I dare not, with-hold neither of them from public view any longer; but by publishing of them in print, I shall expose them to the public view of all men, as far as in me lies.[109]

These works demand to be read together, and Cary has carefully considered her publication strategy to ensure that her readership is ready to receive the truths she's been called to reveal. She also explicitly connects them to her earlier publications.

Another note, in postscript to the book, unusually offers errata and corrections—*not* to the current work but to one of the author's previous books, *Resurrection of the Witnesses*. "Having often referred the reader" to that publication in the current volume, Cary writes that she wants to eliminate any possible confusion, "there being in that Book a mistake of the Emperor's name, by reason of trusting to memory, and neglecting to consult the history about it."[110] She goes on to quote Socrates by book and verse, as well as to make reference to several other historians, and to insist that despite her slip, her original timeline for the reign of the saints is correct, and that "two or three other faults escaped in printing," but they are "not material" to her larger message.[111] This is not merely the conscientious work of a scrupulous writer, but of a woman who recognized that female print authorship would bring special scrutiny. Cary published her first works anonymously, but when her sex became known, *The Resurrection of the Witnesses* was instantly mocked in print by a critic who took it upon himself to expose "this Female-Minister M. Cary" for her ignorance or neglect of writings by church fathers and historians in her explication of Revelations.[112] Without naming him, Cary answers his critique in the postscript to *Little Horn's Doom* and quietly upends his notion that she's too unlearned to have read the historians he cites. She presents herself as gracefully but prodigiously learned, working from memory at the cost of an occasional, immaterial error.

In *Little Horn's Doom* Cary took other steps to insulate herself from being labeled a mere "Female Minister" and to gather up her earlier publications into an authoritative body of work. First, she included a tranche of testimonials by well-credentialed male ministers: Hugh Peters, who was a counselor to Fairfax and Cromwell and chaplain to the Council of State; Henry Jessey, who held millenarian views but was widely respected as a moderating voice within a radical movement; and Christopher Feake, who helped initiate the Fifth Monarchist movement but who had not yet fully embraced the radical positions that would bring him into conflict with the Cromwellian regime.[113] All were products of Cambridge, all were ordained in the church before coming into conflict with its leadership, and together they represent nearly the full spectrum of Independent religious thought during the interregnum. They all explicitly defend Cary as a female author writing within a traditionally male discourse (although Hugh Peters's compliments can be more than a bit backhanded, such as his suggestion that Cary writes and interprets the scriptures "so well, that you might easily think she plow'd with another's heifer"[114]).

Feake's testimonial implies that Cary sought him out specifically to hedge against criticisms that would attempt to marginalize her as a female author, noting that "the ensuing Discourse ... (being a Gentlewoman's thoughts put into form and order by her self) was brought to me to peruse, with this desire added, That (if I judged it meet) I would prefix a few words, to signify my judgement concerning the usefulness thereof."[115] Surprisingly, although Feake is by far the most radical of the men to provide testimonials for Cary, he praises her not for her boldness but for her caution in moderating and supporting her claims, her "vigilant care" in providing evidence that he believes will find favor with saints and skeptics alike.[116] That seems to have been exactly the effect Cary sought. The diversity of viewpoints represented by the three men—from a member of the "Puritan establishment" like Peters to a radical like Feake—is as important as their authority: Cary was placing her works at the center of debates over the interregnum church and the new Jerusalem.

And she did so in a way that emphasized, rather than downplayed, her identity as a female author. Preceding the ministers' testimonials, and preceding her note to the reader, Cary includes a testimonial to "the Virtuous, Heroical, and Honourable Ladies": Elizabeth Cromwell, Bridget Ireton, and Margaret Rolle. Cary praises them as chosen among God's women:

> Observing, how that among the many pious, precious, and sage Matrons, and holy women, with which this Common wealth is adorned; as with so many precious jewels, and choice gems ... God hath selected and chosen out your Ladyships, and placed you in some of the highest places of honour.... I have therefore choosen, (being of your own sex) to dedicate these Treatises to your Ladyships ... and under your favorable aspects, to publish them to the world.[117]

Elizabeth Cromwell was married to the army general and future Lord Protector; Bridget Ireton was her daughter, married to the illustrious parliamentary officer and chief architect of the commonwealth Henry Ireton; Margaret Rolle was married to Chief Justice Henry Rolle, a member of the Council of State who commanded broad respect and who retained his position even after refusing to take part in the king's trial. These are not women who are necessarily invested in millenarian thinking, but Cary is eager to remind readers that the commonwealth will be built on their "heroical" virtues as well as their husbands' efforts.

This careful paratextual display casts some retrospective light on the earlier publications in which Cary eased into her role as a female author, gradually revealing her identity and modulating her claims to authority. These early works were published under initials rather than her name, sometimes in ways that seem deliberately misleading. The title page of her first work, *The Glorious Excellencie of the Spirit of Adoption*, identifies the author as "M. G., Minister of the Gospel," which may have been a slip by the printer Jane Coe, who had recently taken over the printshop after her husband's death and who continued to produce important newsletters and pamphlets in the subsequent years of the Civil War. But the false identification of Cary as "M. G., Minister of the Gospel" seems just as likely to have been an obfuscation by Cary and her collaborators. Coe had already been placed under arrest earlier in the year for illicit printing. And the radical publisher Henry Overton sold the book in a shop that was becoming notorious, as one contemporary put it, for carrying "All kind of unlicensed books that make any ways for the Sects."[118] In *A Word in Season*, published in 1647, Cary was identified only as the "meanest of the Servants of Jesus Christ, M. Cary." She was "M. Cary, a Minister or Servant of Jesus Christ" in *Resurrection of the Witnesses*, in 1648. It seems significant that she finally reveals herself most fully as a wife and woman only in *Little Horn's Doom*, the work that also calls on a community of women to help perpetuate her message, turning a potential vulnerability into a strength. For the first time, she also explicitly connects her argument about the "freeness of the spirit" to the status of women, who she suggests must participate fully in the coming Reformation.

In explaining the tightrope that visionary women had to walk between asserting bold ideas and disclaiming personal responsibility for those ideas, Phyllis Mack notes that the "overall effect on most observers was probably to reinforce traditional preconceptions of the volatile, essentially uncivilized nature of all womanhood," adding that "if respectable women were constrained by convention to behave with humility and modesty, the female visionary was constrained to behave as though she were literally out of her mind."[119] Cary deftly sidesteps that constraint, and in doing so she positions her works at the center of Civil War discourse in a way that allows her simultaneously to address Hartlib's improvers, England's lawmakers, and Calvert's expansive radical readership. In short, she fashions precisely the sort of authorial identity that in 1653 will help make *Twelve Humble Proposals* one of the most central texts of the Civil War era.

The text is a multi-point plan for complete social reform, addressed to the Rump Parliament and holding obvious appeal for audiences of women, Hartlibian projectors, and radical sectarians. In it, Cary once again shuns ecstatic style in favor of numbered headings, footnotes, and cross-references to her other works, which stand as a body of work authorizing her recommendations for church and state. The tract's proposals for new workhouses, improved land use, and modernized, expanded universities would sit entirely at home within the canon of works written and promoted by Hartlib, from Comenius's *Reformation of the Schooles* to Milton's *Of Education*. The universities will be entirely "new modelled" to provide funding to those with the greatest financial need and to increase practical education so that graduates "may be useful to Church or Commonwealth."[120] She proposes a new, public postal service and says "the portage of all inland letters a price should be fixed at 3d a letter, or as your Honors shall think fit," with any profits going toward poor relief. She recommends a system of public notaries so that contracts can be verified for a fixed rate. She calls for a complete revision of the legal code ("wholly abolish and repeal those great and tedious volumes of Law, that are either in a strange tongue or otherwise") and the implementation of a simplified system of arbitration.[121] She proposes a salary cap for civil servants, the abolition of tithes, and the opening of pulpits to all ministers who can gather a congregation under their roofs, transforming the existing church infrastructure to facilitate a public sphere of conversation and debate. All ministers shall be able to "bring their people into each public meeting place that is most commodious for such a congregation, and nearest their habitations, both in the City and Country, that so the people of that parish, and as many as shall desire to hear the word there, may be made partakers of it freely without any charge"; this may entail multiple congregations meeting under the same roof, where multiple ministers preach at different times of the day, and it will be this flourishing debate, rather than enforced belief, that will allow the truth to reveal itself.[122]

Once again, Cary used Calvert as her bookseller. Mario Caricchio has argued for "the centrality of Calvert's bookshop in the experience of the English Revolution"; its "pluralistic" identity was instrumental in forming "a cluster of social networks, which had one nexus at Calvert's bookshop," from the web of relationships that clustered around the families of members of the Council of State, like Henry Vane, to the radical visionaries associated with Jacob Boheme and the improvers associated with Hartlib.[123] If Calvert's shop was central in this way, then Cary's text embodied the spirit of the place, but there are also indications that she was working to ensure a still broader distribution of her ideas, or that she'd successfully positioned this text in a way that expanded its potential audience and reach. Her printer, Henry Hills, was above all an establishment man and a survivor who printed pro-monarchist texts during the Civil War, later convinced the Cromwell regime to make him an official printer and give him a monopoly on printing Bibles, and still later ended his career as a Catholic convert and official printer to King James II.[124] He was not, in other words, a committed ideologue, but he was interested in making a profit and finding an audience for his work among the powerful.

*Twelve Humble Proposals* also names "R. C." as the publisher, and while his identity is not certain, the most likely suspect is Richard Collings, who wrote and published the newsletters *Mercurius Civicus* and *The Weekly Intelligencer of the Common-Wealth*, and who appears to have been the only person publishing under those initials during this period.[125] Collings was by no means a radical, but he was well positioned to aid in distributing the work to a broad, ideologically diverse audience. That was especially important in the uncertain waning days of the Rump Parliament, when allegiances were in flux. The status of *Twelve Humble Proposals* as the fourth-ranking text of the era, by betweenness centrality, seems like a perfectly reasonable consequence of Cary's style, her arguments for broad toleration of dissent and debate, and her authorial identity, which was the culmination of a concerted effort to situate herself and her books effectively within communities that could support and disseminate her ideas.

The next and final known time Cary appeared in print, in an enlarged and updated edition of *Resurrection of the Witnesses* printed by Henry Hills in 1653, the title page names her as "Cary, *alias* Rande," and the book contains a complete list of "books already published by this Author," with instructions for finding them in the shops of Calvert, his former apprentice and sometimes partner Thomas Brewster, and the Fifth Monarchist bookseller Livewell Chapman.[126] It is unclear what happened to Cary after this, but for a moment at least she had established her works at the very center of the interregnum print network.

In attempting to understand the unusually high betweenness of Cary's text, I have perhaps given her too much agency in creating bridges between disparate communities and readerships. After all, the most comprehensive and theoretically coherent approach would emphasize Cary's status as one actor among many—including Henry Overton, Giles Calvert, Thomas Brewster, and Livewell Chapman, who all sold her works, and Henry Hills, Robert White, and Jane Coe, who all printed them. But I hope this book has made it clear that agency for any individual work is broadly distributed within complex networks, with printers, publishers, and booksellers all playing an important role. With that understanding as background, it seems worth exploring how the unusual network behavior of texts relates to decisions made by their authors, especially when those authors have been largely ignored or dismissed as lacking impact and influence. In the case of both Mary Cary and Eleanor Davies, we find authors who worked to situate their texts as both rhetorically and materially central to the debates of their day, and in doing so they cultivated a web of connections that can help explain their works' unusual status in the print network. Self-proclaimed mediators between God and man, they embraced betweenness as an authorial strategy and used it to articulate radical connections between past and future, the world as it was and the world as it could be.

## CHAPTER 5   WEAK TIES AND THE MAKING OF A STRONG POET

John Milton's Early Publishers

THE PRECEDING CHAPTERS OF THIS BOOK have suggested that analysis of the early modern print network can reveal the hidden histories of important but unsung actors. This final chapter takes a different approach, asking how analysis of network structures and behaviors might reshape our understanding of one of England's most highly celebrated—and even dominant—poetic voices. Far from hidden, John Milton has long been the ultimate example of the "strong poet" whose influence threatens to overshadow his ancestors and overawe his poetic descendants.[1] This at least is how Harold Bloom describes him, proclaiming Milton "incapable of suffering the anxiety of influence, unlike all his descendants," and although that account may be infected with Bloom's own preoccupations, this impression of "strength" has been a consistent response to Milton's work from his day to the present.[2] Andrew Marvell famously described Milton as a kind of poetic Samson, so "strong" that Marvell initially worried *Paradise Lost* might ruin the very "sacred Truths" it sought to preserve.³ But ultimately the "Mighty Poet" was completely in control, a singularity whose success led Marvell to conclude that "no room is here for Writers left, / But to detect their Ignorance or Theft."⁴ Milton's enemies also acknowledged this strength, even as they denounced him as one of the "subtile Samsons" that had helped "to pull down Monarchy, and set up Anarchy."⁵

Literary histories of both the old and new varieties have typically approached strong literary voices by exploring the strong ties that shaped them: The closest family members, the dearest friends, the most persistent patrons and mentors. In Milton's own case, this has led to much focus and psychological speculation around a few key people—his parents, his boyhood friend Charles Diodati, his vexed marriage to Katherine Powell, and his relationships with a handful of doomed republicans like Henry Vane. It has also led to the corresponding sense that his strong poetic voice emerged from a place of relative isolation. John Shawcross, for example, describes the young Milton of the 1630s as "isolated" with few exceptions; he depicts the older Milton of the 1670s as an invalid who had "not many visitors, and some called only once."⁶ Neil Forsyth likewise emphasizes that young Milton "made no special friend" at Cambridge and that an older Milton was left lonely and at the mercy of his hostile daughters after 1663, with "no regularity or reliability about the visits of any of Milton's friends."⁷ Such impressions are supported by Milton's own statements in works such as *Prolusion* VII, where he admits that love of learning produces "secluded and withdrawn" men "with little knowledge of and experience in human affairs," or his letters to Charles Diodati and Carlo Dati, where he says he lives "obscurely" and complains that he is so tortured by the company of neighbors and family that he is "forced to live in almost perpetual solitude."⁸ Even those scholars who have protested (perhaps too much?) that "Milton in person could be gregarious, fun-loving, and sociable," have tended to see his poetry as a more lonely pursuit, since "the writing of poetry inclined one toward being solitary, moody, introspective, thoughtful, serious, and deep."⁹

But network science has shown that the most powerful voices are enabled by weak ties, rather than strong ones, and I will argue that many of the very documents that seem to imply Milton's isolation actually show him actively establishing and cultivating such ties. A "weak" tie is one that may be infrequent or unusual—a rare visit with a distant acquaintance or a letter to a friend of a friend—as opposed to an intimate bond to a member of one's family or close social group. This chapter will begin with an overview of the research that has shifted our understanding of social networks by demonstrating that such weak ties are surprisingly crucial at bridging gaps between smaller communities that would otherwise remain disconnected. It then turns to Milton's early work, which has been described as indicating his increasing isolation but which actually shows him using print to cultivate and maintain weak but crucial ties to a cosmopolitan literary world. I conclude by exploring Milton's role as a singular bridge between two of the most connected members of the book trade in the 1640s and 1650s: Humphrey Moseley and Matthew Simmons. In connecting them, he connects the political and poetic discourses of his day and emerges both as the self-proclaimed voice of his nation and as a profoundly social writer.

### I. Weak Ties and Structural Holes

The "'strength' of an interpersonal tie," as Mark Granovetter defines it, is "a combination of the amount of time, the emotional intensity, the intimacy (mutual confiding), and the reciprocal services which characterize the tie."[10] From that definition alone, it will be clear that "strong" ties are the subject of most literary and historical analysis, at least insofar as it applies to a particular individual like a Caesar, a Shakespeare, or a Milton. But as Granovetter notes, we need something more than a focus on strong ties to connect a "large and increasing body of data and theory" about "what happens within the confines of the small group" with the "large scale, statistical, as well as qualitative studies . . . into such macro phenomena as social mobility, community organization, and political structure."[11] The solution, which made Granovetter's 1973 article one of the most-cited in social science, was to focus on the bridges between intimate groups and to recognize that those bridges were typically weak rather than strong ties.[12]

Granovetter's argument is based on the principle of *triadic closure*, illustrated in Figure 5.1. Simply put, if A is strongly tied to B in a social network, and B is strongly tied to C, then A will likely also be connected to C. Returning to Granovetter's definition of tie strength as a measure of time, emotional intensity, or intimacy, triadic closure makes both intuitive and probabilistic sense: If I spend time with someone every day, I will also encounter their other close friends, contacts, and connections. This is what it means to "move in the same circles" (perhaps we should say we move in the same triangles). Triadic closure is now a widely established principle in studies of social networks, which have also shown that when such a triangle forms, the ties among A, B, and C are more likely to survive over time than ties in dyads without a third shared partner.[13] Granovetter coyly dubs a situation like the one illustrated in Figure 5.2 a "forbidden triad" and notes that "except under unlikely conditions, no strong tie is a bridge" between otherwise disconnected nodes.

By contrast, "all bridges are weak ties" is an initially surprising argument that once again makes both intuitive and mathematical sense.[14] If I see someone not daily, but only once every few years, nearly *all* of that person's connections will be new or novel to me. These distant contacts are doorways to entirely new worlds, which is why in academia or business, "networking" happens at far-flung conferences rather than within our own departments. "Whatever is to be diffused," writes Granovetter,

> ... can reach a larger number of people, and traverse greater social distance (i.e., path length), when passed through weak ties rather than strong. If one tells a rumor to all his close friends, and they do likewise, many will hear the rumor a second and third time, since those linked by strong ties tend to share friends. If the motivation to spread the rumor is dampened a bit on each wave of retelling, then the rumor moving through strong ties is much more likely to be limited to a few cliques than that going via weak ones; bridges will not be crossed.[15]

On a practical level, this means we are more likely to learn about new ideas, or communicate our own ideas more broadly, if our social network includes many weak ties. Counterintuitively—as recent, statistical analysis

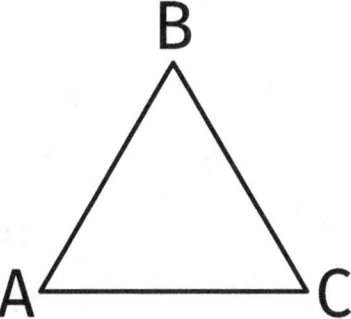

**Figure 5.1** A typical closed triad.

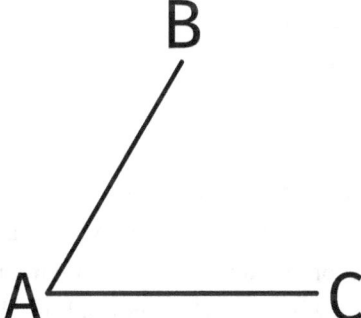

**Figure 5.2** A forbidden triad. If node A has strong connections to both B and C, B and C are likely connected to each other as well.

of vast mobile-phone networks has confirmed—we can remove strong ties from a giant connected component without much impact, but removing only a few weak ties will cause the network to collapse.[16]

Because they offer pathways to new communities, weak ties tend to span "structural holes" in a network, as Ronald Burt has shown.[17] Burt emphasizes the importance of ties that span gaps in a network, whatever their strength or degree, as the most important factor in the spread of "new" and "good" ideas, since "[n]ew ideas emerge from selection and synthesis across the structural holes between groups."[18] In Figure 5.3, for example,

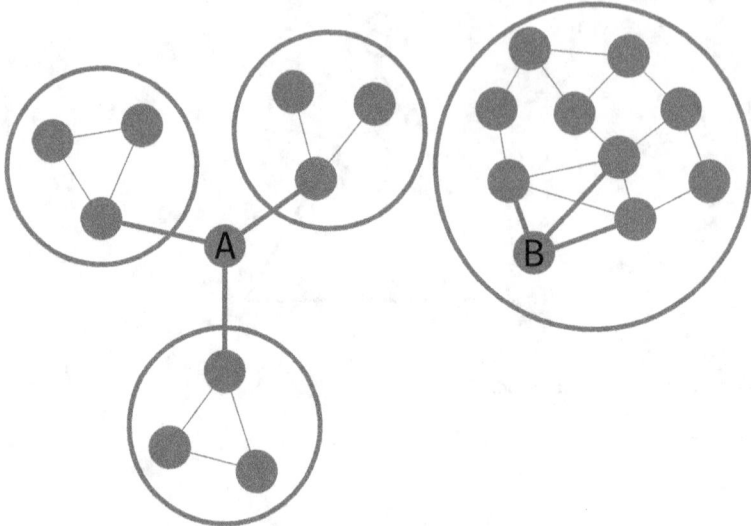

**Figure 5.3** Although they have the same degree (degree three), node A bridges structural holes while node B does not.

both node A and node B have three connections (degree three), but A is a broker for three distinct sections of the network, uniquely positioned to receive, recombine, suppress, and transmit novel information from each.[19]

"People whose networks span structural holes have early access to diverse, often contradictory, information and interpretations," Burt notes, giving them "a competitive advantage in seeing good ideas."[20] John Padgett and Christopher Ansell invoke a version of this theory to describe Cosimo de Medici's rise to political power through his use of contacts to opposing family factions, and others have analyzed modern industry, Bronze Age trade routes, and the twentieth-century art world in similar terms.[21] More broadly, Randall Collins suggests that the ability to bridge gaps in intellectual networks is at the heart of creativity, with innovators in philosophy and other fields achieving most renown when they most successfully broker the friction between competing ideas, schools, and ideologies: "New ideas are created as combinations of old ones; and the intellectual's creative intuitions are feelings of what groups these ideas are appealing to (and against which intellectual enemies)."[22]

According to such theories of influence, a strong poet needs an abundance of weak ties at least as much as close personal attachments. If a poet experiences a flood of inspiration, encounters a new formal possibility, or becomes aware of a paradigm-shifting idea, this is likely to happen via weak ties rather than strong. Conversely, if a poet seeks to communicate these ideas in a way that will influence either contemporaries or posterity, she will need bridges across the divides of culture, space, and time. To borrow a phrase from Milton's description of his own desired readership, the strong poet needs bridges, "few perhaps, but those few, of such value and substantial worth, as truth and wisdom, not respecting numbers and big names, have bin ever wont in all ages to be contented with."[23] The quote comes from *Eikonoklastes*, and this chapter will conclude by showing how that tract and others printed by Matthew Simmons helped forge a bridge from one of the era's most important polemical publishers to one of its most important poetic publishers. But first I want to turn to Milton's earlier career to see how works that have been associated with his increasing isolation actually show him cultivating a remarkably rich and diverse network.

## II. Early Works: The Case of the *Epitaphium Damonis*

The pastoral elegy *Epitaphium Damonis*, which was written and printed around 1639, is not one of Milton's most loved or discussed poems, but it has major implications for understanding his later career, announcing his epic ambitions more explicitly than any other work before *Paradise Lost*. "Give place, woods" (*Vos cedite sylvae*), sings the narrator Thyrsis, as he abandons his pastoral pipe and projects a poetic career in which he will sing the history of his nation instead.[24] This future epic will tell of Trojan conquest—of Igraine, Arthur, and Merlin—as the poet's pipe, "transformed by my native muses, sounds out a British tune" (*patriis mutata camœnis / Brittonicum strides*).[25] Epic achievement will not come without sacrifice and loss, however, and Thyrsis admits that "one man cannot do everything, or even hope to do everything" (*omnia non licet uni / Non sperasse uni licet omnia*).[26] To become a new poet, he will need to leave his pastoral preoccupations behind, and most critics believe Milton himself does this by shrinking his social world.

The *Epitaphium Damonis* is also Milton's "most autobiographical poem," as Barbara Lewalski describes it, "filled with anguish for the loss of his oldest, and perhaps only, truly intimate friend."[27] And in this regard no poem better exemplifies the view of Milton as an isolated or antisocial poet. Milton had appeared in print before: His poem "On Shakespeare" was printed anonymously in the second Shakespeare folio of 1632, and Henry Lawes had helped bring an edition of *A Maske, commonly known as Comus,* into print in 1637 without Milton's name attached. But the *Epitaphium Damonis* was the first work Milton brought into print himself. In the poem, Milton, in the pastoral persona of Thyrsis, not only bids farewell to Charles Diodati, who died a year earlier in 1638, but also to the Italian poets and poetry he encountered on his continental tour. As it depicts "the unbridgeable gap between the protagonist of the poem and the society in which he finds himself," another critic notes, Milton turns inward "to fulfill his destiny in England."[28] The narrator Thyrsis claims with little ambiguity that he does not care if his epic finds readers in the outside world ("externo ... orbi")—an early, more nationalistic version of the "fit audience ... though few" that Milton addressed in *Paradise Lost.*[29] If we think of Milton as an asocial or antisocial author—producing poetry the way a silkworm produces silk, as Marx described him—then this critical understanding of the *Epitaphium Damonis* as a lonely and isolated work is the most obvious beginning of that thread.

But the epitaph was not merely the product of private grief, and by drawing on the work's material history we can demonstrate the ways the poem carefully affirms, reconstitutes, and expands the social, poetic, and political networks that Milton established during his schooling in England and his travels abroad during the 1630s. Recent scholarship on Milton and print has begun to challenge long-held views of him as a singular and somewhat antisocial genius. Chief among this work is Stephen Dobranski's *Milton, Authorship, and the Book Trade,* which argues that the "persona of the independent author that Milton implies in many of his texts paradoxically required a collaboration among" amanuenses, acquaintances, printers, distributors, and retailers.[30] Anne Baynes Coiro has likewise argued that "Milton's success in constructing himself as English literature's great, solitary author" obscures an important story about "collaborative, theatrical, and historically and culturally embedded work" such as *Comus*.[31] But we need to rebalance the agencies implied when Coiro suggests that Milton "was clearly not yet ready to be a public writer" when *Comus* was published without his name on it in 1637.[32]

To understand the emergence of Milton the author, it is useful to explore not just when Milton was ready to be a public writer, but what conditions made members of the book trade receptive to printing works by this little-known and formerly anonymous young man. By the same token, Dobranski understandably focuses most of his attention on the named and famed works that establish Milton's persona, such as *Areopagitica* and the 1645 *Poems*. He has far less to say about the network of printers, publishers, and booksellers who produced Milton's anonymous early works, and about the way Milton used those works to facilitate connections to a wider world and become "The Author John Milton," as he was eventually identified on his title pages. Considered as an instrument of connection, it quickly becomes apparent that the *Epitaphium Damonis* is less a lonely cry than a bridge between richly social worlds of cosmopolitan poetic achievement and oppositional print.

*Epitaphium Damonis* was first printed in quarto, on a single sheet. Survival rates for single-sheet publications are generally low, and this was likely a limited edition, with only one known surviving copy, held by the British Library, where it was not discovered until the twentieth century.[33] John Shawcross convincingly dates the publication to 1639–40, less than a year after Milton's return from Italy.[34] Two years earlier, Henry Lawes had helped bring an edition of *Comus* into print, and, based on a thorough comparison of fonts, Shawcross proposes that *Epitaphium Damonis* shares the same printer: Augustine Mathewes.[35] "It seems natural," as Shawcross notes, that Milton "would have sought out his 'recent' printer" for this new work, and examination of these and other texts printed by Mathewes around this time confirms that attribution.[36] We find an unusual double-cuspated "A," for example, not only on the title pages of *Comus* and the *Epitaphium*, but also Peter Heylyn's *A Coale from the Altar*, which Mathewes printed between 1636 and 1637. The type is worn in both, and it

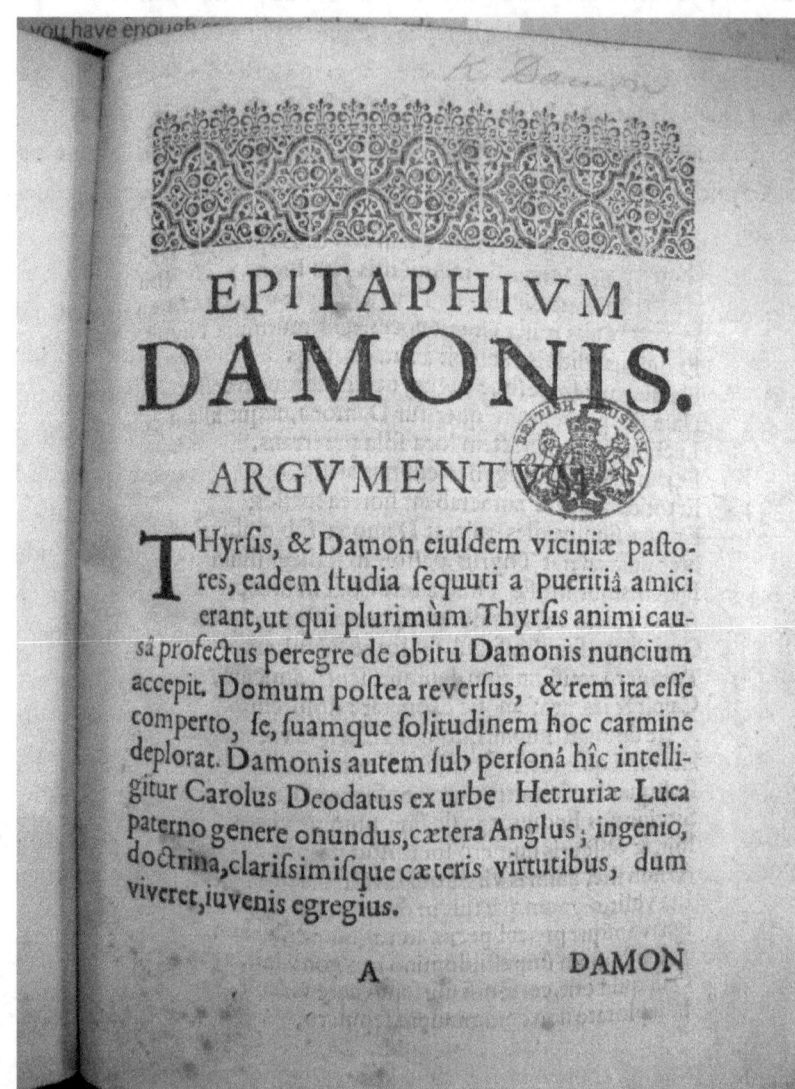

# EPITAPHIVM DAMONIS.

## ARGVMENTVM

Thyrsis, & Damon eiusdem viciniæ pastores, eadem studia sequuti a pueritiâ amici erant, ut qui plurimùm. Thyrsis animi causâ profectus peregre de obitu Damonis nuncium accepit. Domum postea reversus, & rem ita esse comperto, se, suamque solitudinem hoc carmine deplorat. Damonis autem sub personâ hîc intelligitur Carolus Deodatus ex urbe Hetruriæ Luca paterno genere onundus, cætera Anglus; ingenio, doctrina, clarissimisque cæteris virtutibus, dum viveret, iuvenis egregius.

A          DAMON

**Figure 5.4** The only remaining copy of the first printing of *Epitaphium Damonis*. The ornamental border reappears in later works printed by Augustine Mathewes.

SOURCE: The British Library, BL C.57.d.48. Reprinted with permission.

is especially clear that the type used in the 1637 impression of *Coale* derives from the same type fount as *Comus*. They share a battered question mark and a misplaced italic question mark that may have resulted from foul case, while the ornaments shared by the *Epitaphium* (Figures 5.4 and 5.5) and *Comus* also appear in other works Mathewes printed, including *The Wits*, by William Davenant, and *A Collection of Such Sermons and Treatises*, by Samuel Ward.[37]

One adjustment should probably be made to Shawcross's account: It isn't clear that Milton would have viewed Mathewes as "his" printer or vice versa. The 1637 *Comus* did not include the name of Milton or Mathewes. It was advertised as having been performed before "John Earle of Bridgewater" and included an effusive dedication to the earl's son by the musician Henry Lawes, who composed the work's songs. It also announced that it was printed for Humphrey Robinson, a rising publisher who would later become a warden of the Stationers' Company and who is best known for his partnership in publishing literary works of some prestige with Humphrey Moseley. Milton and Mathewes's connection through the 1637 publication of *Comus*, in other words, was a distant and weak one. But it seems to have been enough to prompt Milton to seek out Mathewes when he decided the poem should be printed rather than circulated in manuscript.

Why did he make that decision? Henry Lawes's printing of *Comus* in 1637 is a useful comparison: Lawes explains in the dedication that he undertook its printing in response to a clear demand, as the "often copying of it hath tir'd my pen to give my severall friends satisfaction."[38] But Lawes was at this point a far more renowned name than Milton (his own name would appear alongside Milton's on the title page of Milton's 1645 *Poems*, to bolster the work of the lesser-known poet), and the publisher presumably agreed that demand for his work would recoup the cost of printing *Comus*. By contrast, Milton does not seem to have been struggling to keep up with demand with the *Epitaphium Damonis*, and there are no indications that it was published as a commercial venture or ever sold. However, private printing like this was probably more common than we realize, and while it was not exactly cheap, it would have likely been

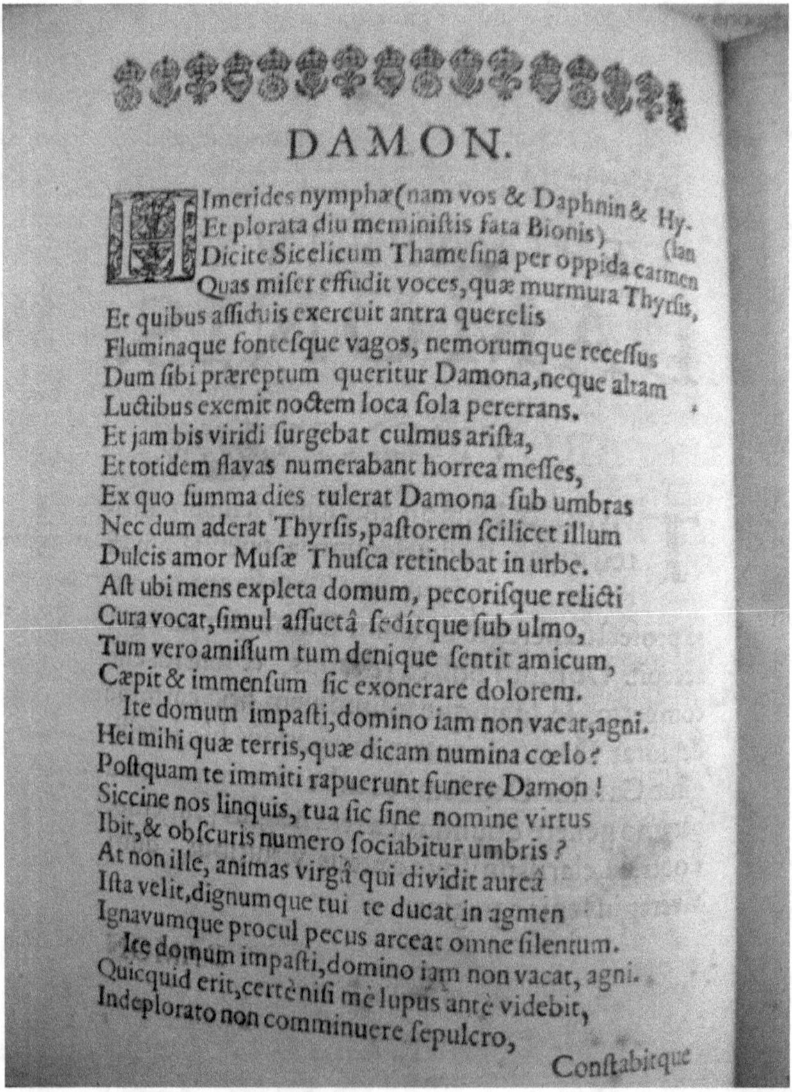

## DAMON.

Imerides nymphæ(nam vos & Daphnin & Hy-
Et plorata diu meministis fata Bionis) (Iam
Dicite Sicelicum Thamesina per oppida carmen
Quas miser effudit voces, quæ murmura Thyrsis,
Et quibus assiduis exercuit antra querelis
Fluminaque fontesque vagos, nemorumque recessus
Dum sibi præreptum queritur Damona, neque altam
Luctibus exemit noctem loca sola pererrans.
Et jam bis viridi surgebat culmus arista,
Et totidem flavas numerabant horrea messes,
Ex quo summa dies tulerat Damona sub umbras
Nec dum aderat Thyrsis, pastorem scilicet illum
Dulcis amor Musæ Thusca retinebat in urbe.
Ast ubi mens expleta domum, pecorisque relicti
Cura vocat, simul assueta seditque sub ulmo,
Tum vero amissum tum denique sentit amicum,
Cæpit & immensum sic exonerare dolorem.

Ite domum impasti, domino iam non vacat, agni.
Hei mihi quæ terris, quæ dicam numina cœlo?
Postquam te immiti rapuerunt funere Damon!
Siccine nos linquis, tua sic sine nomine virtus
Ibit, & obscuris numero sociabitur umbris?
At non ille, animas virga qui dividit aurea
Ista velit, dignumque tui te ducat in agmen
Ignavumque procul pecus arceat omne silentum.

Ite domum impasti, domino iam non vacat, agni.
Quicquid erit, certe nisi me lupus ante videbit,
Indeplorato non comminuere sepulcro,

Constabitque

**Figure 5.5** The verso of the *Epitaphium Damonis* title page, with an ornamental pattern that appears frequently in works printed by Augustine Mathewes.

SOURCE: The British Library, BL C.57.d.48. Reprinted with permission.

possible to print 100 pages of a single-sheet publication like this for just under 8 shillings. As Ian Gadd notes, this was less than half the purchase price of Shakespeare's first folio.[39] And for a relatively affluent young man like Milton, this would have provided an avenue into print without the need to persuade a publisher to take a chance on turning a profit off of this rather rarefied Latin elegy by an essentially unknown writer.

His production and distribution of the *Epitaphium Damonis* implies that print publication was an important part of Milton's strategy of cultivating distant relationships. The work of Harold Love and others has accustomed us to thinking about manuscript circulation in terms of gift exchange, community formation, and prestige.[40] But for Milton, printed works were routinely part of such exchanges. "I beg you to send me Giustiniani, Historian of the Veneti," Milton implores his friend Charles Diodati at the closing of a 1637 letter, in a typical request. "On my word I shall see either that he is well cared for until your arrival, or, if you prefer, that he is returned to you shortly."[41] He thanks his friend and former instructor Thomas Young for sending him a Hebrew Bible in 1628.[42] He sends his former instructor and friend Alexander Gill some unspecified printed verses in 1629, and he offers to send the Dutch poet and diplomat Leo Van Aitzema copies of his tracts in 1654.[43] Although Milton's name did not appear on the printed version of the 1637 *Comus*, he also clearly valued the statement it made about his authorial achievements, circulating copies as gift texts to people who were not close intimates but whose association he valued, like Sir Henry Wotton. Milton's 1645 *Poems* would later include a letter from Wotton acknowledging the gift and vouching, implicitly and explicitly, for Milton's membership in a distinguished cultural community.[44]

As Michel Callon, John Law, and Arie Rip note, "the production and distribution of texts . . . constitutes a vital method for building worlds."[45] Writing a letter, sending a book, publishing a newsletter—all of these textual practices help compose and maintain social networks through processes Callon dubs "interessement" and "enrolment."[46] To "interest" an actor is to create some device that makes the creator essential to access other entities in the network—to produce a poem or a newsletter, for example, that establishes a unique pathway of communication between a reader and a writer. "Enrolment" happens when "*interessement*" succeeds, and an actor is translated into my network on the terms to which we have agreed—becoming a reader, a news consumer, or a friend. Although he does not use the term in quite this technical a sense, Cedric Brown has shown that Milton uses texts in exactly this way as he "enrolls himself in the company of Tasso and Marino" and others through the exchange of letters and gift texts.[47]

These were by definition distant connections, often removed by thousands of miles and rarely connected by more than a handful of letters over many years. But Milton explicitly recognized the value of such weak ties, writing to the Italian scholar Carlo Dati that he cherishes their distant tie more than those who are "closely bound" to him "by the chance of proximity of neighborhood or some other tie of no real importance" (*vicinae aut aliqua nullius usus necessitudo mecum . . . conglutinavit*).[48] We have Milton's letter, written nearly 10 years after his Italian journey, because Milton had just belatedly learned that Dati received a copy of the printed *Epitaphium Damonis* that was sent at some much earlier date. In his letter to Dati, Milton draws on the metaphor of texts as funerary monuments, which was familiar from commemorative editions like the 1632 folio of Shakespeare's plays where Milton's own work first appeared in print. The *Epitaphium Damonis* is the "tomb of Damon" (*Damonis tumulum*), which he has worked to adorn.[49] Milton says he took "care" to send it as a "proof of talent, however small, and love to you," and its material form matters both as commemoration and as announcement of poetic ambition.[50]

He also makes it clear that he had not sent the poem as a private act, but because "I thought in this way, that I would either allure you or some of the others to write" (*Existimabam etiam fore hoc modo, ut vel te vel alium ab scribendum allicerem*).[51] Estelle Haan notes that when Milton writes of sending the poem "to you" he uses the plural (*ad vos*), which shows "that it was to the academy as a whole rather than to Dati personally, as has generally been assumed hitherto, that Milton sent the separate *Epitaphium Damonis*."[52] Although the poem proclaims that men's "minds are alien" to one another" (*aliena animis*), in other words, Milton clearly had it printed in order to circulate it and cultivate just these sorts of connections. The gesture worked, prompting Dati's reply, as well as his own request that Milton contribute to a collection of poems on Francesco Rovai, a recently deceased member of the academy. He attempts to persuade Milton by telling him that the Dutch scholars Nicolas Heinsius and Isaac Vossius have agreed to produce such verses, and although we have no evidence that Milton complied, we can already see Milton's *Epitaphium Damonis* opening up a wider social network rather than confirming its collapse.[53]

Understood in the context of its dissemination, the poem itself makes this obvious. In the poem, Milton/Thyrsis says he still has the gifts ("munera") he received from the Tuscan shepherds, specifically naming Dati and Antonio Francini, another of the Florentine intellectuals Milton befriended on his Italian journey.[54] The gifts he names—reed baskets, bowls, and pipes—are all prizes traditionally given to pastoral poets, and Milton elsewhere says that these gifts include the verses Dati and Francini exchanged with him in the Florentine academies during his visit.[55] The *Epitaphium* continues and extends this social world. The poem invokes the poet Giovanni Battista Manso, the subject of Milton's "*Mansus*," in even more elaborate terms (he is "mirandus"), praising the "wonderful artwork" (*mirum artis opus*) of two cups he has given to Milton.[56] These cups ("pocula,"[57]), are a likely allusion to Manso's books, *Poesie Nomiche* and *Erocallia*, which contain the neoplatonic imagery of Cupid and the Phoenix that Milton uses in his own poem to describe their elaborate engraving and to set the scene for Damon's final apotheosis among the gods.[58] In his 1647 letter, Milton is delighted to learn that all these men, through Dati, have received his poetic missive and he promises to send the 1645 *Poems*, which prominently featured testimonials by each of them. Understood as an intermediary in this exchange, Milton's initial foray into print authorship reads as an explicit effort to maintain and cultivate social connections.

The printer of Milton's poem, Augustine Mathewes, was himself an opportune connection for an aspiring author who had an interest in the commemorative and social powers of print, connecting Milton both to a rich field of literary publications and to a growing oppositional print network at a crucial moment in his career. Mathewes worked regularly with Humphrey Robinson, the influential publisher of the 1637 *Comus* and the frequent partner of Humphrey Moseley, who would later publish Milton's 1645 *Poems*.[59] Mathewes had printed important works of drama and literature by writers including John Donne, George Wither, William Davenant, Michael Drayton, Francis Beaumont, Tom May, William Rowley, and John Marston. Mathewes was a careful printer of Latin verse, such as the miscellany *Parentalia*, which included poems by various Oxford and Cambridge wits, including William Cartwright and Thomas Randolph, and *Parerga* by Milton's friend and former instructor at St. Paul's, Alexander Gill. As William Riley Parker observes, "In the eight years 1630–7, if we may judge from surviving books with his name or initials on the imprint, he was, although unlicensed, one of the most important and active of London printers. Only Thomas Cotes, Thomas Harper, and Miles Flescher can be compared with him in quantity of output."[60]

But Parker's observation points to a paradox: Although Mathewes produced a fairly high volume of titles, when we analyze a graph of the English print network during the years 1630–1637, he appears to be neither central nor strongly connected to leading members of the book trade. In a ranking of the top 150 members of the book trade network during this period by degree—or their absolute number of connections—Mathewes rounds out the bottom of the list at number 146, which is extraordinarily low for a printer, especially considering his prodigious output. Further analysis of the records attributed to him in the English Short Title Catalogue explains his apparently anomalous position: Mathewes was a master of kinds of underinformed title pages discussed in Chapter 1, in which printers and publishers intentionally erased or masked their identity in order to deal in matters of political or religious controversy. In Chapter 1, I showed that this form of anonymized printing does not impact our analysis of the overall network or our ability to identify its major hubs or bridges. But Mathewes's standing within the network is certainly influenced by his deliberate strategies of concealment: His publications were more than twice as likely to be missing information about his own name, or that of the authors, booksellers, or publishers involved, than those by Miles Flescher. They are four times more likely to be missing such information than the other printers Parker mentions as comparable in terms of output: Thomas Cotes and Thomas Harper.[61]

If Mathewes was connected to a respectable field of authors and publishers, he was also associated with the world of unlicensed and increasingly oppositional print. As one study put it, he seems to have avoided asking "awkward questions" about licensing or ownership when authors or publishers brought him material.[62] And he began to find himself at odds with both the state and authorities in his own trade as early as 1621, when he was fined for printing George Wither's *Motto*, an unlicensed political satire that violated the royal proclamation "Against excess of lavish and licentious speech of matters of state."[63] During his war with the Stationers' Company in the 1620s and 1630s, Wither worked with Mathewes more consistently than any other member of the book trade. Wither must have had him in mind when he argued in 1624 that an "honest Stationer is he, that exercizeth his Mystery (whether it be in printing, binding, or selling of Books) with more respect to the glory of God, & the public advantage, then to his own commodity," taking care with controversial works "like a discreet Apothecary in selling poisonous drugs."[64] Mathewes had the skill and discretion to produce controversial works like Wither's *Collection of Emblems*, which appeared without the printer's name attached in 1635. And sometimes that discretion extended to printing under pseudonyms—"Jan Maast," for example, when producing Middleton's controversial *Game at Chess* with the false imprint "Ghedruckt in Lydden by Ian Masse."[65] But it ultimately cost him professionally. He was censored early in his career for illegally operating multiple presses.[66] And after the "great error" of printing a forbidden book brought down the wrath of Star Chamber, he was called in again in 1637, ultimately losing his status as Master Printer.[67]

That book was *The Holy Table, Name and Thing, More Anciently, Properly and Literally Used, Under the New Testament, Then That of an Altar*, published anonymously by John Williams, Bishop of Lincoln. It openly challenged Laud's controversial directives to standardize the placement of communion altars on the east wall of the church, surrounded by rails. Although it was a more diplomatic and ambivalent salvo than those launched by William Prynne, Henry Burton, or John Bastwick, Laud attacked the book in his speech censuring them before the Star Chamber, using the language of explosive conflagration to warn that "I am fully of opinion, this Book was thrust now to the Press, both to countenance these Libellers, and as much in him lay, to fire both Church and State."[68] Indeed, Mathewes may have slyly stoked the coals of this controversy in ways that have not been noticed. Just before printing *The Holy Table,* Mathewes printed the book to which it was replying, *A Coale from the Altar,* by Peter Heylyn, the Laudian apologist. Heylyn himself was responding to a letter that Williams had circulated in manuscript, and Mathewes prefaces Heylyn's work with an unusual note from the "Printer to the Reader" in which he explains that

> howsoever the Letter by him here replied unto, be scattered up and down, and in divers hands; Yet because possibly, the Copy of the same hath not hitherto been seen of all, who may chance cast their eyes upon this Treatise . . . the very Letter it self is herewith Printed, and bound together with it.[69]

Printing the letter has the effect of giving Laud's opponents the final word even in a text ostensibly meant to defend his position.

Considering Mathewes's subsequent punishment for printing Williams's work, it is hard to read this as an entirely innocent gesture, and it is certainly clear that printing Heylyn's work did not ingratiate Mathewes with the Laudian establishment. When the Dean of Arches, John Lambe, surveyed the printing trade in preparation for the new 1637 Star Chamber decree to regulate printing, he recommended that Mathewes should be excluded from the list of licensed printers thanks to his role in the controversy, with Marmaduke Parsons admitted "in his room."[70] Mathewes petitioned the commissioners to intercede with Laud later that year, describing himself as "poor" and "destitute of any other calling whereby he may maintain his wife and family" and begging to be reinstated and admitted as a Master Printer.[71] But his petition was not granted, and in fact when Williams was forced to recant his book, he cast the blame squarely on Mathewes and the others involved who produced it. A document from 1638 in the Lambeth Palace library, endorsed with an order from King Charles that it be delivered to the High Commission, begins with Williams's admission that his first offense was "permitting the Copy thereof to fall into the hands of a Stationer, who caused the same to be printed in London without full and Lawful Authority."[72]

The episode drove Mathewes into the shadows. He may have worked briefly under Parsons until that man's death in 1639/40, and shortly after the printing of the *Epitaphium Damonis*, he reappears briefly in the Stationers' Register in 1641 to transfer his "estate, right, title and interest" in various texts to other printers, always with the proviso that "the said Mr Mathewes is to have the workmanship of printing them (if hereafter he shall keep a printing house) and shall doe them as reasonably as any other printer will doe the same."[73] But it would seem he continued working with his own or others' equipment until at least June 1653, when he entered a text in the Stationers' Register, before disappearing once more from the records.[74] This is one reason he may have been receptive to the kind of small, private, unlicensed work that Milton apparently brought him.

Mathewes's contracts to transfer his texts included one with John Raworth, whose widow Ruth would be responsible for printing Milton's 1645 *Poems* and, with her second husband John Newcomb, seven of his prose tracts between 1650 and 1660.[75] But the shop where the fonts and ornaments used in the *Epitaphium Damonis* show up most frequently in the 1640s is that of Thomas Paine. Paine worked with Matthew Simmons on Milton's *Doctrine and Discipline of Divorce* and *Tetrachordon*, as well as on other Simmons publications. He often worked with the radical bookseller Giles Calvert (as did Raworth), and we find the fonts, ornamental borders, and crowned national emblems from *Epitaphium Damonis* used in Paine's printing of the Leveller William Walwyn's defense of religious nonconformity, *A Parable, or Consultation of Physitians upon Master Edwards*.

It is impossible to know whether Mathewes was working as a journeyman under Paine and Simmons or whether they had simply acquired his materials. It is clear, however, that Mathewes's clash with church, state, and company authorities thrust him into the midst of a growing oppositional print network just as Milton was seeking a printer for the *Epitaphium Damonis*. Milton's publications to this point—an unnamed appreciation for Shakespeare in the second folio, an anonymous masque with music by the royal musician Henry Lawes, and a poem in a genteel Cambridge memorial volume—showed few signs that he would soon emerge as a critic of the unholy alliance between an overweening church and "old patentees and monopolizers in the trade of book selling," as he later attacked them in *Areopagitica*.[76] But even as *the Epitaphium Damonis* announced Milton's grand poetic ambitions and affirmed a cosmopolitan intellectual community, it was a link to a constellation of book producers who had their own reasons for helping him make that case.

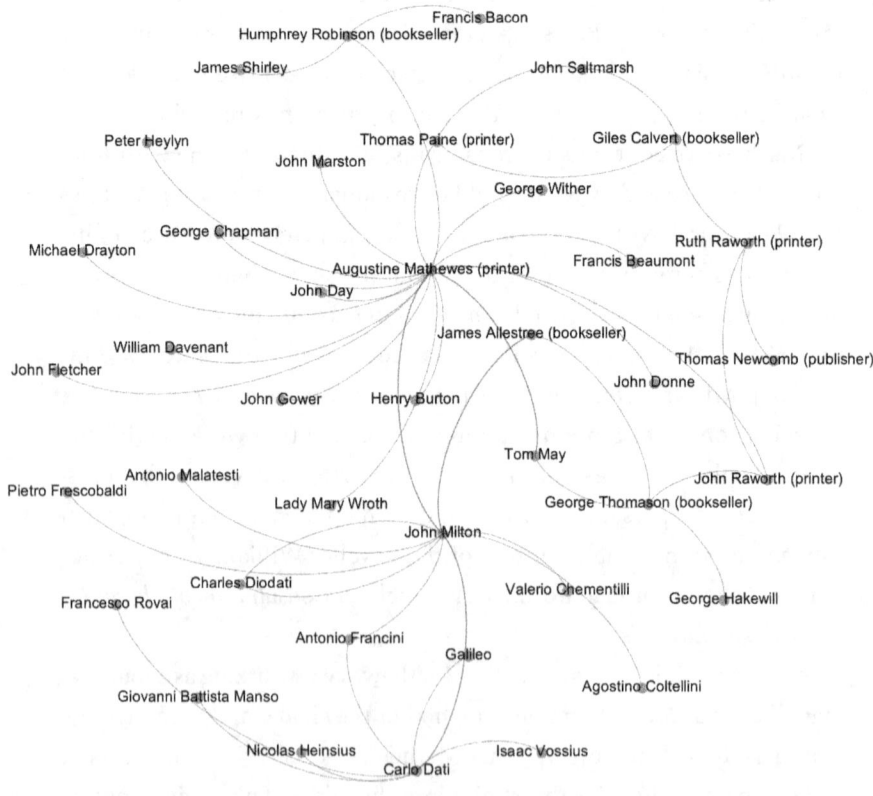

**Figure 5.6** Network of people connected within two degrees of separation to the printing and circulation of Epitaphium Damonis.

Figure 5.6 is one possible visualization of that constellation—tracing Milton's connections to some of the printers and publishers mentioned above, to the some of the other authors they printed, and to Milton's own correspondence involving the poem. It only includes people within two degrees of separation, and for the sake of visibility it is only a small sample of the possible connections that we could trace, to make it easier to see that they include some of the foremost authors and intellectuals of Milton's era. But despite these limitations—or because of them—it helps make the point that although *Epitaphium Damonis* has most typically been seen as marking Milton's isolation, it was in fact establishing ties to a much wider world.

### III. Moseley, Simmons, and the Prophetic Voice

In large networks, Granovetter notes, "it probably only happens rarely, in practice, that a specific tie provides the *only* path between two points."[77] But, as the graph in Figure 5.7 shows, that's exactly the kind of unique path Milton appears to provide between two of the most important members of the book trade between 1641 and 1660: Humphrey Moseley and Matthew Simmons. Actually this appearance is somewhat deceiving: If we removed Milton, we could trace other paths between the two men, but Milton is the only author who worked with both of them, and therefore he provides the shortest and only *direct* path. Both Moseley and Simmons have been mentioned above because they were weakly connected to Milton through his earliest publications: Moseley often produced literary works in partnership with Humphrey Robinson, who published *Comus* in 1637; Simmons worked with Thomas Paine and other members of the radical print network that absorbed Augustine Mathewes after the Laudian establishment had made it impossible for Mathewes to maintain his own shop. These weak ties would prove enormously consequential for Milton's career as a poet, polemicist, and public person.

That the names Moseley and Simmons would appear in Milton's early publication network is not exactly surprising since they were, respectively, two of the most well-connected members of the book trade from 1641–1660. Figure 5.8 shows the highest-degree members of the print

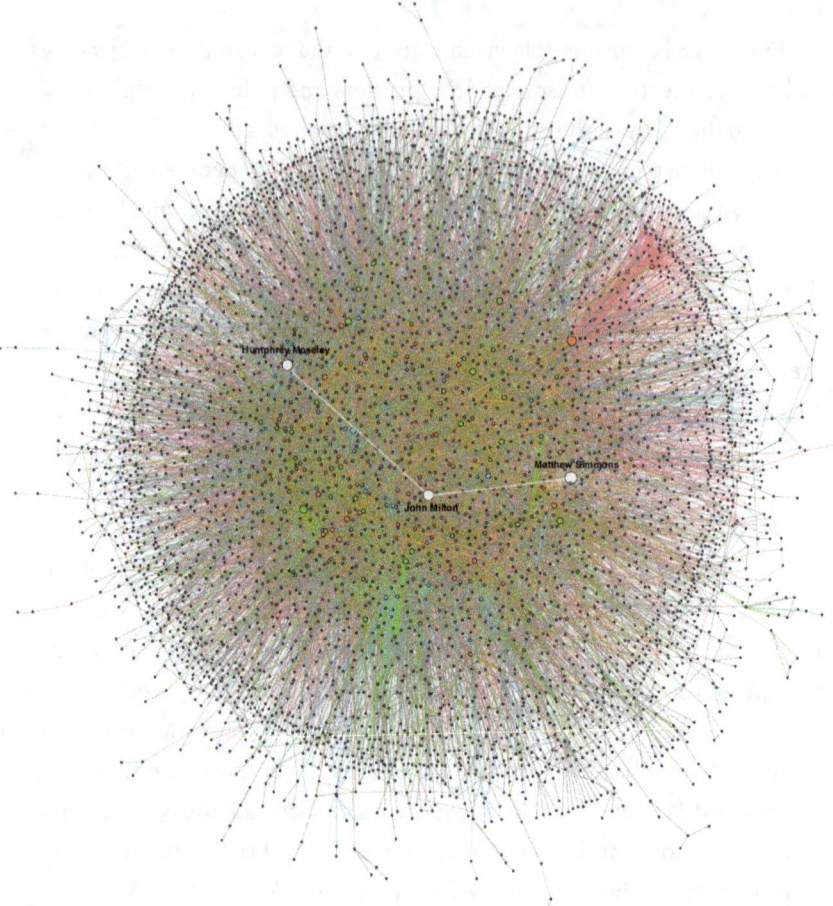

**Figure 5.7** John Milton provides the shortest and only direct path between the radical political print network of Matthew Simmons and the literary and royalist one of Humphrey Moseley between 1641–1660.

network during this period, and Simmons is ranked second only to the prolific radical bookseller Giles Calvert, who was discussed in Chapter 4 and with whom he did frequent business. Like Thomas Ratcliffe, who ranks near him, Simmons produced polemic, news, and official publications for Parliament and the Westminster Assembly. Moseley stands out as the only person on this list known primarily for literary publications—his shop was the place to find poetry and plays by Sir John Suckling, John Donne, James Shirley, Francis Beaumont, William Davenant, Abraham

Cowley, Thomas Carew, and more. He was a "major figure within the seventeenth-century world of printing," notes Dobranski, whose "catalogues read like the syllabus to a survey course in Renaissance literature."[78] In a small-world network where the rich-get-richer effect applies, neither Simmons nor Moseley would ever be more than a short path away from a given author, printer, or bookseller.

And yet Moseley's book list, which has a distinctly royalist bent, highlights a fascinating and nearly complete division between the people in Figure 5.8. Neither Moseley nor John Grismond, who dealt in royalist propaganda including King Charles's *Eikon Basilike*, have any *direct* links to the other three most-connected members of the book trade, who were known for their anti-monarchist output. As represented by its most highly connected members, the worlds of royalist and anti-monarchist publishing are completely distinct, as are the worlds of what we might consider "high" literary culture, on the one hand, and news and polemic on the other. This is what makes Milton's status as a bridge between Moseley and Simmons so striking, and as we come to understand the processes that formed and

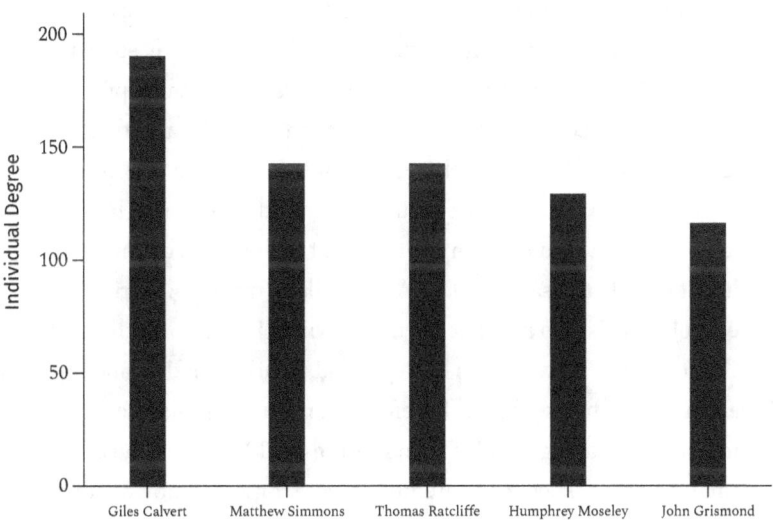

**Figure 5.8** The top five members of the English book trade by degree, 1641–1660. There are no direct links between the hubs associated with royalism (Moseley and Grismond) and the hubs associated with anti-monarchism (Calvert, Simmons, and Ratcliffe).

sustained his connection to these important stationers, we gain insight into the making of a distinctive authorial voice.

Although *Epitaphium Damonis* had announced Milton's intention to compose a British epic, the outbreak of anti-prelatical sentiment the following year, and perhaps some personal encounters with Laudian church officials, compelled him to dedicate his next publications to the cause of church reformation.[79] In 1641 he published three anonymous tracts with Thomas Underhill: *Of Reformation*, *Of Prelatical Episcopacy*, and *Animadversions*. In March of that year his former tutor and old friend Thomas Young, along with four other anti-prelatical clergy, began to publish reformist tracts under the name "*Smectymnuus*," taken from their initials, and Milton likely contributed anonymously to their effort.[80] Their target, Bishop John Hall, answered in kind, and the first two of Milton's tracts obliquely engaged with the dispute, while his third responded directly, in a point-by-point rebuttal of Hall. So it makes sense that by 1642 he had switched to the *Smectymnuus* publisher, John Rothwell, to issue his first work under his own name, *The Reason of Church Government*.[81] In this work, however, the subtle and largely apolitical poet of *Comus* and *Epitaphium Damonis* expresses real ambivalence about associating his name with the cut and thrust of polemical debate. In a long biographical digression, he describes his gentlemanly education, his travels in Italy, and his poetic vocation, and he laments that in prose "I have the use, as I may account it, but of my left hand."[82] But he also finds himself in a conundrum as he admits that the troubled times are not suited to the higher literary pursuits that he would prefer and that he still has in mind. It is all quite lofty for a fledgling author, and Bishop Hall dismisses Milton at almost exactly the same time as "a scurrilous mime . . . a grim, lowring, bitter fool" who is also pathetically unknown.[83] "I have no further notice of him," notes Hall, "than he hath been pleased, in his immodest and injurious Libell to give of himself: and therefore . . . must fetch his character from some scattered passages in his own writings."[84] Milton's name did not yet command either respect or contempt. It was simply unknown—or at least obscure enough to make for a good jab.

By the summer of 1642, the king was in the field and the country at open war, and Milton took a leap into truly dangerous waters that would make him both known and notorious. Recently married, and even more recently abandoned by a wife who returned to live with her royalist family, he penned *The Doctrine and Discipline of Divorce*, an unlicensed work advocating a position that shocked and outraged both his enemies in the Laudian church and his former Presbyterian allies.[85] As with his earlier tracts, his central argument was that laws of church or state must not interfere with liberty of spirit and conscience. Specifically, "tender pitty might be had of those who have unwarily in a thing they never practiz'd before, made themselves the bondmen of a luckless an helpless matrimony" by allowing divorce based on mutual incompatibility and remarriage based on natural affection.[86]

To advocate this position, which would be quickly caricatured as libertinism and even polygamy, Milton returned to anonymous publication and to his contacts in the oppositional print network who were most invested in challenging press restrictions: Thomas Paine and Matthew Simmons. As mentioned earlier, Milton's first printer— Augustine Mathewes—was involved in their growing network by this time, and he may have provided the crucial link. But rather than marking the continuation of this earlier relationship, *The Doctrine and Discipline of Divorce* began Milton's "life-long relationship with the Simmons family, who worked with [Milton] over a thirty-one year period," culminating with Simmons's son publishing the first editions of *Paradise Lost*.[87] Anna Beer perhaps goes too far to describe Simmons as Milton's "life-long friend," since we find no familiar letters between them, no autographed gift copies like the ones Milton gave to the bookseller George Thomason, and no dedicatory poems.[88] But Simmons was a rising printer whose professional and ideological interests aligned very well with the project of making of "The Author John Milton," as he would soon be presented on the title pages of Simmons's books.

Sharon Achinstein and Benjamin Burton note that Simmons was "a lightning rod for political scrutiny" in the early 1640s, during a time of "fracturing ideological consensus" among the forces who had risen up against Charles and his Laudian church.[89] Milton's own *Doctrine and Discipline of Divorce* was both a cause and a symptom of this fracturing and the subsequent Presbyterian "crackdown on the press," which led to Parliament's reinstitution of pre-publication licensing in 1643.[90] The instantly controversial work found a ready readership and was the first of Milton's works to reach a second edition. This augmented edition of 1644 flouted the new licensing order even as it boldly announced Milton's authorship. The title page, in an era when title pages were not merely for decoration but were the primary space for advertising and promoting books, placed the single word "DIVORCE" in large letters on its own line, followed by its dedication to Parliament, the Westminster assembly, and the initials of "The Author J. M.," which were followed by a prefatory address to Parliament signed with his full name.

If Milton and his publishers were courting controversy, the strategy worked—this time igniting a firestorm among the Presbyterian clergy, including Herbert Palmer, who denounced Milton by name in a sermon in Parliament. The sermon was also quickly printed, decrying the "wicked booke . . . abroad and uncensored, though deserving to be burnt, whose Author has been so impudent as to set his name to it."[91] In a mark of how far apart Milton now found himself from his erstwhile Presbyterian colleagues, the sermon was published by Thomas Underhill, who had also published Milton's earliest, anonymous anti-prelatical tracts. Another book-length response, *An Answer to a Book Intituled, The Doctrine and Discipline of Divorce, or, A Plea for Ladies and Gentlewomen*, agreed that Milton's new work was "worthie to be burnt by the Hangman."[92]

Both Milton and Simmons, however, leaned into the controversy rather than turning away.[93] In November 1644, Milton published *Areopagitica*, again without a license, but with his own name stretching across the title page as boldly as "DIVORCE" had stretched across the front of his previous pamphlet. The printer was anonymous and has long remained so, but as Nicholas von Maltzahn has recently shown, it was once again Matthew Simmons, who had his own reasons for taking another risk on the suddenly notorious author.[94] *Areopagitica* famously makes the case against licensing by arguing that it is as good almost to "kill a man as kill a good book."[95] But less famously it is also deeply invested in matters that would concern an upstart member of the book trade like Simmons, whose "careful ideological positioning" in the works he printed was placing him "at the heart of oppositional printing networks."[96] Milton attacks the "old *patentees* and *monopolizers* in the trade of book-selling," suggesting that they promoted the licensing order as a way of protecting their entrenched business interests.[97] And Simmons was clearly making a move on those interests. As Achinstein and Burton note, even as Parliament and the Stationers' Company attempted to reinstitute control over print, "Simmons' output did not slow down," and "on the contrary, his individual output soared," with 22 works for 1644, 39 for 1645, and 57 for 1646.[98]

Shortly after the publication of *Areopagitica*, in December 1644, the Stationers' Company requested the House of Lords conduct an inquiry into "Printing of scandalous Books by divers, as *Hezechia Woodward* and *Jo. Milton*."[99] Simmons was the connective thread: Earlier in 1644 he had had printed Hezekiah Woodward's *Inquiries into the Causes of Our Miseries* even after "the refusal of Mr. Carroll, minister of Lincoln's Inn, to grant a license."[100] Both Milton and Woodward were summoned by Westminster Assembly to be examined. Woodward's deposition made it clear that Simmons knew of the parliamentary order against unlicensed printing but did it anyway (there is no record of Milton's appearance). No doubt Milton's argument in *Areopagitica* was true to his own beliefs about the necessity of open debate and the need for trial "by what is contrary" to forge true virtue. But it was also part of a campaign by Simmons in which Milton played a part without necessarily writing the entire script.

Simmons's ability to operate at the center of an oppositional print network where he not only evaded serious consequences, but also thrived on controversy, helped ensure that a schoolmaster formerly known for a handful of lofty poems was now thrust very much into the center of the era's most consequential political debates. Milton's "name was now on the target list of the Presbyterian propaganda campaign and under scrutiny by Parliament."[101] In 1645 he was denounced by Robert Baillie in *A Dissuasive from the Errours of the Time* as exemplifying "this unhappy love toward liberty," and in 1646 he was excoriated in *Gangraena* by Thomas Edwards, who complained that female preachers were using Milton's works to spread dangerous heresies and act out against their husbands.[102] Both called for the burning of Milton's books, but such outrage seems only to have fueled Simmons's business.

During this time, Simmons's establishment became one of the best-known shops for news and for polemic at the bleeding edge of the radical cause, and he benefited as that cause prevailed. He printed Milton's *Tenure of Kings and Magistrates* in 1649, defending the regicide against its critics, and both Milton and Simmons shortly began working for the new regime in an official capacity. Milton was named Secretary for Foreign Tongues—essentially, its chief public defender and propagandist—and in 1649 Simmons printed both his first work for the commonwealth's Council of State, *Articles of Peace*, as well as Milton's *Eikonoklastes*, which responded to Charles's wildly popular and dangerous hagiography, *Eikon Basilike*. In the following years, Simmons regularly worked as an official printer to the commonwealth, building one of London's most prosperous firms, which his wife, and then his son, would continue to operate after his death in 1654.

Milton had gone from anonymous poet to household name, even if that name was often invoked as a bugbear by critics like Baillie and Edwards. After penning the *Defense of the English People* in 1651, he wrote that "All Europe talks from side to side" of his work as the voice of the fledgling republic.[103] The talk was not always positive: Christopher Wase prefaced his translation of Sophocles's *Electra* with a polemical poem in which he made Milton the emblem of a government that had crossed the line into licentiousness and tyranny by forcing subjects to renounce their former allegiance to the king and take an oath to the new regime:

> While like the forward Miltonist,
> We our old Nuptial knot untwist:
> And with the hands, late faith did joyn,
> This Bill of plain Divorce now signe.
> Here their New Kingdom must commence
> And sinn conspire with Conscience.[104]

Wase's poem was printed in the Hague, since its aggressive royalism and overt calls for Prince Charles to avenge his father's death made it too dangerous to be printed at home. But it must have been sold by Humphrey Moseley, who curiously included an advertisement in the final pages notifying the "courteous reader" that he could also find the "Poems of Mr *John Milton,* with a Masque presented at *Ludlow* Castle before the Earle of *Bridge-water,* then president of *Wales,*" in octavo "*at his shop at the Prince's Armes in St. Paul's Church-yard.*"[105] This is where Milton's role as a bridge between two of the most prominent people on the most bifurcated sides of the print network is both fascinating and important: All the time that Simmons was building Milton's brand as a controversialist and defender of liberty, Moseley was cultivating an image of Milton as a gentleman poet.

Milton's links to Moseley were weak, but powerful. Henry Lawes, who wrote the music to *Comus* and published it with Moseley's partner Humphrey Robinson, subsequently became a regular feature on Moseley's book list and so provided the most obvious tie. But Milton also became a feature on Moseley's list in a more minor way when his poem on Shakespeare was included in *Poems: Written by Wil. Shakespeare, Gent,* a 1640 miscellany that contains an appendix of poems by "other Gentlemen," including Milton, Francis Beaumont, Ben Jonson, Robert Herrick, and Thomas Carew.[106] For an aspiring poet who wanted to highlight the products of his right hand, this was auspicious company, and Milton no doubt saw the value in maintaining such connections as he was preparing his first major collection of poetry. Nevertheless, we should be wary of the dominant scholarly account of Milton's 1645 *Poems,* which still depicts Milton presiding over nearly every aspect of that work in a careful, autonomous, and ultimately solitary act of authorial self-presentation.[107] At the opposite extreme, Warren Chernaik memorably argues that in the 1645 edition of his *Poems,* Milton was "virtually kidnapped by Moseley and transformed against his will into a royalist."[108] Milton's complicated aesthetic alliances should make us skeptical that he was such a passive victim, but Chernaik's strong language usefully reminds us just how oddly the 1645 *Poems* sits alongside Milton's other publications of 1640–50 and just how much agency Moseley had in shaping his poetic persona.

Milton's works appeared together with Moseley volumes by Edmund Waller, Thomas Carew, James Shirley, and John Suckling that all looked like part of a series. The tile pages of the Waller, Milton and Carew books were all essentially identical, calling attention to the settings of poems by

Henry Lawes, "Gentleman of the Kings Chapel." The Milton, Carew, and Shirley volumes also follow the same basic design, starting with poems in rough chronological order and finishing with a masque. And although Milton famously groused about the engraved portrait of him by William Marshall that appeared as a frontispiece to his *Poems*, this too was part of a house style, with Marshall's engravings appearing in Moseley publications of Shirley, Suckling, Edmund Gregory, and Robert Stapylton. Indeed, as represented by Marshall, all the men bear something of a gnomish family resemblance.[109]

Moseley also routinely prefaced his volumes with dedications very much like the one he added to Milton's poems, where he presents himself as a collector of exemplary English verse ("such dainties") and emphasizes his access to original manuscript sources (the "Authors . . . papers").[110] In these prefaces, he very explicitly distinguishes the fine literature he publishes from the pamphlets and polemics pouring off the presses of men like Simmons, decrying "this age of Paper-prostitutions" where "a man may buy the reputation of some Authors into the price of their Volume."[111] In this way, Milton the poet is presented as a direct repudiation of Milton the pamphleteer, with Moseley complaining in the preface to the 1645 *Poems* that "the slightest Pamphlet is now adayes more vendible than the Works of learnedest men" and protesting that he brings these works to light only because of the "love I have to our own Language."[112]

Despite his philanthropic protestations, however, Moseley was a savvy businessman; the advertisement of Milton's collection in Christopher Wase's poem attacking Milton was merely the oddest manifestation of a long-running and pervasive promotional campaign. J. Milton French notes that Moseley's advertisements for Milton's 1645 *Poems* "were constantly before the eyes of many readers" until 1660, when Moseley died.[113] French identifies at least 23 books over 11 years with Moseley's advertisements in them. Each time they place Milton in the company of cavalier poets and royalist musicians. In the last version of the catalogue and advertisement Moseley printed in his lifetime, for example, we find Milton nestled securely among the crème of the royalist crop:

91. Poems with a Masque by *Thomas Carew* Esq; Gentleman of the Privie Chamber to his late Majestie, revived and enlarged with Aditions, 80.

92. Poems of Mr. *John Milton*, with a Masque presented at *Ludlow Castle before the Earle of Bridgewater*, then President of *Wales*, 80.

93. Poems, &c. with a Masque called The Triumph of Beauty, by *James Shirley*, Gent. 80.

94. The Mistriss, or several Copies of love-verses written by Mr. *Abraham Cowley.* 80.[114]

Many of the advertisements also include *Poems: Written by Wil. Shakespeare, Gent*, with its appendix of poems by "other Gentlemen," including Milton, Beaumont, Jonson, Herrick, and Carew.[115]

Moseley's efforts to present Milton as a cavalier poet and an heir to Shakespeare appear to have worked, at least if we can trust the evidence of a rather strange edition that appeared just after the publisher's death, *Cupid's Cabinet Unlock't*, purportedly by "W. Shakespeare." As Lukas Erne has noted, although the book had Shakespeare's name on the cover, it was part of "Shakespeare's reconfiguration as a cavalier poet" during the period and included many poems by other writers, including five by Milton.[116] Erne finds it "ironic that a text like *Cupids Cabinet Unlock't*, with its royalist resonance," contains these poems by "a very prominent republican English poet," and this is true except that Milton was not at this time very prominent as a republican poet.[117] He was prominent in the prose published by Simmons and others as a republican, and in the poetry published and promoted by Moseley as a gentleman poet who composed "dainties" of exactly the type that found their way into this book—lines from "L'Allegro," a song from *Arcades,* and the echo song from *Comus.* He was highly unusual, and even unique, in bridging these two print communities, at least in a way that connected the dominant printers and publishers in each. But like the invention of Shakespeare, Spenser, and Greene as print authors, as discussed in Chapter 2, the agency was not entirely Milton's own.

This too is what constitutes Milton's strong poetic voice as it is most realized in *Paradise Lost,* which he had been composing and contemplating during the interregnum but which he turned to in earnest after the restoration. In it, Milton positions himself as a prophetic vessel, mediating between earth and heaven, as he describes in the invocation to the muse in Book 7:

> Into the Heav'n of Heav'ns I have presum'd
> An Earthlie Guest, and drawn Empyreal Aire,
> Thy tempring; with like safetie guided down
> Return me to my Native Element:
> Least from this flying Steed unrein'd (as once
> Bellerophon, though from a lower Clime)
> Dismounted, on th' Aleian Field I fall
> Erroneous there to wander and forlorne.
> Half yet remains unsung, but narrower bound
> Within the visible Diurnal Spheare;
> Standing on Earth, not rapt above the Pole . . .[118]

Standing in the spaces between human and divine, "rapt above the Pole," Milton justifies the ways of God to men by uniting those aspects of his writing that threaten to pull apart: systematic theology and dramatic poetry, republican polemic and religious allegiance to an omnipotent being, classical models and Christian ethics. The result is an epic in which readers still cannot agree whether Satan is the hero or the villain, whether he is an allegory of King Charles or Oliver Cromwell, whether God exemplifies tyranny or benevolence.[119] But in one way or another, many have agreed with Gordon Teskey that in the poem Milton himself is "a sort of Janus figure, looking at once into the culture of the past, which he mastered and possessed, and into the culture of the future, which he unintentionally prophesied."[120]

Before his voice had bridged such divides, I would like to suggest, in conclusion, that Milton's authorial persona had bridged structural holes of equal magnitude, and he invoked this persona just as clearly as he invoked the muse when he wrote *Paradise Lost.* Or perhaps we should say that it was invoked for him by the poem's printer, Samuel Simmons, who had taken over the family business and whose publication of "A Poem, Written in Ten Books, by John Milton," brought two distinct sides of Milton's authorial identity together. It was a voice forged over a lifetime of connections that have often been easy to overlook because they appear weak. But as Milton himself wrote in a personal motto he began to inscribe in autograph albums in the 1650s, "My strength is made perfect in weakness."[121]

# EPILOGUE  FUTURE DIRECTIONS IN NETWORKING THE PAST

IN EARLY MODERN ENGLAND, preachers were fond of warning their flocks that "flattery is the Devil's invisible net, by which he catcheth and holdeth men fast in the snare."[1] Although it too has mostly remained invisible, the net described in this book is by contrast a record of the relationships through which humans act and express their agency. This is why Bruno Latour has impishly suggested that the term "network" should really be inverted to "worknet or action net"—when we act in the world, we do so by cultivating, extending, and maintaining networks.[2] I've attempted to show that analyzing these networks can yield important historical and cultural insights, such as the fact that a gradual evolution of the printing trade led to a sudden revolution in the print network around the end of the sixteenth century. In the small new world that emerged, nearly everyone could be connected to everyone else within a few steps, and information could seem to spread like an epidemic or "public fire." Hyperconnected hubs played an outsized role in this network's connectivity, although they have not necessarily played such a role in our historiography—printers like Nicholas Okes and booksellers like Michael Sparke and Giles Calvert reconfigured their trades in ways that made them structurally and culturally significant. Also underrepresented in histories of the period are the texts and authors that linked disparate communities in the print network, and by turning our attention to the high- betweenness texts of female prophets like Mary Cary and Eleanor Davies we can appreciate the unusual publication strategies that made their texts important bridges. Finally, even authors at no risk of being forgotten, like John Milton, look very different when we understand the weak ties that shaped and enabled their emergence as strong voices. Like the other figures in this book, Milton may have lacked the language of network analysis, but he was sensitive to the evolving communications landscape and adept at networking strategies that allowed him to speak, with some authority, as the voice of a wider spiritual, intellectual, and national community.

But this book is an opening, rather than a final word, on the questions that network analysis can pose within the field of literary studies and book history, and I would like to conclude by pointing to ongoing projects and developments that might expand, deepen, and complicate my own work. Although this is one of the first books to develop and use digital analysis to investigate early modern networks, it could not have been written without a large and growing community of scholars who are investigating other, related networks and associations. Just naming the projects and institutions that have provided important support, feedback, and inspiration as we created the Shakeosphere website could fill a chapter: the University of Iowa's Atlas of Early Printing, the University of Victoria's Map of Early Modern London (MoEML), the Medici Archive, the Center for Spatial and Textual Analysis at Stanford, Early Modern Letters Online (EMLO), Six Degrees of Francis Bacon, Networking Archives, and many more. Our understanding of and ability to analyze complex, multilayered networks will become more powerful as we connect such related but distinct projects through Linked Open Data frameworks—after all, a member of the print network may also be engaged in an epistolary network, a scientific society, a particular geographical community, and an extended kinship circle. Linking projects will not only provide more context for the networks of persons, places, and things found in each of these resources, but will also lend more power to methods of network analysis such as link prediction, which may allow us to identify missing collaborators and anonymous authors by their likely association with known figures. But in order to talk about the future of this work, I also need to address a question that has become urgent as many humanities programs have come to face the dire realities of funding scarcity: Are the digital humanities a salvation, or a threat?

After rapturous early coverage, including a short-lived *New York Times Book Review* column called "The Mechanic Muse" that was devoted exclusively to covering forms of "distant reading," we have arguably entered the phase of backlash and corrective.[3] Timothy Brennan gleefully announced the "digital humanities bust" in the *Chronicle of Higher Education* in 2017, explaining that "For all its resources, the digital humanities makes a rookie mistake: It confuses more information for more knowledge."[4] Tom Eyers similarly accuses the digital humanities of "uncritical positivism," creating an entire academic subculture that is "thrusting, confident, often garlanded with money, and finds an especially welcoming home in those largely private universities that snap at the heels of the very top tier of institutions of higher learning."[5] And Nan Z. Da has attacked the digital humanities, or "Computational Literary Studies" (CLS), for failing to deliver on their early promise, for a lack of statistical sophistication, and for "the exorbitant funding that CLS has garnered."[6] Some of these arguments—such as Da's case that digital humanities projects are too often opaque and should make their data more openly available so others can interrogate or reproduce their results—are fair and becoming the norm, including with my own project, where underlying data are available through Github as well as through the Shakeosphere website. But others are frankly wrong in ways that are nevertheless illuminating for thinking about future development of the field, and I think they merit brief mention here.

Through the account presented in Chapter 1 of the ESTC's history and our transformation of it into a new kind of data source, I hope I've already shown that the notion of the digital humanities as either a new and exciting phase in the discipline, or an existential threat to it, is something of a false dichotomy. First, the oft-repeated idea that digital humanities is some radical upstart relies on a strangely truncated view of scholarly history. Although literary studies labeled "distant reading" or "macroanalysis" are fairly new, we are well into the third or fourth generation of digital humanities work; the earlier phases of "humanities computing," which included ambitious projects of digitization and database construction, emerged along with consumer computing in the 1960s and 70s.[7] Even before that, Roberto Busa worked with Thomas Watson and IBM in the 1940s and 50s to create the searchable corpus of Aquinas's works known as the *Index Thomisticus*—a work that belongs equally to the history of computing and to the tradition of indexing, annotating, and organizing that Ann Blair describes as fundamental to the humanist tradition from its inception.[8] Like early computers themselves, early digital projects were costly and limited, but they laboriously laid the groundwork for much of what we do today. Incidentally, and against the idea that digital humanities scholarship today is larded with money, the analysis made possible by that early, costly work can typically now be done on a laptop, which is how I conducted all of the network analysis for this book (although sometimes the laptop needed to be left running overnight).

Nearly all humanities scholarship today, including that which openly rejects computational methods of analysis, is made possible by the digital finding aids, catalogues, and archives that have in many cases been built over previous decades. One of my goals throughout the book has been to show how such tools and data can silently inflect our knowledge of the field and to suggest that we actively need to engage, and sometimes repurpose them, to understand areas where that knowledge needs revision. As Marlene Manoff argues, library collections and "digital archives represent the entanglement of matter and meaning, content and device, and human and machine elements," with "content produced and selected by individuals in particular social and historical contexts, but it is also shaped by multiple additional factors, including the hardware and software that enable access to and manipulation of that content."[9] The elucidation and analysis of those factors seems to me an especially appropriate goal in a book about the early modern period, which was marked by curiosity and skepticism about the ways in which telescopes, microscopes, and other instruments might reform or distort our view of the objects we study.[10]

To use any scholarly tool uncritically—whether it is the *Short Title Catalogue of Books Printed in England, Scotland, and Ireland* (STC), the British Library's online catalogue (ESTC), or the NetworkX Python package—is to risk the kind of mistake made by the astronomers in Samuel Butler's parodic poem, "The Elephant in the Moon," as they cluster around a telescope and witness "two mighty armies" on the moon, "in a bloody fight engaged. . . . As by the glass 'tis clear, and plain."[11] While they rush off to publish their accounts of the celestial battle, a footboy discovers the deflating truth that flies, gnats, and a mouse have become trapped between the telescope's lenses, and that their grotesque and distorting magnification has proven the "virtuous occasion / Of all this learned dissertation."[12] Many a learned dissertation has been written in the same way, under the influence of catalogues and archives that magnify certain categories—such as the work, the subject, and above all, the author—at the expense of others, such as the printer, the community, or the network. The analysis I've done offers an alternative perspective, although I've also tried to approach it with the footboy's curiosity about both what he sees and why.

Of course, doing digital analysis does not exempt one from the charge of using tools uncritically or ineffectively. But in this regard, too, critiques of the digital humanities tend to rely on a narrow definition of digital scholarship that simply does not represent the field as it exists today. Eyers admits to an "inevitable flattening" of approaches before arguing that Franco Moretti's version of "distant reading" emblematizes the entire field.[13] Da states plainly that

> CLS papers are all more or less organized the same way, detecting patterns based in word count (or 1-, 2-, n-grams, a 1-gram defined as anything separated by two spaces) to make one of six arguments: (1) the aboutness of something; (2) how much or how little of something there is in a larger body, (3) the amount of influence that something has on something else; (4) the ability of something to be classified; (5)

if genre is consistent or mixed; and (6) how something has changed or stayed the same.¹⁴

Da's claims led to a lively debate, hosted by *Critical Inquiry*, in which the scholars she cites as representatives of such arguments have defended their own work, and I will let them make their own case for the value of their methods.¹⁵ But I should add that my book and its underlying digital analysis departs completely from the kind of corpus analytics that Da and Eyers discuss, and it is hardly the only digital humanities project to do so. Indeed, the "digital humanities" is less a specific set of methodologies or a distinct field than a "tactical term," as Matthew Kirschenbaum has put it, deployed to "get things done."¹⁶ None of the projects I mentioned above rely on "detecting patterns based in word count" or anything like "distant reading" as it is usually described by its critics.

The Atlas of Early Printing, for example, documents, maps, and visualizes the output of paper mills and printshops throughout Europe from 1450 to 1500.¹⁷ The Map of Early Modern London uses a digitized version of the 1633 "Agas map" of London to visualize literary and historical data, with layers depicting locations like chapels and playhouses, an encyclopedia of named places from literary and historical documents, and editions of topographical texts.¹⁸ The Translation and the Making of Early Modern English Print Culture project at the University of Montreal analyzes and maps the communities of translators, publishers, and printers who often played multiple roles in reproducing continental works in England.¹⁹ The Women in Book History Bibliography²⁰ aggregates resources about female printers, publishers, and booksellers and has led to revisions in the new, more flexible ESTC 21 being developed by Brian Geiger and Carl Stahmer.²¹ Six Degrees of Francis Bacon mines the *Oxford English Dictionary*—and increasingly, the contributions of its users—to construct probabilistic maps of social connections during the early modern period.²² The English Broadside Ballad Archive reproduces, transcribes, and records around 9,000 early English Broadside ballads, as well as using metadata and text from the archive for topic modeling and other forms of analysis (such as documenting the number of ballads with tunes versus those without).²³ Networking Archives uses data collected in Early Modern

Letters Online and the Gale State Papers Online to visualize and analyze the connections between people in those databases.[24] All of these projects offer tools for discovery that ultimately direct users back to practices of reading, researching, and writing that are neither flat, nor deterministic, nor particularly distant.

Attending a panel on digital scholarship at just about any academic conference will immediately make it clear that this field is far too big tent for "all CLS papers" to be "more or less organized the same way." The field includes network analysis, topic modeling, and vast projects of digitization and preservation, as well as projects that do not fit into any of these categories; for example, "IDEA: Isabella d'Este Archive" describes itself as an "exercise in imagination, discovery, and critical engagement" and attempts to give users insights into the life and times of the powerful and influential Renaissance marchesa of Mantua by providing access to her texts, musical compositions, art collection, and an immersive 3D reconstruction of her palazzo.[25] Such projects are truly interdisciplinary—often involving librarians, faculty, and members of the public—and they are far more representative of digital scholarship today than the straw man version of digital-humanities-as-word-counting often cited by detractors.

New databases are also being built in ways that will allow researchers to download, explore, manipulate, and analyze the data using some of the tools and methods I've employed, but without the more laborious data transformation and cleanup processes that were required for the ESTC MARC records. Although it does not incorporate tools of network analysis and visualization into the interface, the 4 million letters in the Medici Archive, spanning 1537–1743, could be analyzed with the tools I've outlined in this book, yielding new views of networks of power and patronage in early modern Tuscany and Europe. The same is true of the ambitious Universal Short Title Catalogue (USTC), which proposes to provide a "digital bibliography of early modern print culture" across Europe and which currently includes 740,000 volumes. Although it is still in development, network analysis of the USTC should eventually allow researchers to ask the same sorts of questions of the French, Dutch, Italian, or pan-European printing networks that I've been able to ask of anglophone printing using the data in the ESTC. Scholars who are interested in American print culture, or the networks of producers and musicians involved in twentieth-century popular music, or the names associated with Persian manuscripts, can access that data through World-Cat, which consolidates entries and metadata for 2 billion items held in libraries worldwide. Network analysis of such metadata would make it possible for researchers to ask the same sort of questions I've asked here: Did these networks change over time, and if so, how? Are links distributed evenly, and if not, who are the most connected figures? Who are the bridges, and why?

Moreover, the future of digital scholarship will be defined not by the infinite proliferation of sites organized to investigate such questions, but by their integration with one another. With the advent of the Semantic Web, in which data in web pages can be structured and tagged in ways that make it directly readable by computers, Linked Open Data allows researchers to conduct more powerful forms of analysis, working at scale. As Alan Liu pointed out as early as 2012,

> [E]arly digital humanities projects . . . scaled up more or less accidentally, with the result (to the best of my knowledge) that every one of them ran up against the same virtual supersonic barrier. The barrier took the form of the following impasse: either a project retains established practices of scholarly quality-control (e.g., hierarchically-organized editing teams led by authorities, whose work is peer-reviewed in the traditional way by other authorities) . . . *or* a project uses some combination of algorithmic means and crowd sourcing to take the brakes off . . . whereupon quality-control no longer meets the standards of scholarship.[26]

Liu suggested that one way to address this issue was for digital humanities projects to engage more rigorously with theories of scale, and I've tried to model that in the opening chapter of this book, drawing on existing work in network analysis to discuss acceptable amounts of data loss. But another way to address scalability issues is Linked Data, which can allow for bigger, more robust analysis across datasets that have been hand-curated.

Carl Stahmer, who works with both the ESTC and the English Broadside Ballad Archive, sums up the possibilities this way:

> Linked Data provides the technological framework for the creation of such a common interface without pulling or duplicating data from external sources and storing it in a local silo. A Linked Data architecture would take user queries from the common interface, run them against existing and reputable external sources, aggregate the results, including combining with local records, and return this aggregation to the user. It would also offer a mutually accessible endpoint or API to its own locally created records that others could query and likewise aggregate. It would, in other words, operate as part of a "share and share alike" community of bibliographers.[27]

A Linked Data architecture, in short, allows for the efficient distribution of scholarly labor, making it possible to scale up—through aggregation—without compromising local expertise and quality control. Several projects have begun to demonstrate the possibilities. Amsterdam's Rijksmuseum, for example, released as Linked Open Data the digital images and full metadata for over 350,000 objects in its collection.[28] This data can be explored, curated, and analyzed in connection with records from 3,500 other museums, galleries, libraries, and archives through the Europeana Foundation and various interfaces in the Europeana Labs, including a SPARQL endpoint that allows users to connect data to outside sources like VIAF, Shakeosphere, and Wikidata.[29]

The Advanced Research Consortium has similarly created the Big Data Visualization Application (BigDIVA) to allow users to browse, search, and visualize data from member nodes of the consortium, rather than viewing results of individual catalogues in list form. The BigDIVA visual interface is appealing, but as is the case with the Europeana Labs, the project's most remarkable innovation is that it provides a single endpoint through which users can explore, and pivot between, resources as diverse as 18th Connect (which aggregates nearly a million texts and other digital objects from 60 federated websites on eighteenth-century literature and culture), Nines.org (which does the same thing for nineteenth-century literature), MESA (aggregating 112,000 medieval texts and digital objects from 32 sites), and ModNets (nearly 100,000 modernist texts and digital objects from 69 sites). A completely realized Linked Data architecture would go further by allowing even deeper interoperability. The locations of printshops mentioned on one website that specializes in print culture, for example, could be mapped onto another partner website that specializes in period-specific cartography; a project mapping the connections between artists could link to the museums holding their works; an epistolary network could be combined with a print network, a network of members in a scientific society, and a biographical database that allowed users to learn more about any of the figures in these overlapping communities.

My Shakeosphere project has experimented with these sorts of functions as part of the Linked Data for Libraries (LD4L) initiative.[30] LD4L is a collaboration between Cornell, Harvard, the Library of Congress, Stanford, and the University of Iowa—organized to pilot the use of Linked Data to improve the discovery, use, and understanding of scholarly information. Shakeosphere served as a proof of concept tool. Shakeosphere's data can be retrieved and manipulated with the SPARQL query language, which allowed us, for example, to match the locations of printshops and bookstalls in our database to places identified by the Map of Early Modern London. The record for the 1609 edition of Shakespeare's *Troilus and Cressida, As It Was Acted by the Kings Maiesties Servants at the Globe*, which was sold "at the Spred Eagle In Paules Church-Yeard," contains links to three MoEML locations—"The Globe," "St. Paul's Cathedral," and "St. Paul's Church Yard"; users who find the record in Shakeosphere can pivot through our site to view the locations in MoEML, or vice versa.

Using the same types of query, the developers at Wikidata matched 20,405 Shakeosphere IDs with their own and linked them to the other resources queried by the data clearinghouse. To take just one random example, the English antiquary Andrew Ducarel's Shakeosphere ID is linked via Wikidata to an image on Wikipedia, a record in Early Modern Letters Online, an ID and set of records in the UK National Archives, a file and ID in the National Portrait Gallery, VIAF, the Cambridge Alumni Database, the National Library of Wales, and the *Dictionary of Art Historians*. To demonstrate the ways that such cross-linkage could aid scholarly inquiry, I also worked with James Lee and several students at Grinnell College to create a system that would allow users to toggle between his Global Renaissance project, which does topic modeling and mapping of full texts, and the Shakeosphere project, which identifies people involved in the production of those texts. We published the results of this collaboration in *Cultural Analytics*, where we described a "methodology we call 'Linked Reading' that embeds topic models and vector space models within historical book networks, allowing us to explore both the language associated with race in texts that mention Moors and the extensive networks of booksellers, printers, and publishers who produced these texts."[31] By pivoting between both datasets, we were able to make two key observations: first, that the language of race ranged across multiple topics including "trade, geography, and militarization," and second that the network of printers, publishers, and booksellers involved in producing early editions of *Othello* was particularly invested in these topics.[32] Both datasets informed each other, making the collective conclusions we were able to draw from them far more meaningful for understanding *Othello's* place in the history of early modern race than if we would have been working in isolation. As digital projects have proliferated in recent years, so have the opportunities for this sort of data sharing and collaboration, which will be integral to the next phase of digital scholarship in the humanities.

Finally, contrary to arguments that the digital humanities offer shortcuts and easy answers, our paper on the Linked Reading project concluded that "At every stage, the process of Linked Reading involved interpretive *work*, as the researchers puzzled over results, debated them, read, recalibrated tools, puzzled over the relationship between our findings and the existing scholarly and primary literature, debated some more, and finally agreed on an argument that we think can make sense of it all."[33] This has also been consistent throughout the process of researching and writing this book, and it is what makes me optimistic about the future of humanities research using network analysis and other digital methods. If it were true that digital scholarship threatened "the displacement of a critical humanities praxis with one that announces its resistance to interpretation and to engaging with virtually every canon of existing interpretive thought," then this book wouldn't have been nearly as difficult, frustrating, or fun to write.[34]

*Networking Print in Shakespeare's England* began with the idea that the labor of cultural production matters and that network analysis offers a promising tool to learn more about the figures and communities responsible for that labor. However capacious an author's vision, in other words, it can only be realized through the efforts of a whole universe of other figures, including publishers, booksellers, and printers, who have their own motives and constraints. It has been more fascinating than I could have predicted to learn about printers like Nicholas Okes and booksellers like Michael Sparke, who reconfigured their respective businesses in ways that made them hubs in the network and serious dangers to the Laudian establishment. It has been a revelation to read the works of Mary Cary and to piece together the publishing practices that made her works, along with those of Eleanor Davies, unusually powerful bridges in the print network before both women slipped into obscurity. And I am hopeful that by turning attention to the weak ties that enabled Milton's strong poetic voice I have offered a model that will be compelling for other canonical figures. But the most gratifying aspect of the project was the way it merged theory and practice, requiring collaboration, discussion, and debate at every stage.

As John Paget contemplated his own personal conclusion in the 1630s, the aging, exiled, leader of the English reformed church in Amsterdam paused to remark on the miracle of life, emblematized by the body's system of veins and arteries: "a curious network & woven together . . . of subtle threads & thousands of them, more fine & small then hairs . . . & all these held and upheld in their severall functions by the finger of God, extending his quickening power unto every one of them."[35] This is yet another case of a "network" used as a metaphor, deriving from the visual similarity of a net to the venous system. But as it imagines quickening power pulsing through that net, sustaining the action of the whole, it also demonstrates the capacity of metaphor to advance our understanding. Through the collective action of thousands of threads, work gets done. And even as we've gained the capacity to quantify and analyze such networks, their curiosity and subtlety has not been diminished.

# NOTES

### Introduction

1. Edmund Spenser, "Muiopotmos," *The Minor Poems: Volume Two*, vol. 8 of *The Works of Edmund Spenser: A Variorum Edition*, eds. Edwin Greenlaw et al., 11 vols. (Baltimore: Johns Hopkins University Press, 1932–1945), line 368.

2. Albert-László Barabási, *Linked: The New Science of Networks* (New York: Plume/Penguin, 2002); Duncan J. Watts, *Six Degrees: The Science of a Connected Age* (New York: W. W. Norton, 2003).

3. Nicholas A. Christakis and James H. Fowler, *Connected: The Surprising Power of Our Social Networks and How They Shape Our Lives* (New York: Little, Brown and Company, 2009); Jonah Berger, *Contagious: Why Things Catch On* (New York: Simon and Schuster, 2013).

4. Paul Erdős and Alfred Rényi, "On the Evolution of Random Graphs," *Publications of the Math Institute of the Hungarian Academy of Sciences* 5 (1960): 18.

5. Ibid., 52, 19–20.

6. C. S. Lewis, *English Literature in the Sixteenth Century, Excluding Drama* (Oxford: Clarendon Press, 1954), 1.

7. Robert K. Merton, "The Matthew Effect in Science: The Reward and Communication Systems of Science Are Considered," *Science* 159 (1968): 56–63.

8. Ibid., 50n8.

9. Herbert A. Simon, "On a Class of Skew Distribution Functions," *Biometrika* 42 (1955): 425–440.

10. Alex Bavelas, "A Method for Investigating Individual and Group Ideology," *Sociometry* 5 (1942): 371–377.

11. Alex Bavelas, "A Mathematical Model for Group Structures," *Applied Anthropology* 7 (1948): 23–24.

12. Mark Granovetter, "Citation Classic," *Current Contents: Arts and Humanities* 49 (1986): 24.

13. Ibid., 24.

14. William Shakespeare, *Hamlet*, in *The Norton Shakespeare, 3rd* ed., ed. Stephen Greenblatt (New York: W. W. Norton, 2016), 3.1.112–113; Mark Granovetter, "The Strength of Weak Ties," *American Journal of Sociology* 78 (1973): 1364.

15. Milgram published his work in several venues, but the most detailed early account of the project was in Jeffrey Travers and Stanley Milgram, "An Experimental Study of the Small World Problem," *Sociometry* 32 (1969): 425–443.

16. Two hugely influential papers to this effect were published within a year of one another: Duncan J. Watts and Steven H. Strogatz, "Collective Dynamics of 'Small-World Networks," *Nature* 393 (1998): 440–442, which demonstrated that the small-world effect existed in many large networks found in nature, and Albert-László Barabási and Réka Albert, "Emergence of Scaling in Random Networks," *Science* 286 (1999): 509–512, which demonstrated that the "preferential attachment model" could lead to rich-get-richer effects in real-world systems ranging from power grids, to citation networks of scientific papers, to actor collaboration networks. Empirical studies of large dynamic networks have since tested and augmented these findings, such as J.-P. Onnela et al., "Structure and Tie Strengths in Mobile Communication Networks," *Publications of the National Academy of Sciences* 104 (2007): 7332–7336, and Matjaž Perc, "The Matthew Effect in Empirical Data," *Journal of the Royal Society Interface* 11 (2014). doi: 10.1098/rsif.2014.0378

17. Abdul Khaleque and Parongama Sen, "An Empirical Analysis of the Ebola Outbreak in West Africa," *Scientific Reports* 7 (2017): 1–8.

18. See former director of the NSA and CIA Michael Hayden's admission that "we kill people based on metadata" in the article of the same title by David Cole in the *New York Review of Books* (10 May 2014).

19. See Watts, *Six Degrees*, 93–95. The challenge is now much diminished thanks to a website, http://oracleofbacon.org/, which instantly traces these connections.

20. John Sutherland, "Publishing History: A Hole at the Centre of Literary Sociology," *Critical Inquiry* 14 (1988): 574–589.

21. Natalie Zemon Davis, "Printing and the People," in *Society and Culture in Early Modern France: Eight Essays* (Stanford: Stanford University Press, 1975), 190.

22. Marshall McLuhan suggests the network is an important object of analysis in *The Gutenberg Galaxy* (1962; reprint, Toronto: University of Toronto Press, 2011), 5. Networks are implicit in Walter J. Ong's discussion of revolutionary technology in *Orality and Literacy: The Technologizing of the Word* (London: Methuen, 1982), 127. And the "formation of syndicates and far-flung trade networks" motivates discussion of cultural changes in Elizabeth L. Eisenstein's *The Printing Press as an Agent of Change* (1979; reprint, Cambridge: Cambridge University Press, 1997), 140. Eisenstein's book was followed by many others about the ways these networks ushered in a new "print culture."

23. Arthur F. Marotti, *Manuscript, Print, and the English Renaissance Lyric* (Ithaca: Cornell University Press, 1995), 129. See also Marotti's *John Donne, Coterie Poet* (Madison: University of Wisconsin Press, 1986), and Harold Love, *Scribal Publication in Seventeenth-Century England* (Oxford: Clarendon Press, 1993).

24. Joseph A. Dane shows that much evidence used to assert a revolutionary "print culture" is not supported by fact in *The Myth of Print Culture: Essays on Evidence, Textuality, and Bibliographic Method* (Toronto: University of Toronto Press, 2003). See also Adrian Johns, *The Nature of the Book: Print and Knowledge in the Making* (Chicago: University of Chicago Press, 1998), 5, and Johns's debate with Eisenstein in the *American Historical Review* 107 (2002): 106–125.

David McKitterick, *Print, Manuscript, and the Search for Order: 1450–1830* (Cambridge: Cambridge University Press, 2003), 4. For more on the persistence of coterie scribal culture see Betty A. Schellenberg, *Literary Coteries and the Making of Modern Print Culture: 1740–1790* (Cambridge: Cambridge University Press, 2016).

25. Richard A. McCabe, *"Ungainefull Arte": Poetry, Patronage, and Print in the Early Modern Era* (Oxford: Oxford University Press, 2016), 6.

26. Kirk Melnikoff, *Elizabethan Publishing and the Makings of Literary Culture* (Toronto: University of Toronto Press, 2018), 13.

27. Jeffrey J. Cohen, *Medieval Identity Machines* (Minneapolis: University of Minnesota Press, 2003), xxiv–xxv.

28. Drew Daniel, *The Melancholy Assemblage: Affect and Epistemology in the English Renaissance* (New York: Fordham University Press, 2013), 30. See also Julian Yates, *Error, Misuse, Failure: Object Lessons from the English Renaissance* (Minneapolis: University of Minnesota Press, 2003), and Gail Kern Paster, *Humoring the Body: Emotions and the Shakespearean Stage* (Chicago: University of Chicago Press, 2004).

29. John Law, one of the founders of ANT, claims that there is "little difference" between Deleuze's assemblage and the "actor network"; see "Actor

Network Theory and Material Semiotics," in *The New Blackwell Companion to Social Theory*, ed. Bryan S. Turner (Oxford: Blackwell, 2008), 147. Latour also sees similarities but suggests that where "assemblage" thinking offers a philosophical perspective, ANT offers an empirically grounded approach to that philosophy; see Andrew Iliadis, "Interview with Bruno Latour," *Figure/Ground* (24 September 2013). http://figureground.org/fg/interview-with-bruno-latour/

30. Bruno Latour, *Reassembling the Social: An Introduction to Actor-Network-Theory* (Oxford: Oxford University Press, 2005), 29.

31. Michel Callon, "Some Elements of a Sociology of Translation: Domestication of the Scallops and the Fishermen of St. Brieuc Bay," in *Power, Action and Belief: A New Sociology of Knowledge?*, ed. John Law (London: Routledge, 1986), 211.

32. Bruno Latour, "The Powers of Association," *Sociological Review* 32 (1984): 273.

33. See Michael Witmore on the power of "fictions" in *Pretty Creatures: Children and Fiction in the English Renaissance* (Ithaca: Cornell University Press, 2007), 12; Jonathan Gil Harris's discussion of "polychronic agency" in *Untimely Matter in the Time of Shakespeare* (Philadelphia: University of Pennsylvania Press, 2009), 143; and Miriam Jacobson, *Barbarous Antiquity: Reorienting the Past in the Poetry of Early Modern England* (Philadelphia: University of Pennsylvania Press, 2014), 16.

34. Carl Knappett, *An Archaeology of Interaction: Network Perspectives on Material Culture and Society* (Oxford: Oxford University Press, 2011), 8.

35. Latour, *Reassembling*, 129.

36. Knappett, *An Archaeology*, 8.

37. Ruth Ahnert, "Maps Versus Networks," in *News Networks in Early Modern Europe*, eds. Joad Raymond and Noah Moxham (Leiden: Brill, 2016), 133.

38. Lindsay O'Neill, *The Opened Letter: Networking in the Early Modern British World* (Philadelphia: University of Pennsylvania Press, 2014); Stanford Project (Dan Edelstein, Paula Findlen, and Nicole Coleman), *Mapping the Republic of Letters*: http://republicofletters.stanford.edu

39. Franco Moretti, "Network Theory, Plot Analysis," *Literary Lab Pamphlet 2* (2011): 11. https://litlab.stanford.edu/LiteraryLabPamphlet2.pdf

40. Johanna Drucker, "Humanistic Theory and Digital Scholarship," in *Debates in the Digital Humanities*, ed. Matthew K. Gold (Minneapolis: University of Minnesota Press, 2012), 86.

41. Johanna Drucker, "Non-Representational Approaches to Modeling Interpretation in a Graphical Environment," *Digital Scholarship in the Humanities* 33 (2018): 248–263.

42. Johanna Drucker, "Why Distant Reading Isn't," *PMLA* 132 (2017): 633.

43. Alex H. Poole, "The Conceptual Ecology of Digital Humanities," *Journal of Documentation* 73 (2017): 91.

44. Matthew L. Jockers, *Macroanalysis: Digital Methods and Literary History* (Urbana-Champaign: University of Illinois Press, 2013), 151-152.

45. Patrik Svensson, "Sorting out the Digital Humanities," in *A New Companion to the Digital Humanities,* eds. Susan Schreibman, Ray Siemens, and John Unsworth (Chichester: Wiley, 2016), 560, 551.

46. Jerome J. McGann, *The Textual Condition* (Princeton: Princeton University Press, 1991), 21.

47. D. F. McKenzie, *Bibliography and the Sociology of Texts* (Cambridge: Cambridge University Press, 1999), 15.

48. See Ann M. Blair, *Too Much to Know: Managing Scholarly Information Before the Information Age* (New Haven: Yale University Press, 2011); Jeffrey Todd Knight, *Bound to Read: Compilations, Collections, and the Making of English Renaissance Literature* (Philadelphia: University of Pennsylvania Press, 2013); William W. E. Slights, *Managing Readers: Printed Marginalia in English Renaissance Books* (Ann Arbor: University of Michigan Press, 2001); Peter Stallybrass et al., "Hamlet's Tables and the Technologies of Writing in Renaissance England," *Shakespeare Quarterly* 55 (2004): 379-419.

49. Cecile M. Jagodzinski, *Privacy and Print: Reading and Writing in Seventeenth-Century England* (Charlottesville: University Press of Virginia, 1999), 11. See also Schellenberg, *Literary Coteries.*

50. Joseph Loewenstein, *The Author's Due: Printing and the Prehistory of Copyright* (Chicago: University of Chicago Press, 2002), 63. See also Stephen B. Dobranski, *Milton, Authorship, and the Book Trade* (Cambridge: Cambridge University Press, 2009); Wendy Wall, *The Imprint of Gender: Authorship and Publication in the English Renaissance* (Ithaca: Cornell University Press, 1993).

51. McCabe, *"Ungainefull Arte,"* 2.

52. Joad Raymond, "News Networks: Putting the 'News' and 'Networks' Back in," in *News Networks in Early Modern Europe,* eds. Joad Raymond and Noah Moxham (Leiden: Brill, 2016), 113.

53. Harold Bloom, *The Anxiety of Influence: A Theory of Poetry,* 2nd ed. (Oxford: Oxford University Press, 1997), 33.

54. Andrew Marvell, "On Paradise Lost," in *Paradise Lost,* ed. Barbara K. Lewalski (Oxford: Wiley-Blackwell, 2007), lines 7-8. All subsequent references to *Paradise Lost* are from this edition.

**Chapter 1**

1. David L. Vander Meulen, "ESTC as Foundational and Always Developing," *Age of Johnson* 21 (2011): 265.

2. Thomas Tanselle, "A History of the ESTC in North America," in *The*

*English Short-Title Catalogue: Past, Present, Future. Papers Delivered at a Conference at the New York Public Library on January 21, 1998*, eds. Henry L. Snyder and Michael S. Smith (New York: AMS Press, 2003), 10.

3. Henry L. Snyder, "The Future of the ESTC: A Vision," in *The English Short-Title Catalogue: Past, Present, Future. Papers Delivered at a Conference at the New York Public Library on January 21, 1998*, eds. Henry L. Snyder and Michael S. Smith (New York: AMS Press, 2003), 24. See also David McKitterick, "'Not in STC': Opportunities and Challenges in the ESTC," *The Library*, series 7 vol. 6 (2005): 178-194.

4. See, for example, Diana Kichuk, "Metamorphosis: Remediation in *Early English Books Online (EEBO)*," *Literary and Linguistic Computing* 22 (2007): 291-303; and William Proctor and William Baker, "Caveat Lector. English Books 1475-1700 and the Electronic Age," *Analytical & Enumerative Bibliography* 12 (2001): 1-29.

5. Ian Gadd, "The Use and Misuse of *Early English Books Online*," *Literature Compass* 6 (2009): 686.

6. http://eebo.chadwyck.com/about/about.htm#online

7. Stephen Tabor, "ESTC and the Bibliographical Community," *The Library*, series 7 vol. 8 (2007): 368.

8. Robin C. Alston, "The History of ESTC," *The Age of Johnson* 15 (2004): 271.

9. Alfred W. Pollard et al., *A Short-Title Catalogue of Books Printed in England, Scotland, and Ireland, and of English Books Printed Abroad, 1475-1640*, 2nd ed. Revised and enlarged by Katharine F. Pantzer. 3 vols. (London: Bibliographical Society, 1976-1991); Donald G. Wing, *Short-Title Catalogue of Books Printed in England, Scotland, Ireland, Wales, and British America, and of English Books Printed in Other Countries, 1641-1700*, 2nd ed. Revised and enlarged by Timothy J. Crist et al. 4 vols. (New York: Modern Language Association of America, 1972-1998).

10. Alston, "History," 281, 288.

11. Ibid., 298.

12. Snyder, "Future of the ESTC," 22.

13. Tabor, "ESTC," 367-386.

14. Ibid., 370-371.

15. McKitterick, "Not in STC," 185.

16. Alston, "History," 319.

17. Ibid., 320.

18. McKitterick, "Not in STC," 183.

19. For an assessment of some of the differences between this sort of specialized database and the comprehensive ambitions of resources like the ESTC, see the article by DEEP's creators, Alan B. Farmer and Zachary Lesser, "Early Modern Digital Scholarship and *DEEP: Database of Early English Playbooks*," *Literature Compass* 5/6 (2008): 1139-1153.

20. Joseph A. Dane and Rosemary A. Roberts, "The Calculus of Calculus: W. W. Greg and the Mathematics of *Everyman* Editions," *Studies in Bibliography* 53 (2000): 124–125.

21. Rudolf Hirsch, *Printing, Selling and Reading, 1450–1550* (Wiesbaden: Otto Harrassowitz, 1967), 11; Jonathan Green, Frank McIntyre, and Paul Needham, "The Shape of Incunable Survival and Statistical Estimation of Lost Editions," *Papers of the Bibliographical Society of America* 105 (2011): 141–175. This latter article adopts a negative binomial distribution that allows for the possibility that survival is correlated rather than independent, to deal with the issues raised by Dane and Roberts in "The Calculus of Calculus."

22. Alan B. Farmer, "Playbooks and the Question of Ephemerality," in *The Book in History, the Book as History,* eds. Heidi Brayman, Jesse M. Lander, and Zachary Lesser (New Haven: Yale University Press, 2016), 95.

23. See Tiffany Stern, *Documents of Performance in Early Modern England* (Cambridge: Cambridge University Press, 2009), 40.

24. Farmer, "Playbooks," 106.

25. Anthony Trollope, *An Autobiography,* in *An Autobiography and Other Writings,* ed. Nicholas Shrimpton (Oxford: Oxford University Press, 2014), 60. One of the most prominent early projects to begin using network visualization and analysis in literary and historical study, for example, is *Mapping the Republic of Letters,* hosted by Stanford University in collaboration with Oxford, the National Endowment for the Humanities, and others. See http://republicofletters.stanford.edu/index.html

26. D. F. McKenzie examines the productive capacity of typical printshops, in terms of presses and labor, versus the number of known titles from those shops, to determine that anonymous and jobbing work such as blank forms, licenses, advertisements, and other ephemera that have since disappeared may have constituted the majority of a typical shop's output. See D. F. McKenzie, "Printing and Publishing 1557–1700: Constraints on the London Book Trades," in *The Cambridge History of the Book in Britain* (vol. 4, pp. 1557–1695), eds. John Barnard, D. F. McKenzie, with Maureen Bell (Cambridge: Cambridge University Press, 2002). See also James Raven, *The Business of Books: Booksellers and the English Book Trade 1450–1850* (New Haven: Yale University Press, 2007).

27. Albert-László Barabási, *Network Science* (Cambridge: Cambridge University Press, 2016), 284.

28. This derives from the Molloy-Reed criterion, which states that a random network will have a giant connected component if $k = \frac{\langle k^2 \rangle}{\langle k \rangle} = \frac{\langle k \rangle(1+\langle k \rangle)}{\langle k \rangle} > 2$. See Barabási, *Network Science,* 279, and Michael Molloy and Bruce Reed, "A Critical Point for Random Graphs with a Given Degree Sequence," *Random Structures and Algorithms* 6 (1995): 161–179.

29. See Barabási, *Network Science,* 280, for the formula, critical threshold $f_c = 1 - \frac{1}{\frac{<k^2>}{<k>}-1} =$. 65. As Barabási notes, the larger the network, the closer its critical threshold to $f_c = 1$.

30. Sabrina A. Baron, "Licensing Readers, Licensing Authorities in Seventeenth-Century England," in *Books and Readers in Early Modern England,* eds. Jennifer Andersen and Elizabeth Sauer (Philadelphia: University of Pennsylvania Press, 1992), 224.

31. David R. Adams, "The Secret Printing and Publishing Career of Richard Overton the Leveller, 1644-46," *The Library,* series 7 vol. 11 (2010): 3-88.

32. Matthew A. Peeples, "Network Science and Statistical Techniques for Dealing with Uncertainties in Archaeological Datasets" (2017): http://www.mattpeeples.net/netstats.html. Peeples's methodology draws from Elizabeth Costenbader and Thomas W. Valente, "The Stability of Centrality Measures When Networks Are Sampled," *Social Networks* 25 (2003): 283-307.

33. Stephen Karian, "The Limitations and Possibilities of the ESTC," *The Age of Johnson* 21 (2011): 293.

34. Ibid., 293-294.

35. Paddy Bullard, "Digital Humanities and Electronic Resources in the Long Eighteenth Century," *Literature Compass* (2013): 756.

36. Terry Reese, MarcEdit website: http://marcedit.reeset.net

37. See Eric Brill, "A Simple Rule-Based Part of Speech Tagger," in *Proceedings of the Third Conference on Applied Natural Language Processing* (Stroudsburg, PA: Association for Computational Linguistics, 1992), 152-155.

38. The Brill Tagger is available in various enhanced versions; a standard distribution is at https://www.cs.cmu.edu/Groups/AI/areas/nlp/parsing/taggers/brill/0.html

39. For documentation of the parser rules and principles, see http://www.link.cs.cmu.edu/link/. Ongoing development of the parser in many languages besides English is at https://www.abisource.com/projects/link-grammar/#download

40. https://linguistics.stanford.edu/resources/corpora/corpus-tools. Our own implementation is at https://github.com/shakeosphere

41. https://mapoflondon.uvic.ca/gazetteer_about.htm

42. Lukas Erne, *Shakespeare and the Book Trade* (Cambridge: Cambridge University Press, 2013), 138.

43. Ibid., 138n27.

44. See D. F. McKenzie, "Stationers' Company Liber A: An Apologia," in *The Stationers' Company and the Book Trade 1550-1990,* eds. Robin Myers and Michael Harris (Winchester St. Paul's Bibliographies, and New Castle, DE: Oak Knoll Press, 1997), 39-59.

45. Michael Treadwell, "London Trade Publishers, 1675-1750," *The Library*, series 6 vol. 4 (1982): 99.

46. M. A. Shaaber notes that there "can be no doubt about the usual meaning" of this formula, although he also notes that it is relatively infrequent, in "The Meaning of the Imprint in Early Printed Books," *The Library, series 4 vol. 24* (1944): 120-141.

47. Ibid., 127.

48. Ibid., 132-133.

49. See Erne, *Shakespeare*, 138.

50. Peter W. M. Blayney, "The Publication of Playbooks," in *A New History of Early English Drama, eds.* John D. Cox and David Scott Kastan (New York: Columbia University Press, 1997), 391, 417.

51. Vincent D. Blondel, Jean-Loup Guillaume, Renaud Lambiotte, and Etienne Lefebvre, "Fast Unfolding of Communities in Large Networks," *Journal of Statistical Mechanics: Theory and Experiment* 10 (2008): 1-12.

52. Constance Brown Kuriyama, "Marlowe Biography: Fact, Inference, Conjecture, Speculation," in *Christopher Marlowe at 450*, eds. Sara Munson Deats and Robert A. Logan (Abingdon: Routledge, 2016), 327.

53. https://networkx.github.io/documentation/stable/index.html. See Aric A. Hagberg, Daniel A. Schult, and Pieter J. Swart, "Exploring Network Structure, Dynamics, and Function Using NetworkX," in *Proceedings of the 7th Python in Science Conference*, eds. Gäel Varoquaux, Travis Vaught, and Jarrod Millman (Pasadena, 2008), 11-15.

54. https://github.com/shakeosphere

## Chapter 2

1. Andrew McRae, *Literature and Domestic Travel in Early Modern England* (Cambridge: Cambridge University Press, 2009), 96.

2. James Daybell, *The Material Letter in Early Modern England, 1512-1635* (New York: Palgrave, 2012), 232.

3. C. G. A. Clay, *Economic Expansion and Social Change: England 1500-1700* (Cambridge: Cambridge University Press, 1984), 1:197-213.

4. Daybell, *Material Letter*, 120.

5. See Harold Love, *Scribal Publication in Seventeenth Century England* (Oxford: Clarendon Press, 1993); Arthur F. Marotti, *Manuscript, Print, and the English Renaissance Lyric* (Ithaca: Cornell University Press, 1994). See also David R. Carlson, *English Humanist Books: Writers and Patrons, Manuscript and Print, 1475-1525* (Toronto: Toronto University Press, 1993).

6. Julia Crick, "The Art of the Unprinted: Transcription and English Antiquity in the Age of Print," in *The Uses of Script and Print, 1300-1700*, eds. Julia Crick and Alexandra Walsham (Cambridge: Cambridge University Press, 2004),

116–134; M. D. Reeve, "Manuscripts Copied from Printed Books," in *Manuscripts in the Fifty Years After the Invention of Printing*, ed. J. B. Trapp (London: Warburg Institute, 1983), 12–20.

7. David Scott Kastan, *Shakespeare and the Book* (Cambridge: Cambridge University Press, 2001), 116.

8. Adrian Johns, *The Nature of the Book: Print and Knowledge in the Making* (Chicago: University of Chicago Press, 1998), 5. See also Johns's debate with Eisenstein, and restatement of this position, in the *American Historical Review* 107 (2002): 106–125.

9. David McKitterick, *Print, Manuscript, and the Search for Order, 1450–1830* (Cambridge: Cambridge University Press, 2003), 4. For more on the persistence of coterie scribal culture deep into the world of eighteenth-century print, see Betty A. Schellenberg, *Literary Coteries and the Making of Modern Print Culture, 1740–1790* (Cambridge: Cambridge University Press, 2016).

10. See also Richard A. McCabe, *"Ungainefull Arte": Poetry, Patronage, and Print in the Early Modern Era* (Oxford: Oxford University Press, 2016), 6.

11. Stephen Davis et al., "The Abundance Threshold for Plague as a Critical Percolation Phenomenon," *Nature* 454 (2008): 634–637.

12. Ricard V. Solé, *Phase Transitions* (Princeton: Princeton University Press, 2011), 99–106.

13. Ibid., 54–55.

14. Peter Blayney, *The Stationers' Company and the Printers of London, 1501–1557*, 2 vols. (Cambridge: Cambridge University Press, 2013), 2:842.

15. Susannah Fox and Lee Rainie, "The Web at 25 in the U.S." (Washington, DC: Pew Research Center, 2014), 5–10: https://www.pewresearch.org/internet/2014/02/27/the-web-at-25-in-the-u-s/

16. Blayney, *Stationers' Company*, 2:914.

17. Ibid., 2:915.

18. Credit for the pun goes to Daniel Shore and Chris Warren, whose Six Degrees of Francis Bacon project mines the *Oxford Dictionary of National Biography* to establish probable links between Bacon and other early modern figures: http://www.sixdegreesoffrancisbacon.com/?ids=10000473&min_confidence=60&type=network

19. A. E. B. Coldiron, *Printers Without Borders: Translation and Textuality in the Renaissance* (Cambridge: Cambridge University Press, 2015), 5. As I discuss in the Epilogue, in the future it should be possible for researchers to adapt the analytical tools and methods here to catalogues like the Universal Short Title Catalogue (USTC), in order to demonstrate how these dynamics played out on the continent.

20. See Coldiron, *Printers Without Borders*, 35–41.

21. Neil Rhodes and Jonathan Sawday, "Introduction," in *The Renaissance Computer: Knowledge Technology in the First Age of Print*, eds. Neil Rhodes and Jonathan Sawday (New York: Routledge, 2000), 2.

22. Matthew D. Lincoln, "Social Network Centralization Dynamics in Print Production in the Low Countries, 1550-1750," *Digital Art History* 2 (2016): 144-145.

23. Ibid., 145.

24. Ibid., 145.

25. Stephen Greenblatt, *Will in the World: How Shakespeare Became Shakespeare* (New York: W. W. Norton, 2005), 200, 203.

26. Robert Greene, *Greene's Groatsworth of Wit* (London, 1592), sig. E2v.

27. Thomas Nashe, *Strange Newes of the Intercepting Certaine Letters*, in *The Works of Thomas Nashe*, 3 vols., ed. R. B. McKerrow (Oxford, 1958), 1:287-288.

28. Kirk Melnikoff and Edward Gieskes, "Introduction: Re-Imagining Robert Greene," in *Writing Robert Greene: Essays on England's First Notorious Professional Writer*, eds. Kirk Melnikoff and Edward Gieskes (Aldershot: Ashgate, 2008), 8.

29. Robert Greene, *Perimedes the Blacke-smith* (London, 1588), sig. B1v.

30. Ibid., sig. G4v.

31. John Clark Jordan, *Robert Greene* (New York: Columbia University Press, 1915), 201-202.

32. Thomas Overbury, *Sir Thomas Overbury, His Wife, with Additions of New News, and Divers More Characters* (London, 1618), sig. G8r.

33. Melnikoff and Gieskes, "Introduction," 24.

34. Lori Humphrey Newcomb, "A Looking Glass for Readers: Cheap Print and the Senses of Repentance," in *Writing Robert Greene: Essays on England's First Notorious Professional Writer*, eds. Kirk Melnikoff and Edward Gieskes (Aldershot: Ashgate, 2008), 153.

35. See H. R. Woudhuysen, *Sir Philip Sidney and the Circulation of Manuscripts, 1558-1640* (Oxford: Clarendon Press, 1996), 210-213. J. W. Saunders popularized the idea that Sidney and his ilk actively avoided the "stigma of print," in "The Stigma of Print: A Note on the Social Bases of Tudor Poetry," *Essays in Criticism 1* (1951): 137-164. But Woudhuysen and others have modified this assessment and shown that it was poetry and publicity, as much as print, that aroused suspicion. See also Nita Krevans, "Print and the Tudor Poets," in *Reconsidering the Renaissance*, ed. M. A. Di Cesare (Binghamton, NY: Medieval and Renaissance Texts and Studies, 1992), 301-13.

36. Michael Brennan, "William Ponsonby: Elizabethan Stationer," *Analytical and Enumerative Bibliography* 7 (1983): 92-93.

37. Ibid., 91.

38. See Joel Davis, "Multiple 'Arcadias' and the Literary Quarrel Between Fulke Greville and the Countess of Pembroke," *Studies in Philology* 101 (2004): 401–430.

39. Andrew Zurcher, "Printing *The Faerie Queene* in 1590," *Studies in Bibliography* 57 (2005), 115.

40. McCabe, *"Ungainfull Arte,"* 239–252.

41. Zurcher, "Printing *The Faerie Queene*" in 1590," 116.

42. Ibid., 133.

43. Ibid., 135.

44. Edmund Spenser, *The Faerie Queene*, eds. A. C. Hamilton, Hiroshi Yamashita, and Toshiyuki Suzuki (Harlow: Longman, 2001), 714.

45. See Park Honan, who argues that Shakespeare had "little to gain" from seeing his name in print, in *Shakespeare: A Life* (Oxford: Oxford University Press, 1998), 114–115; and Kastan, who claims that Shakespeare's investments in the theatre meant that he treated the printing of his plays with "indifference," in *Shakespeare and the Book*, 16.

46. For the "socially suspect cultural domain" of theatrical texts, see Wendy Wall, *The Imprint of Gender: Authorship and Publication in the English Renaissance* (Ithaca: Cornell University Press, 1993), 89.

47. Adam G. Hooks, *Selling Shakespeare: Biography, Bibliography, and the Book Trade* (Cambridge: Cambridge University Press, 2016), 136–177.

48. Lukas Erne, *Shakespeare and the Book Trade* (Cambridge: Cambridge University Press, 2013), 18.

49. Katherine Duncan-Jones, *Ungentle Shakespeare: Scenes from His Life* (London: Arden, 2001), 114.

50. Hooks, *Selling Shakespeare*, 37.

51. Duncan-Jones, *Ungentle Shakespeare*, 115.

52. Robert Greene, *Greene's Groats-worth of Witte* (London, 1592), sig. F1v. Authorship of the text—released posthumously in the year of Greene's death—has long been disputed, with Thomas Nashe a likely candidate.

53. Nancy Peters Maude, "The Extended Collaboration of John Danter and Edward Allde," *The Library*, series 7 vol. 16 (2015): 329–342.

54. Hooks, *Selling Shakespeare*, 27.

55. Rhodes and Sawday, *Renaissance Computer*, 12.

56. Ann M. Blair, *Too Much to Know: Managing Scholarly Information Before the Modern Age* (New Haven: Yale University Press, 2010), 13.

57. "To the Most Illustrious Princes of Germany" (the legation of the pontifical ambassador to the Diet of Nuremberg, 1622), in *One Hundred Grievances: A Chapter from the History of Pre-Reformation Days*, ed. Charles Hastings Collette (London, 1869), 123–132.

58. Thomas More, *The Confutacyon of Tyndales Answere* (London, 1532), sig. Aa3r-v.

59. William Marshall, trans. and ed., *A Prymer in Englyshe* (London, 1534), sig. B1r.

60. Charles I, *Eikon Basilike* (London, 1648), sig. K4r.

61. Michael Sparke, *A Second Beacon Fired by Scintilla* (London, 1652), sig. B1v.

62. Ibid., sig. A3r; Johns, *The Nature of the Book*, 152.

63. Michael Sparke, *Scintilla, Or a Light Broken into Dark Warehouses* (London: 1641), title page. For the Bible's central role in the nevertheless feckless Royal Printing House, see David Norton, *A Textual History of the King James Bible* (Cambridge: Cambridge University Press, 2005), 62-81; for the Bible as one of Cambridge University Press's "mainstays" and primary "generator of profits" see David McKitterick, *History of Cambridge University Press*, 3 vols. (Cambridge: Cambridge University Press, 1992), 1:195; for the English Stock see Cyprian Blagden, "The English Stock of the Stationers' Company: An Account of Its Origins," *The Library*, series 5 vol. 10 (1955): 163-185, and "The English Stock of the Stationers' Company in the Time of the Stuarts," *The Library*, series 5 vol. 12 (1957): 167-186.

64. Sparke, *Scintilla*, 5-6.

65. Ibid., 5-6.

66. William Laud, *History of the Troubles and Trial of the Most Reverend Father in God and Blessed Martyr* (London, 1695), sig. Zz2r.

67. Sparke, *A Second Beacon Fired by Scintilla*, sig. B2r.

68. Firefighters, under the king's supervision, ultimately resorted to this technique during the Great Fire of 1666. See David Garrioch, "1666 and London's Fire History: A Re-Evaluation," *The Historical Journal* 59 (2016): 319-338. See also Roy Porter, *London: A Social History* (Cambridge, MA: Harvard University Press, 1994), 85-87.

69. George Walker, *A Brotherly and Friendly Censure of the Errour of a Dear Friend and Brother in Christian Affection* (London, 1645), sig. A2r-v. It is not clear if Sparke printed Prynne's original *Four Questions*, which was a controversial treatise seeking a Presbyterian form of church discipline, but he did print Prynne's response to Walker, *A Vindication of Foure Serious Questions* (London, 1645).

70. Edward Dacres, "To the Reader," in *Nicholas Machiavel's Prince* (London, 1640), sig. A2v, A4v. See also William Ball, who followed such arguments to their logical end by arguing in *A Briefe Treatise Concerning the Regulating of Printing Humbly Presented to the Parliament of England* (London, 1651):

> Printers . . . ought to have some careful, and exact supervisors over them, even as Apothecaries (who have the College of Physicians, and Doctors of Physique over them, not only to prescribe, but also to peruse their Medicines) lest the first poison the minds of the People by erronious principles in print; as may the last their bodies, by evil Medicines. (22-23)

71. John Milton, *Areopagitica*, in *Complete Prose Works of John Milton*, ed. Ernest Sirluck (New Haven: Yale University Press, 1959), 2:528. This edition is subsequently abbreviated CPW and cited by volume and page.

72. Ibid., 521.

73. Christina Haas, *Writing Technology: Studies on the Materiality of Literacy* (New York: Routledge, 2009), 211.

74. Bruno Latour, *Reassembling the Social: An Introduction to Actor-Network-Theory* (Oxford: Oxford University Press, 2005), 48.

75. Erasmus, *The Adages of Erasmus*, trans. Margaret Mann Phillips, ed. William Barker (Toronto: University of Toronto Press, 2001), II.I.I, 145-146.

76. R.W., *Martine Mar-Sixtus* (London, 1591), sig. A3v.

77. Thomas Nashe, *Pierce Penilesse His Supplication to the Devill* (London, 1592), sig. J3r.

78. See Peter Burke on "the myth of the Renaissance," *The Renaissance*, 2nd ed. (Houndmills: Macmillan, 1991), 1.

79. Henry Chettle, *Kind Harts Dream* (London, 1593), sig. C1r.

**Chapter 3**

1. John Jowett, "Henry Chettle: 'Your Old Compositor,'" *Text* 15 (2003): 144.

2. Henry Chettle, *Kind-hart's Dreame* (London, 1593), sig. C1r-v.

3. Such networks are conventionally called "scale free," but it would be more precise to say that they exhibit scale-free behavior over some range, since the system's finite size means that some node will ultimately have the highest degree, and the long tail will terminate. See Duncan J. Watts, *Six Degrees: The Science of a Connected Age* (New York: W. W. Norton, 2003), 110-112.

4. However, skill, merit, and agency are not entirely absent either, as in the "good get richer" model described by Guido Caldarelli et al. in "Scale-Free Networks from Varying Vertex Intrinsic Fitness," *Physical Review Letters* 89 (2002): 1-4.

5. See Guido Caldarelli, "Geophysical Networks," in *Scale-Free Networks: Complex Webs in Nature and Technology* (Oxford: Oxford University Press, 2007), 148-164.

6. Chettle, *Kind-hart's Dreame*, sig. C1v.

7. http://www.oxforddnb.com/page/about

8. E. A. J. Honigmann, *The Texts of "Othello" and Shakespearean Revision* (London: Routledge, 1996), 24.

9. Michael Neill, Appendix B, in Shakespeare's *Othello, the Moor of Venice*, ed. Michael Neill (Oxford: Clarendon Press, 2006), 407; W. W. Greg, *The Variants in the First Quarto of "King Lear": A Bibliographical and Critical Inquiry* (London: Bibliographical Society, 1939), 47.

10. Brian Vickers, *The One King Lear* (Cambridge, MA: Harvard University Press, 2016), 91, 144, 114.

11. Ibid., 154.

12. Ibid., 114.

13. Adrian Weiss, "Casting Compositors," *Thomas Middleton and Early Modern Textual Culture: A Companion to the Collected Works*, eds. Gary Taylor and John Lavagnino (Oxford: Oxford University Press, 2007), 200n6.

14. See H. R. Woudhuysen, "Early Play Texts: Forms and Formes," in *In Arden: Editing Shakespeare, Essays in Honour of Richard Proudfoot*, eds. Gordon McMullan and Ann Thompson (London: Bloomsbury, 2003), 48–64.

15. See Holger S. Syme, "The Text Is Foolish: Brian Vickers's *One King Lear*," *Los Angeles Review of Books* (6 September 2016): https://lareviewofbooks.org/article/text-foolish-brian-vickerss-one-king-lear/

16. Peter W. M. Blayney, "Quadrat Demonstrandum," *Papers of the Bibliographical Society of America* 111 (2017): 81.

17. Peter W. M. Blayney, *The Texts of King Lear and Their Origins: Volume I, Nicholas Okes and the First Quarto* (Cambridge: Cambridge University Press, 1982), 292.

18. Ibid., 50.

19. Ibid., 27.

20. For the early modern decline of the horner's trade, see Arthur MacGregor, "Antler, Bone, and Horn," in *English Medieval Industries: Craftsmen, Techniques, and Products*, eds. John Blair and Nigel Ramsay (London: Hambledon, 1991), 373–374.

21. Edward Arber, *A Transcript of the Registers of the Company of Stationers of London, 1554–1640 A.D.* (London: 1875–94), 2:209.

22. Lukas Erne, *Shakespeare and the Book Trade* (Cambridge: Cambridge University Press, 2013), 147.

23. Katherine Duncan-Jones, *Ungentle Shakespeare: Scenes from His Life* (London: Arden, 2001), 115.

24. See Adam G. Hooks, *Selling Shakespeare: Biography, Bibliography, and the Book Trade* (Cambridge: Cambridge University Press, 2016), 44.

25. Paul Mulholland, "Nicholas Okes," in *Dictionary of Literary Biography*, vol. 170 of *The British Literary Book Trade, 1475–1700*, eds. James K. Bracken and Joel Silver (Detroit: Gale, 1996), 170:193.

26. Ibid., 170:193.

27. Blayney, *Texts of King Lear*, 49. See also David L. Gants, "A Quantitative Analysis of the London Book Trade," *Studies in Bibliography* 55 (2002): 185–213.

28. Gants calculates that the entire London book trade produced an average of 7,616 edition-sheets per year between 1614–1618, putting the average per shop between 150–200; "A Quantitative Analysis," 187.

29. Another long-lived printer, William Jaggard, shared work with 12 others during his 29-year career (1594–1623).

30. Anonymous, *A True Relation of a Barbarous and Most Cruel Murder* (London, 1633).

31. J. S. Cockburn, *A History of English Assizes, 1558–1714* (Cambridge: Cambridge University Press, 1972), 229.

32. Robert Pricket/Sir Edward Coke, *The Lord Coke His Speech and Charge* (London: for Nathaniel Butter, 1607), sig. C2r.

33. See Blayney, *Texts of King Lear*, 66.

34. Paul Raffield, *The Art of Law in Shakespeare* (Oxford: Bloomsbury, 2017), 237–238. See also A. D. Boyer, *Sir Edward Coke and the Elizabethan Age* (Stanford: Stanford University Press, 2003), 288.

35. William Shakespeare, *M. William Shak-speare: His True Chronicle Historie of the Life and Death of King Lear* (London, 1608), sig. G3v.

36. Tiffany Stern, "'Guilty of Such a Ballad': Shakespeare the Ballad Monger," unpublished talk, Stanford University, 16 April 2016.

37. Katherine Duncan-Jones repeatedly refers to the poem's "unpopularity" in "Ravished and Revised: The 1616 *Lucrece*," *Review of English Studies*, new series 51 (2001): 516–523. But a text that goes through four editions in its first six years can only be called unpopular in comparison with the stunning popularity of a poem like *Venus and Adonis*, which was by far Shakespeare's most successful printed work, reprinted 10 times during his lifetime. By that standard, nothing Shakespeare wrote except *Venus and Adonis* would be popular.

38. Richard Rowland, *Thomas Heywood's Theatre, 1599–1639: Locations, Translations, and Conflict* (Burlington, VT: Ashgate, 2010), 4. Rowland discusses his own initial "distaste" for the play and the way various critics have attempted to explain away this distaste, before arguing that such reactions do not give enough credit to the complicated ways that it must have "amused and troubled its original audiences" (16).

39. In "Ravished and Revised," Duncan-Jones mistakenly states that "Roger Jackson purchased the rights to *Lucrece* from Nicholas Okes in 1614," which would imply that Okes procured them from Harrison when he printed the play (519). But in fact Harrison still held the rights until 1614, when he transferred them to Jackson on 1 March 1613/14. See Arber, *Transcript of the Registers*, 3:248b.

40. Anonymous, *The Merrie Conceited Jests of George Peele, Gentleman* (London, 1607), sig. D1v.

41. David Randall, *Credibility in Elizabethan and Early Stuart Military News* (London: Pickering and Chatto/Routledge, 2008), 89.

42. Zachary Lesser, *Renaissance Drama and the Politics of Publication: Readings in the English Book Trade* (Cambridge: Cambridge University Press, 2004), 42.

43. C. H. Herford, "Introduction to *The Merry Wives of Windsor*," in *The Works of Shakespeare* (London: Macmillan, 1900), 2:233.

44. Gerald D. Johnson, "John Busby and the Stationer's Trade, 1590–1612," *The Library*, series 6 vol. 7 (1985): 15; Erne, *Shakespeare and the Book Trade*, 170–171.

45. Mulholland, "Nicholas Okes," 170:193.

46. Thomas Heywood, *An Apology for Actors* (London, 1612), sig. G4r-v.

47. See James P. Bednarz, "Canonizing Shakespeare: The Passionate Pilgrim, England's Helicon and the Question of Authenticity," *Shakespeare Survey* 60 (2007): 252–267.

48. This is not the only indication that Okes worked closely with authors and understood that "authority" sells: See the eighth edition of John Smith's *Great Assize* (London, 1638), sig. A5r-v, where Okes and/or his son John included a note from the "Printer to the Courteous reader" advertising fresh additions and corrections "by the Author himselfe," who had formerly been living "far distant from the City, and having a Pastorall charge to attend upon, could not attend the Presse."

49. Blayney, *Texts of King Lear*, 28.

50. William A. Jackson, ed., *Records of the Court of the Stationers' Company 1602–1640* (London: Bibliographical Society, 1957), Court Book C: 472.

51. Cyndia Susan Clegg, *Press Censorship in Jacobean England* (Cambridge: Cambridge University Press, 2001), 18. The "hegemonic" view of press censorship was most notably put forward by Christopher Hill, "Censorship in English Literature," in *The Collected Essays of Christopher Hill*, vol. 1 of *Writing and the Revolution in 17th Century England* (Amherst: University of Massachusetts Press, 1987), 1:32–72; and Frederick S. Siebert, *Freedom of the Press in England 1476–1776* (Urbana: University of Illinois Press, 1952).

52. Clegg, *Press Censorship in Jacobean England,* 17. For earlier periods, see also Clegg's argument that "Elizabethan press censorship and control is a crazy quilt of proclamations, patents, trade regulations, judicial decrees, and privy council and parliamentary actions patched together by the sometimes common and sometimes competing threads of religious, economic, political, and private interests" in *Press Censorship in Elizabethan England* (Cambridge: Cambridge University Press, 1997), 5. For the arbitrary and inconsistent nature of censorship in the period, see also Mark Bland, "'Invisible Dangers': Censorship and the Subversion of Authority in Early Modern England," *Papers of the Bibliographical Society of America* 90 (1996): 151–193.

53. Quoted by Jackson, *Records of the Court,* viii. For an excellent account of Wither's conflict with the stationers and his attempts to secure his own patent, see James Doelman, "George Wither, the Stationers Company, and the English Psalter," *Studies in Philology* 90 (1993): 74–82.

54. David Norbrook, *Poetry and Politics in the English Renaissance*, rev. ed. (Oxford: Oxford University Press, 2002), 201. See also Allan Pritchard, "Abuses Stript and Whipt and Wither's Imprisonment," *Review of English Studies* 14 (1963): 337–345.

55. George Wither, *Wither's Motto*, 2nd ed. (London, for John Marriot, 1621), sig. D8r.

56. See Allan Pritchard, "George Wither's Quarrel with the Stationers: An Anonymous Reply to the *Schollers Purgatory*," *Studies in Bibliography* 16 (1963): 28.

57. Norbrook, *Poetry and Politics*, 202.

58. For a good summary of scholarship on the 1621 Parliament and its dissolution, see Michael C. Questier, "Introduction," in *Stuart Dynastic Policy and Religious Politics, 1621–1625* (Cambridge: Cambridge University Press, 2009), 18–25.

59. Arber, *A Transcript of the Registers*, 4:15.

60. Jackson, *Records of the Court*, Court Book C, 135.

61. Wither, *Wither's Motto*, sig. F2v.

62. "Examination of George Wither" (26 June 1621), *State Papers Domestic*, 14/121, fol. 245r-v. The State Papers are subsequently cited in the standard format, for this volume SP 14/121.

63. See the excellent account of "George Wither: The Poet in Prison," in Paul Salzman, *Literary Culture in Jacobean England: Reading 1621* (Houndmills: Palgrave Macmillan, 2002), 117–122.

64. Examination of John Marriot (10 July 1621), SP 14/122 fol. 15v. See also Wither's testimony at SP 14/121 fol. 245r, and Marriot and Grismond at SP 14/122 fol. 15r-v.

65. Note by Thomas Trussell (10? July 1621), SP 14/122 fol. 17r.

66. Examination of John Grismond (12 July 1621), SP 14/122 fol. 22r.

67. Examination of Nicholas Okes (12 July 1621), SP 14/122 fol. 21r. Emphasis added.

68. Ibid., fol. 21r.

69. George Wither, *Schollars Purgatory* (London, 1624), 9–10.

70. Ben Jonson, *Time Vindicated to Himself and to His Honors*, vol. 5 of *The Cambridge Edition of the Works of Ben Jonson*, eds. David Bevington et al. (Cambridge: Cambridge University Press, 2012), 5:135–136.

71. Ibid., 183.

72. *The Petition and Articles Exhibited in Parliament Against Doctor Heywood, Late Chaplen to the Bishop of Canterburie by the Parishioners of S. Giles in the Fields* (London, 1641), sig. B1r.

73. For a comprehensive discussion of this affair and excerpts from all the relevant documents quoted below, see N. W. Bawcutt, "A Crisis of Laudian

Censorship: Nicholas and John Okes and the Publication of Sales's *Introduction to a Devout Life* in 1637," *The Library*, series 7 vol. 1 (2000): 404-438.

74. The engraving served as frontispiece to *A Breviate of the Life of William Laud* (London, 1644), but would have been available for purchase on its own or been bound up with other works in Sparke's shop, as was his common practice. Sparke detailed this practice, and his admiration for Hollar, in the short autobiographical account he offered up in *A Second Beacon Fired by Scintilla* (London, 1652), sig. A3v.

75. The testimony is printed in *The Manuscripts of the House of Lords*, new series, vol. 11 of *Addenda 1514—1714*, ed. Maurice F. Bond (London: HMSO, 1962), 11:436, 448-449.

76. J. V. to his Wife, 1639(?), SP16/437, fol. 86r.

77. See Bawcutt, "A Crisis," 411.

78. Ibid., 410-411.

79. Testimony of Mary Okes (1643), SP16/499, fol. 255r.

80. List in John Lambe's Handwriting (1637), SP16/364, fol. 214r. Okes's petition is at SP16/376, fol. 46r.

81. William Prynne, *Canterburies Doom* (London: Printed by John Macock for Michael Sparke, 1646), 188.

82. Ibid., 188.

83. Testimony of William Laud, *The Manuscripts of the House of Lords*, 436.

84. Ibid., 448-449.

85. William Laud, *The History of the Troubles and Tryal of the Most Reverend Father in God, and Blessed Martyr, William Laud*, ed. Henry Wharton (London, 1695), 363-364.

86. William Laud, *The Second Volume of the Remains of the Most Reverend Father in God . . . William Laud*, ed. Henry Wharton (London, 1700), 129.

87. Franklin B. Williams, "The Laudian Imprimatur," *The Library*, series 5 vol. 15 (1960): 101.

88. Bawcutt, "A Crisis," 419.

89. George Garrard to the Earl of Strafford, *The Earl of Strafforde's Letters and Dispatches*, vol. 2, ed. William Knowler (London, 1739), 74.

90. Autograph Diary of Walter Yonge (1627-1642), BL Add. MS 35331, fol. 66; W. Hawkins to the Earl of Leicester (20 April 1637), reproduced in *Report on the Manuscripts of the Right Honourable Viscount de L'Isle, V. C., Preserved at Penshurst Place, Kent*, vol. 6 ed. G. Dyfnallt Owen (London: Historical Manuscripts Commission, 1966), 102.

91. Bawcutt, "A Crisis," 429.

92. *The Petition and Articles Exhibited in Parliament Against Doctor Heywood*, sig. A2r.

93. Portrait of Archbishop Laud and Mr. Henry Burton, BM Satires 412. For the date, see Antony Griffiths, "The Print in Stuart Britain 1603-1689," BM 1998, cat. 98.

94. Andrew Marvell, *The Rehearsal Transpros'd*, in *The Prose Works of Andrew Marvell*, eds. Martin Dzelzainis and Annabel Patterson (Yale: Yale University Press, 2003), 1:45.

95. Andrew Marvell, *The Rehearsal Transpros'd: The Second Part*, in *The Prose Works of Andrew Marvell*, 1:406.

**Chapter 4**

1. Christopher Hill, *The World Turned Upside Down* (Viking: New York, 1972), 14. See also works like A. L. Morton, *The World of the Ranters* (London: Lawrence and Wishart, 1970).

2. Elaine Hobby, *Virtue of Necessity: English Women's Writings 1649-1688* (Ann Arbor: University of Michigan Press, 1989; Hilary Hinds, *God's Englishwomen: Seventeenth-Century Radical Sectarian Writing and Feminist Criticism* (Manchester: Manchester University Press, 1996); Nigel Smith, *Perfection Proclaimed: Language and Literature in English Radical Religion, 1640-1660* (Oxford: Clarendon Press, 1989); Phyllis Mack, *Visionary Women: Ecstatic Prophecy in Seventeenth-Century England* (Berkeley: University of California Press, 1992). See also Paul Salzman on the "particularly large numbers of women [that] emerged from within the burgeoning radical religious movements that flourished" during the Civil War, in *Reading Early Modern Women's Writing* (Oxford: Oxford University Press, 2006), 109.

3. http://www.womensbookhistory.org/

4. Hobby, *Virtue of Necessity*, 201.

5. Sharon Achinstein, "Women on Top in the Pamphlet Literature of the English Revolution," *Women's Studies* 24 (1994): 135.

6. Carole Pateman, *The Sexual Contract* (Stanford: Stanford University Press, 1988), 78.

7. For simplicity, I'll refer to Eleanor "Davies" even though she remarried a man named Douglas and usually referred to herself only as "Lady Eleanor."

8. Similarly, I'll refer to Mary "Cary" although she also remarried and sometimes went by the name "Mary Rande" or "Mary Rante."

9. Notable exceptions include Esther Cope's biography of Davies, discussed below, and Katharine Gillespie's *Domesticity and Dissent in the Seventeenth Century: English Women's Writing and the Public Sphere* (Cambridge: Cambridge University Press, 2004) and *Women Writing the English Republic, 1625-1681* (Cambridge: Cambridge University Press, 2017), which provide chapters on Cary and Davies, respectively.

10. Stevie Davies, *Unbridled Spirits: Women of the English Revolution, 1640–1660* (London: Women's Press, 1999), 7.

11. Esther S. Cope, *Handmaid of the Holy Spirit: Dame Eleanor Davies, Never Soe Mad a Ladie* (Ann Arbor: University of Michigan Press, 1993), 167.

12. Ruth Ahnert and Sebastian E. Ahnert, "Protestant Letter Networks in the Reign of Mary I: A Quantitative Approach," *English Literary History* 82 (2015): 17.

13. Jana Smith Elford, "Recovering Women's History with Network Analysis: A Case Study of the *Fabian News*," *Journal of Modern Periodical Studies* 6 (2015): 191–213; Hildrun Kretschmer and Isidro F. Aguillo, "New Indicators for Gender Studies in Web Networks," *Information Processing and Management* 41 (2005): 1481–1495.

14. Evan Bourke, "Female Involvement, Membership, and Centrality: A Social Network Analysis of the Hartlib Circle," *Literature Compass* 14 (2017): 1.

15. In the late seventeenth century, a "projector" was a figure who proposed or supported various projects for the public good or improvement of the commonwealth, often through proto-scientific means; "intelligencer" was sometimes a term applied to spies, but just as often to people like Hartlib, who collected and transmitted news and information.

16. John Dury to Messrs. Marshall and Baall (30 June 1635), Sloane MSS 654 fol. 350; transcribed in G. H. Turnbull, *Samuel Hartlib: A Sketch of His Life and His Relations to J. A. Comenius* (Oxford: Oxford University Press, 1920), appendix 5: 79.

17. Gordon Campbell and Thomas N. Corns, *John Milton: Life, Work, and Thought* (Oxford: Oxford University Press, 2008), 267.

18. See Carol Pal, *Republic of Women: Rethinking the Republic of Letters in the Seventeenth Century* (Cambridge: Cambridge University Press, 2012), 116–124.

19. Alfred Harold Wood, *Church Unity Without Uniformity: A Study of Seventeenth-Century English Church Movements and of Richard Baxter's Proposals for a Comprehensive Church* (London: Epworth Press, 1963), 17. Ralph Young, *Dissent: The History of an American Idea* (New York: New York University Press, 2015), 21, 18.

20. Alan Ford, *James Ussher: Theology, History, and Politics in Early Modern Ireland and England* (Oxford: Oxford University Press, 2007), 230–231.

21. David L. Smith, *Constitutional Royalism and the Search for Settlement, 1640–49* (Cambridge: Cambridge University Press, 2002), 138–143.

22. Andrew Hopper, *Turncoats and Renegadoes: Changing Sides During the English Civil Wars* (Oxford: Oxford University Press, 2012), 202–204. Love's dramatic speech from the scaffold was published in Christopher Love, *Mr. Love's Case* (London, 1651), 21.

23. See Margaret Griffin, *Regulating Religion and Morality in the King's Armies, 1639–46* (Leiden: Brill, 2004), 98–100. See also David Cressy, *England on Edge: Crisis and Revolution, 1640–42* (Oxford: Oxford University Press, 2006), 307–308.

24. Robert Devereux Essex, *A Letter from the Earl of Essex to His Highnesse Prince Rupert* (Bristol/Avon, 1645), 6.

25. David R. Como, *Blown by the Spirit* (Stanford: Stanford University Press, 2004), 455–556. For a caution against equating "antinomian" with "radical" during this period, see Tim Cooper, "The Antinomians Redeemed: Removing Some of the 'Radical' from Mid-Seventeenth-Century English Religion," *Journal of Religious History* 24 (2000): 247.

26. Hobby, *Virtue of Necessity*, 48.

27. Mack, *Visionary Women*, 118.

28. Cope, *Handmaid*, 167.

29. Christopher Brooke, Letter to Eleanor Davies (May? 1626), SP 14/130 fol. 174r.

30. Ibid., fol. 174r.

31. Michelle O'Callaghan, "'An Uncivill Scurrilous Letter': 'Womanish Brabb[l]es' and the Letter of Affront," in *Cultures of Correspondance in Early Modern Britain*, eds. James Daybell and Andrew Gordon (Philadelphia: University of Pennsylvania Press, 2016), 181.

32. Brooke, SP 14/130 fol. 174v.

33. Ibid., fol. 174v.

34. O'Callaghan, "Uncivill," 178.

35. Ibid., 182.

36. Eleanor Davies, *Lady Eleanor Her Appeale to the High Court of Parliament* (London, 1641), sig. B3v.

37. Eleanor Davies, *A Warning to the Dragon and All His Angels* (London: Printed by Bernard Alsop, 1625), 99–100.

38. She describes this very public scene retrospectively in *The Lady Eleanor Her Appeal* (London or Amsterdam, 1646), sig. B2r.

39. Davies, *Warning to the Dragon*, 26.

40. Ibid., sig. A3r-v.

41. Davies, *The Lady Eleanor Her Appeal*, sig. B4r.

42. Ibid.

43. Ibid.

44. Cope, *Handmaid*, 44.

45. Davies, *The Lady Eleanor Her Appeal*, sig. C1v.

46. Ibid.

47. See Cope, *Handmaid*, 50–51.

48. Davies, *The Lady Eleanor Her Appeal*, sig. B4v.

49. Ibid.

50. Ibid., sig. C4r.

51. See Dianne Purkiss, *The English Civil War: Papists, Gentlewomen, Soldiers, and Witchfinders in the Birth of Modern Britain* (New York: Basic Books/HarperCollins, 2006) 39-71. For Lucy Percy-Hay's spying, use of encrypted communications, and role as a "major player in contemporary politics," see Nadine Akkerman, *Invisible Agents: Women and Espionage in Seventeenth-Century Britain* (Oxford: Oxford University Press, 2018), 8, 51-52, 91-92.

52. Davies, *The Lady Eleanor Her Appeal*, sig. C3v.

53. Ibid.

54. Eleanor Davies, *The Everlasting Gospell* (Amsterdam? 1649), 8-9.

55. Ibid., 9.

56. Davies, *The Lady Eleanor Her Appeal*, sig. D4v.

57. See Cope, *Handmaid*, 66.

58. Davies, *The Everlasting Gospell*, 10.

59. Ibid., 10.

60. John Milton, *A Masque Presented at Ludlow Castle*, in *The Complete Poetry and Essential Prose*, eds. William Kerrigan, John Rumrich, and Stephen M. Fallon (New York: Modern Library, 2007), 77.

61. The first person to interpret Milton's *Comus* primarily through this lens was Barbara Breasted, "'Comus' and the Castlehaven Scandal," *Milton Studies* 3 (1971): 201-224. John Creaser argued against the scandal as a primary influence in "Milton's *Comus:* The Irrelevance of the Castlehaven Scandal," *Milton Quarterly* 21 (1987): 24-34, but even there he concludes by admitting that Milton "dealt most adroitly with an invidious issue" by creating a work that could defend the family against rumors and implications that were on everyone's mind (32).

62. Gillespie is one exception to this critical neglect, but in her suggestion that "Davies forms one viable prototype for Milton's Lady," she curiously neglects Davies's role as Touchet's chief defender and instead focuses on Davies "as a woman who was literally placed in bondage by her interrogating Comus for believing that the true fifth monarch was Christ and that it was she, not Laud, who sang on his behalf." See Gillespie, *Domesticity and Dissent*, 3-5.

63. Lady Eleanor Davies, *Woe to the House* (Amsterdam, 1633). Facsimile in *The Early Modern Englishwoman: A Facsimile Library of Essential Works*, ser. 1, printed writings, 1500-1640: Part 2, ed. Teresa Feroli (Aldershot: Ashgate, 2000).

64. Lady Eleanor Davies, *Word of God to the Citie of London, from the Lady Eleanor: Of the Earl of Castle-Haven: Condemn'd, and Beheaded: Aprill 25 1631* (London? 1644), sig. A3v. For a major reassessment of the scandal and trial that lends Davies's defense some credibility, see Cynthia Herrup, *A House in Gross Disorder: Sex, Law, and the 2nd Earl of Castlehaven*, rev. ed. (Oxford: Oxford University Press, 2001).

65. Lady Eleanor Davies, *Crying Charge* (London, 1649), 2, 6.

66. See Blaine Greteman, *The Poetics and Politics of Youth in Milton's England* (Cambridge: Cambridge University Press, 2013).

67. Gillespie, *Women Writing*, 72.

68. State Papers Domestic (1637–38), SP 16/380 fol. 138r.

69. Ibid., fol. 138r.

70. State Papers Domestic (1637–38), SP 16/380 fol. 138v.

71. Cope, *Handmaid*, 84–85.

72. Gerrard Winstanley to Eleanor Davies (4 December 1650), 348. Paul H. Hardacre reprints the letter in "Gerrard Winstanley in 1650," *Huntington Library Quarterly* 22 (1949): 345–349, and page numbers here refer to that publication.

73. Ibid., 348.

74. Ibid.

75. Ibid., 349.

76. The account is posthumously told in Peter Heylyn, *Cyprianus Anglicus* (London, 1688), 2.266.

77. The epitaph for the tomb, which no longer exists in St. Martin's Church, is quoted in its original Latin and translated in *The Complete Poems of John Davies*, ed. Alexander Grosart (London, 1876), liii–lvi.

78. Smith, *Perfection Proclaimed*, 32.

79. See *The Lady Eleanor, Her Blessing to her Beloved Daughter* (London, 1644), 7.

80. Michael Mendle, *The Putney Debates of 1647: The Army, the Levellers, and the English State* (Cambridge: Cambridge University Press, 2010), 110. See also Benjamin Woodford, *Perceptions of a Monarchy Without a King: Reactions to Oliver Cromwell's Power* (Montreal: McGill-Queen's University Press), 44.

80. Jason Peacey, "Print, Publicity, and Popularity: The Projecting of Sir Balthzar Gerbier, 1642–62," *Journal of British Studies* 51 (2012): 297–300.

82. Gillespie, *Domesticity and Dissent*, 12.

83. Ibid., 13.

84. As discussed later in the chapter, there is also a third person on the title page, "R. C.," who remains more mysterious but who may be Richard Collings, the editor of the *Mercurius Civicus* newsbook. Between 1645 and 1660, however, "R. C." only appears in the publishing field twice, and both are on Cary's publications.

85. Mary Cary/Rande, *Little Horn's Doom and Downfall* (London, 1651), sig. A8r.

86. David Loewenstein, "Scriptural Exegesis, Female Prophecy, and Radical Politics in Mary Cary," *Studies in English Literature* 46 (2006): 133.

87. Milton, *Reason of Church Government*, CPW 1:795.

88. Milton, *Areopagitica*, CPW 2:543.

89. Mary Cary, *A Word in Season* (London, 1647), sig. B2r, B1r.

90. See Samuel How, *The Sufficiencie of the Spirit's Teaching* (London, 1640).

91. Milton, *Reason of Church Government*, CPW 1:771; *Areopagitica*, CPW 2:554.

92. Cary, *Word in Season*, sig. B1r.

93. Ibid. Cary also cited the parable of the talents in her first work, *The Glorious Excellencie of the Spirit of Adoption* (London, 1645), sig. A3v.

94. Ibid., sig. B2r.

95. Mary Cary, *A New and More Exact Mappe or, Description of New Jerusalem's Glory* (London, 1651), sig. I1v–I2r. This tract has its own title page but is the second part of *Little Horn's Doom*. The two parts have continuous pagination and always seem to have been sold together. Cary herself is listed as the publisher for the tracts, which were sold by the radical bookseller Giles Calvert.

96. Ibid., sig. A8r.

97. Ibid., sig. E1r.

98. Ibid., sig. Q5v.

99. Ibid., sig. S6r.

100. Ibid., sig. U2v.

101. Hinds, *God's Englishwomen*, 97.

102. John Barnard, "London Publishing, 1640–1660: Crisis, Continuity, and Innovation," *Book History* 4 (2001): 3. For more on Calvert's "pluralism" see Mario Caricchio, "News from the New Jerusalem: Giles Calvert and the Radical Experience," in *Varieties of Seventeenth and Early Eighteenth Century Radicalism in Context*, eds. Ariel Hessayon and David Finnegan (Farnham: Ashgate, 2011), 69–86.

103. D. F. McKenzie, "The London Book Trade in the Later Seventeenth Century," Sandars Lectures (Cambridge: Cambridge University Press, 1976), 12.

104. Kate Peters, "The Dissemination of Quaker Pamphlets in the 1650s," in *Not Dead Things: The Dissemination of Popular Print in England and Wales, Italy and the Low Countries*, eds. Roeland Harms, Joad Raymond, and Jeroen Salman (Leiden: Brill, 2013), 218.

105. Cary, *Little Horn's Doom*, sig. A8v.

106. Hill, *World Turned Upside Down*, 260n.84. See also Hill's *Antichrist in Seventeenth-Century England* (Oxford: Oxford University Press, 1971), 119n4.

107. John Beale to Hartlib (26 March 1659), Hartlib Papers, 51/105b.

108. Henry Oldenburg to Hartlib (30 April 1659), Hartlib Papers, 39/3/22b.

109. Cary, *Little Horn's Doom*, sig. A7r–v.

110. Ibid., sig. z4r.

111. Ibid., sig. z4v.

112. John Downame, *The Account Audited, or the Date of the Resurrection of the Witnesses, Pretended to Be Demonstrated by M. Cary, a Minister* (London, 1649), sig. A2v.

113. See Bryan Ball, "Feake, Christopher (1611/12-1682/3), Fifth Monarchist Leader," *Oxford Dictionary of National Biography* (26 July 2018); R. P. Stern, *Hugh Peter: The Strenuous Puritan* (Urbana: University of Illinois Press, 1954); B. R. White, "Henry Jessey: A Pastor in Politics," *Baptist Quarterly* 25 (1973): 98-110.

114. Cary, *Little Horn's Doom*, sig. A2r.

115. Ibid., sig. A7r.

116. Ibid.

117. Ibid., sig. A3v-A5r.

118. The preface to the reader is correctly signed "M. C.," but because of the title page misattribution, the book is still not listed as Cary's in the STC or ESTC as of December 2020; see Alfred Cohen, "Mary Cary's *The Glorious Excellencie Discovered*," *British Studies Monitor* 10.1-2 (1980): 4-7. The quote on Overton is from Thomas Edwards, *The Second Part of Gangraena* (London, 1646), sig. B4r-v. For more on Overton's importance as a publisher of radical and independent books, see Ann Hughes, *Gangraena and the Struggle for the English Revolution* (Oxford: Oxford University Press, 2004), 208-238. For Jane Coe's career and arrest, see David R. Como, *Radical Parliamentarians and the English Civil War* (Oxford: Oxford University Press, 2018), 318-319.

119. Mack, *Visionary Women*, 105-106.

120. Cary, *Twelve Humble Proposals*, sig. B1r.

121. Ibid., sig. B3r.

122. Ibid., sig. A4r.

123. Mario Caricchio, "News from the New Jerusalem: Giles Calvert and the Radical Experience," in *Varieties of Seventeenth- and Early Eighteenth-Century English Radicalism in Context*, eds. Ariel Hessayon and David Finnegan (Abingdon: Routledge, 2016), 72, 71.

124. See Woodford, *Perceptions of a Monarchy*, 43.

125. For the attribution of these newsletters to Collings, see Joad Raymond, *The Invention of the Newspaper: English Newsbooks 1641-49* (Oxford: Oxford University Press, 1996), 27.

126. Cary, *Resurrection of the Witnesses*, 2nd ed. (London, 1653), sig. A4v.

## Chapter 5

1. Harold Bloom, *The Anxiety of Influence: A Theory of Poetry*, 2nd ed. (Oxford: Oxford University Press, 1997), 33.

2. Ibid., 34. The theme of Milton's "grand" and "sublime" style (and the question of whether it may be "too grand for its own good") rings throughout John Leonard's *Faithful Labourers: A Reception History of Paradise Lost, 1667-1970* (Oxford: Oxford University Press, 2013), 1: ix.

3. Andrew Marvell, "On Paradise Lost," in *Paradise Lost*, ed. Barbara K. Lewalski (Oxford: Wiley-Blackwell, 2007), lines 7–8; all subsequent references to *Paradise Lost* are from this edition, edited by Lewalski.

4. Ibid., 23, 29–30.

5. Clement Walker, *Anarchia Angliacana, the Second Part* (London, 1649), 199–200.

6. John Shawcross, *John Milton: The Self and the World* (Lexington: University Press of Kentucky, 2001), 67, 273.

7. Neil Forsyth, *John Milton: A Biography* (Oxford: Lion Hudson, 2008), 34, 154. See also Barbara K. Lewalski's account of Milton's "lonely and difficult" years of blindness in *The Life of John Milton: A Critical Biography* (Oxford: Blackwell, 2000), 280.

8. My translations are from volume 12 of *The Works of John Milton*, ed. Frank Allen Patterson et al. (New York: Columbia University Press, 1936) 262, 28, 46. All citations of Milton's Latin prose are from this edition, hereafter abbreviated C and cited by volume.

9. Roy C. Flannagan, *John Milton: A Short Introduction* (Oxford: Blackwell, 2002), 36.

10. Mark Granovetter, "The Strength of Weak Ties," *American Journal of Sociology* 78 (1973): 1361.

11. Ibid., 1360.

12. Granovetter discusses the genesis and impact of the article in, "Citation Classic," *Current Contents: Arts and Humanities* 49 (1986): 24.

13. See Stanley Wasserman and Katherine Faust, *Social Network Analysis: Methods and Applications* (Cambridge: Cambridge University Press, 1994), 556–584; David Krackhardt and Mark S. Handcock, "Heider vs. Simmel: Emergent Features in Dynamic Structures," *Proceedings of the 2006 Conference on Statistical Network Analysis* (Pittsburgh: Springer-Verlag, 2007), 14–27.

14. Granovetter, "Strength of Weak Ties," 1364.

15. Ibid., 1366.

16. J. P. Onnela et al., "Structure and Tie Strengths in Mobile Communications Networks," *Proceedings of the National Academies of Sciences* 104 (2007): 7332–7336.

17. Ronald S. Burt, *Structural Holes: The Social Structure of Competition* (Cambridge, MA: Harvard University Press, 1992).

18. Ronald S. Burt, "Structural Holes and Good Ideas," *American Journal of Sociology* 110 (2004): 350.

19. See Stephen P. Borgatti and Virginie Lopez-Kidwell, "Network Theory," in *The Sage Handbook of Social Network Analysis*, eds. John Scott and Peter J. Carrington (London: Sage, 2011), 42.

20. Burt, "Structural Holes," 356.

21. John F. Padgett and Christopher K. Ansell, "Robust Action and the Rise of the Medici, 1400-1434," *American Journal of Sociology* 98 (1993): 1259-1319. For a discussion of structural holes in the biotech industry, see Gordon Walker, Bruce Kogut, and Weijian Shan, "Social Capital, Structural Holes, and the Formation of an Industry Network," *Organization Science* 8 (1997): 109-125; for Bronze Age trade routes, see Viviana Amati, Termeh Shafie, and Ulrik Brandes, "Reconstructing Archaeological Networks with Structural Holes," *Journal of Archeological Method and Theory* 25 (2018): 226-253; for art, see Katherine Giuffre, "Sandpiles of Opportunity: Success in the Art World," *Social Forces* 77 (1999): 815-832.

22. Randall Collins, "A Micro-Macro Theory of Intellectual Creativity: The Case of German Idealist Philosophy," *Sociological Theory* 5 (1987): 67. Collins expanded and elaborated in *The Sociology of Philosophies: A Global Theory of Intellectual Change* (Cambridge, MA: Harvard University Press, 1998).

23. Milton, *Eikonoklastes*, CPW 3:339-340.

24. John Milton, *Epitaphium Damonis, Complete Shorter Poems*, ed. Stella P. Revard (Chichester: Wiley Blackwell, 2009), line 160. Translations are mine.

25. Ibid., lines 170-171.

26. Ibid., lines 171-172.

27. Lewalski, *The Life of John Milton*, 109.

28. Stephen Guy-Bray, *Homoerotic Space: The Poetics of Loss in Renaissance Literature* (Toronto: University of Toronto Press, 2002), 121, 125.

29. Milton, *Epitaphium*, line 174; *Paradise Lost*, 7.31.

30. Stephen B. Dobranski, *Milton, Authorship, and the Book Trade* (Cambridge: Cambridge University Press, 1999), 9.

31. Ann Baynes Coiro, "Anonymous Milton, or *A Maske* Masked," *English Literary History* 71 (2004): 609.

32. Ibid., 612.

33. Leicester Bradner, "Milton's *Epitaphium Damonis*," *Times Literary Supplement* (18 August 1932): 531.

34. John T. Shawcross, "The Date of the Separate Edition of Milton's 'Epitaphium Damonis,'" *Studies in Bibliography* 18 (1965): 262-265. Shawcross writes contra Harris Fletcher, "The Seventeenth-Century Separate Printing of Milton's 'Epitaphium Damonis,'" *Journal of English and Germanic Philology* 61 (1962): 788-796.

35. Shawcross, "Date of the Separate," 263-264.

36. Ibid., 264.

37. I have inspected these works at the British Library and the University of Illinois Special Collections. The italic question mark mentioned by Shawcross

also appears throughout *Coale from the Altar*; the battered question mark appears at sig. B3v., sig. D1v, sig. E2r, and elsewhere. The ornaments at the top of sig. A2r in the 1637 *Maske (Comus)* and sig. A1v in *Epitaphium* appear identical, with only slight variants in the pattern. If we represent the patterns alphabetically, they are ABCDEABCDFABCDE (*Maske)* and ABCDABCDABCDABCE (*Epitaphium*). That is, Shawcross in "Date of the Separate" explains

> *A Maske* is headed by five ornaments printed one after the other in a row three times except that what would have been the fifth ornament in the second grouping is a different (or sixth) ornament, probably as a result of foul case; and the elegy is headed by the identical first four ornaments printed one after the other in a row four times, except that what would have been the fourth ornament in the fourth grouping is the identical fifth ornament used in the *A Maske* row. (264)

This is a characteristic pattern for Mathewes—it is not included, for example, on the 1626 edition of Samuel Ward's sermons printed by Miles Flescher, but it appears, in the familiar pattern (ABCDABCDBA) in Mathewes's 1636 reprint (sig. A3r) and Edward Norris's 1636 "Treatise Maintaining That Corporeal Blessings Are to Be Sought" (ABCDABC, sig. B1r).

38. Henry Lawes, dedicatory epistle, *A Maske Presented at Ludlow Castle*, sig. A2r–v.

39. Private communication, 4 September 2017. Gadd extrapolates his estimate of private printing costs from Peter W. M. Blayney, "The Publication of Playbooks," in *A New History of Early English Drama*, eds. John D. Cox and David Scott Kastan (New York: Columbia University Press, 1997), 405–410.

40. See Harold Love, *Scribal Publication in Seventh-Century England* (Oxford: Clarendon Press, 1993); Arthur F. Marotti, *Manuscript, Print, and the English Renaissance Lyric* (Ithaca: Cornell University Press, 1995); and Jason-Scott Warren, "Reconstructing Manuscript Networks: The Textual Transactions of Sir Stephen Powle," in *Communities in Early Modern England: Networks, Place, Rhetoric*, eds. Alexandra Shepard and Phil Withington (Manchester: Manchester University Press, 2000), 18–37.

41. Milton to Diodati, *C* 12:28–29.

42. Milton to Thomas Young, *C* 12:7.

43. Milton to Alexander Gill, *C* 12:11; Milton to Leo Van Aitzema, *C* 12:71.

44. When Milton sent a gift copy of *Comus* to Henry Wotton, it turned out the elder man had already received another copy of the work, anonymously bound with Thomas Randolph's works, as discussed by Coiro, "Anonymous," 609–629.

45. Michel Callon, John Law, and Arie Rip, "How to Study the Force of Science," in *Mapping the Dynamics of Science and Technology*, eds. Michel Callon, John

Law, and Arie Rip (Houndmills: Macmillan, 1986), 14. See also Bruno Latour, who argues that while texts look "like miserable pathways to move between the many contradictory frames of reference ... their efficacy is unmatched," in *Reassembling the Social: An Introduction to Actor-Network-Theory* (Oxford: Oxford University Press, 2005), 140.

46. Michel Callon, "Some Elements of a Sociology of Translation: Domestication of the Scallops and the Fishermen of St. Brieuc Bay," *Power, Action, and Belief*, ed. John Law (London: Routledge, 1986), 196.

47. Cedric C. Brown, "Letters, Verse Letters, and Gift-Texts," in *Milton in Context*, ed. Stephen B. Dobranski (Cambridge: Cambridge University Press, 2010), 42.

48. Milton to Dati, *C* 12:44.

49. Ibid., 12:48.

50. Ibid.

51. Ibid.

52. Estelle Haan, *From Academia to Amicitia: Milton's Latin Writings and the Italian Academies* (Transactions of the American Philosophical Society, 88.6) (Philadelphia: American Philosophical Society, 1998), 55.

53. See also Mandy Green, "Reaching a European Audience: Milton's Neo-Latin Poems for Charles Diodati, 1625-39," *European Legacy* 17 (2012): 165-184.

54. Milton, *Epitaphium*, line 134.

55. Milton related his success reading his poems at the Florentine academies, where they "were receiv'd with written encomiums," in *The Reason of Church Government*, *CPW* 1:809-810.

56. Milton, *Epitaphium*, line 183.

57. Ibid., line 181.

58. See Michele de Filippis, "Milton and Manso: Cups or Books?" *PMLA* 51 (1936): 745-756.

59. See William R. Parker, "Contributions Toward a Milton Bibliography," *The Library*, series 4 vol. 16 (1936), 425-438, and Dobranski, *Milton, Authorship, and the Book Trade*, 77-78.

60. Parker, "Contributions," 427.

61. Of the 260 records attributed to Augustine Mathewes (and variants of his name), 51% in the ESTC lack identifying information. This compares with 25% of 514 for Miles Flescher, 12.5% of 327 for Thomas Cotes, and 14% of 390 for Thomas Harper.

62. Margaret Anne Witten-Hannah, "Lady Mary Wroth's Urania: The Work and the Tradition," PhD dissertation, University of Auckland, 1978, 73.

63. James I, *A Proclamation Against Excesse of Lavish and Licentious Speech of Matters of State* (London, 1620).

64. George Wither, *The Schollers Purgatory* (London, 1624), sig. H2v–H3r.

65. See Diane K. Jakacki, "Title Page Engravings and Re-Ordering the Quartos of *A Game at Chess*," *Romard* 50 (2011): 58.

66. David McKitterick, *History of Cambridge University Press*, 3 vols. (Cambridge: Cambridge University Press, 1992), 1:166.

67. "Petition of Augustine Matthews to Sir John Lambe, Sir Nathaniel Brent, and Dr. Duck, Commissioners Concerning the Printers of London." Calendar of State Papers Domestic, Charles I (July 1637), 364:345.

68. William Laud, *A Speech Delivered in the Starr-Chamber* (London, 1637), sig. I3v. See also Kenneth Fincham and Nicholas Tyacke, *Altars Restored: The Changing Face of English Religion, 1547–1700* (Oxford: Oxford University Press, 2007), 158–159.

69. Peter Heylyn, *A Coale from the Altar* (London, 1637), sig. A3r-v.

70. Edward Arber, *A Transcript of the Registers of the Company of Stationers of London, 1554–1640 A.D.* (London: 1875–94), 4:528.

71. State Papers Domestic (1637–38) SP 16/363, fol. 217r.

72. Lambeth MS. 1030/92, transcribed in H. T. Blethen, "Bishop John Williams's Recantation of His 'Holy Table, Name and Thing,' 1638," *Journal of Theological Studies* 29 (1978): 157–160.

73. H. R. Plomer, *A Transcript of the Registers of the Worshipful Company of Stationers: From 1640–1708* (London: private printing, 1913), 1:29.

74. Ibid., 1:419.

75. See Dobranski, *Milton, Authorship, and the Book Trade*, 128.

76. Milton, *Areopagitica*, CPW 2:570.

77. Granovetter, "Strength of Weak Ties," 1364.

78. Dobranski, *Milton, Authorship, and the Book Trade*, 87.

79. See Gordon Campbell and Thomas N. Corns, *John Milton: Life, Work, and Thought* (Oxford: Oxford University Press, 2008), 95–96, and archival evidence presented by Edward Jones, "'Church-Outed by the Prelats': Milton and the 1637 Inspection of the Horton Parish Church," *Journal of English and Germanic Philology* 102 (2003): 42–58.

80. David L. Hoover and Thomas N. Corns, "The Authorship of the Postscript to *An Answer to a Booke Entituled, An Humble Remonstrance*," *Milton Quarterly* 38 (2004): 59–75.

81. William Riley Parker, "Milton, Rothwell, and Simmons," *Huntington Library Quarterly*, series 4 vol. 18 (1937): 89–103.

82. Milton, *Reason of Church Government*, CPW 1:808.

83. Anonymous, *A Modest Confutation* (London, 1642), sig. A3r. The tract is anonymous but was likely by Hall himself or by his son, as Milton assumed.

84. Ibid.

85. See Lewalski, *Life of John Milton*, 182–184.

86. Milton, *Doctrine and Discipline of Divorce*, CPW 2:240.

87. Dobranski, *Milton, Authorship, and the Book Trade*, 126.

88. Anna Beer, *Milton: Poet, Pamphleteer, and Patriot* (London: Bloomsbury, 2008), 309.

89. Sharon Achinstein and Benjamin Burton, "Who Printed Milton's *Tetrachordon?*" *The Library*, series 7 vol. 14 (2013): 33.

90. Ibid.

91. Herbert Palmer, *The Glasse of Gods Providence* (London, 1644), 57.

92. Anonymous, *An Answer to a Book Intituled, The Doctrine and Discipline of Divorce, or, A Plea for Ladies and Gentlewomen* (London, 1644), 44.

93. See Campbell and Corns, *John Milton*, 159–161.

94. Nicholas von Maltzahn "Who Printed *Areopagitica?*: The Press and Milton's Paper Work," Modern Language Association (9 January 2015), Vancouver. Von Maltzahn's findings are based on extensive comparison of paper stock and other bibliographical evidence and constitute one of the major findings of his forthcoming edition of *Areopagitica* for Oxford University Press, *Complete Works of John Milton*.

95. Milton, *Areopagitica*, CPW 2:492.

96. Achinstein and Burton, "Who Printed Milton's *Tetrachordon?*" 22.

97. Milton, *Areopagitica*, CPW 2:570. See also Cyndia Susan Clegg, *Press Censorship in Jacobean England* (Cambridge: Cambridge University Press, 2001), 218–231.

98. Achinstein and Burton, "Who Printed Milton's *Tetrachordon?*" 35.

99. *Journals of the House of Lords: Volume 7, 1644* (28 December 1644) (London: His Majesty's Stationery Office, 1767–1830), 116.

100. D. F. McKenzie and Maureen Bell, *A Chronology and Calendar of Documents Relating to the London Book Trade* (Oxford: Oxford University Press, 2006), 1:129.

101. Achinstein and Burton, "Who Printed Milton's *Tetrachordon?*" 35.

102. Robert Baillie, *A Dissuasive from the Errours of the Time* (London, 1645), 115; Thomas Edwards, *The First and Second Parts of Gangraena* (London, 1646), sig. C1r.

103. John Milton, Sonnet 22, in *The Complete Poetry and Essential Prose*, eds. William Kerrigan, John Rumrich, and Stephen M. Fallon (New York: Modern Library, 2007), 12.

104. Christopher Wase, "Epilogue," *Electra of Sophocles, Presented to her Higness the Lady Elizabeth* (The Hague, 1649), sig. E8r.

105. The advertisement is in the British Library copy.

106. Milton's poem in this edition is on sig. K8r-v.

107. For the best summary of this argument, and of recent efforts by Michael Wilding, Leah Marcus, and Gary Spear to reinsert Moseley into the conversation about Milton's authorial presentation, see Dobranski, *Milton, Authorship, and the Book Trade*, 82-85.

108. Warren Chernaik, "Books as Memorials: The Politics of Consolation," *Yearbook of English Studies* 21 (1991): 210.

109. See James Shirley, *Six New Plays* (London, 1653); Robert Stapylton, *De Bello Belgico* (London, 1650); John Suckling, *Fragmenta Aurea* (London, 1646).

110. Humphrey Moseley, "The Stationer to the Reader," *Poems of Mr. John Milton* (London, 1645), sig. a3v-a4r. See for example his preface to Edmund Waller's *Poems* (London, 1645), William Cartwright's *Comedies, Tragicomedies, and Poems* (1651), and Francis Beaumont and John Fletcher's *Comedies and Tragedies* (1647).

111. Humphrey Moseley, "To the Reader," *Fragmenta Aurea* (London, 1646), sig. A3v.

112. Humphrey Moseley, "Stationer," *Poems of Mr. John Milton*," sig. A3r.

113. J. Milton French, "Moseley's Advertisements of Milton's *Poems*, 1650-1660," *Huntington Library Quarterly* 25 (1962): 345.

114. See *Two New Plays . . . Written by Tho. Middleton, Gent.* (London, 1657), sig. A3v.

115. Milton's poem in this edition is on sig. K8r-v.

116. Lukas Erne, "*Cupids Cabinet Unlock't* (1662), Ostensibly 'By W. Shakespeare', in Fact Partly by John Milton," in *Canonising Shakespeare: Stationers and the Book Trade, 1640-1740*, eds. Emma Depledge and Peter Kirwan (Cambridge: Cambridge University Press, 2017), 108-129.

117. Ibid., 115.

118. *Paradise Lost*, 7.13-23.

119. For a summary of some of the ways "Satan bridges the gap," see Neil Forsyth, *The Satanic Epic* (Princeton: Princeton University Press, 2003), 63-64. The debate over Milton's God is extensive, but to see the lines drawn most clearly, compare William Empson, *Milton's God* (London: Chatto and Windus, 1965) and C. S. Lewis, *A Preface to Paradise Lost* (Oxford: Oxford University Press, 1961).

120. Gordon Teskey, *Delirious Milton: The Fate of the Poet in Modernity* (Cambridge, MA: Harvard University Press, 2006), 29.

121. For Milton's motto, which derives from 2 Corinthians 12:9-10, see William Kerrigan, *The Sacred Complex: On the Psychogenesis of Paradise Lost*

(Cambridge, MA: Harvard University Press, 1983), 134, and William Riley Parker, *Milton: A Biography* (Oxford: Clarendon Press, 1968), 1:479.

### Epilogue

1. Thomas Taylor, *The Progresse of Saints to Full Holiness, Described in Sundry Apostolical Aphorisms* (London, 1630), 296. See also Edward Leigh, *Annotations of Five Poetical Books of the Old Testament* (London, 1657), 152, and William Gearing, *A Bridle for the Tongue* (London, 1663), 217.

2. Bruno Latour, *Reassembling the Social: An Introduction to Actor-Network-Theory* (Oxford: Oxford University Press, 2005), 132.

3. "Introducing the Mechanic Muse," *New York Times Sunday Book Review* (26 June 2011): BR4. https://www.nytimes.com/2011/06/26/books/review/up-front-introducing-the-mechanic-muse.html

4. Timothy Brennan, "The Digital-Humanities Bust," *Chronicle of Higher Education* (15 October 2017). https://www.chronicle.com/article/the-digital-humanities-bust/

5. Tom Eyers, *Speculative Formalism: Literature, Theory, and the Critical Present* (Evanston: Northwestern University Press, 2017), 34–35. See also Daniel Allington, Sarah Brouillette, and David Golumbia, "Neoliberal Tools (and Archives): A Political History of Digital Humanities," *Los Angeles Review of Books* (1 May 2016).

6. Nan Z. Da, "The Computational Case Against Computational Literary Studies," *Critical Inquiry* 45 (2019): 603.

7. See Alan Liu, "The State of Digital Humanities: A Report and a Critique," *Arts and Humanities in Higher Education* (2011); and Patrick Svensson, "Humanities Computing as Digital Humanities," *DHQ* 3.3 (2009).

8. Roberto Busa, "The Annals of Humanities Computing: The Index Thomisticus," *Computers and the Humanities* 14 (1980) 83–90. Ann M. Blair, *Too Much to Know: Managing Scholarly Information Before the Modern Age* (New Haven: Yale University Press, 2010).

9. Marlene Manoff, "Human and Machine Entanglement in the Digital Archive: Academic Libraries and Socio-Technical Change," *Portal: Libraries and the Academy* 15 (2015): 516–517; see also Marlene Manoff, "The Materiality of Digital Collections: Theoretical and Historical Perspectives," *Portal: Libraries and the Academy* 6 (2006): 311–325.

10. See Joanna Picciotto, *Labors of Innocence in Early Modern England* (Cambridge, MA: Harvard University Press, 2010), 323–399.

11. Samuel Butler, "The Elephant in the Moon," *The Collected Works of Samuel Butler*, vol. 3, ed. René Lamar (Cambridge: Cambridge University Press, 1928), 3:56–57.

12. Ibid., 358–358.
13. Eyers, *Speculative Formalism*, 34.
14. Da, "Computational Case," 605.
15. https://critinq.wordpress.com/2019/03/31/computational-literary-studies-a-critical-inquiry-online-forum. See also Ted Underwood's *Distant Horizons* (Chicago: Chicago University Press, 2019), which offers a model of statistical corpus analytics that departs in overt ways from the one Da describes, since "we have recently graduated from measuring variables to framing models of literary concepts. . . . Instead of starting with, say, the frequency of connective words, quantitative literary research now starts with social evidence about things that really interest readers of literature, like audience, genre, character, and gender" (xii).
16. Matthew Kirschenbaum, "Digital Humanities As/Is a Tactical Term," in *Debates in the Digital Humanities*, ed. Matthew K. Gold (Minneapolis: University of Minnesota Press, 2012), 416.
17. https://atlas.lib.uiowa.edu/
18. https://mapoflondon.uvic.ca/
19. https://www.translationandprint.com/project
20. http://www.womensbookhistory.org/
21. https://estc21.wordpress.com/about/
22. http://www.sixdegreesoffrancisbacon.com/
23. https://ebba.english.ucsb.edu/
24. https://networkingarchives.org/
25. http://isabelladeste.web.unc.edu/
26. Liu, "The State of the Digital Humanities," 20.
27. Carl Stahmer, "The Universal Short Title Catalogue," Spenser Review 45.1 (2015). http://www.english.cam.ac.uk/spenseronline/review/item/45.1.3
28. Chris Dijkshoorn et al., "The Rijksmuseum Collection as Linked Data," *Semantic Web Journal* 9 (2018): 221–230.
29. http://sparql.europeana.eu. To see how this works, visit the "Linked LODer" demonstration site http://apps.dri.ie/locationLODer/locationLODer. Selecting a place name on the map loads available content sourced from the Placename Database of Ireland, Europeana, DBpedia, the National Library of Ireland's Longfield Maps collection, and the Irish Historic Towns Atlas project.
30. See https://www.ld4l.org. For Shakeosphere's role as a proof of concept in LD4L, see https://wiki.duraspace.org/pages/viewpage.action?pageId=76843831#StatementsofWork(LD4LLabs)-6.4IowaStatementofWork
31. James Jaehoon Lee, Blaine Greteman, Jason Lee, and David Eichmann, "Linked Reading: Digital Historicism and Early Modern Discourses of Race

Around Shakespeare's *Othello*," *Journal of Cultural Analytics* (26 January 2018). https://culturalanalytics.org/article/11034

32. Ibid.

33. Ibid.

34. David Golumbia, "Death of a Discipline," *Differences: A Journal of Feminist Cultural Studies* 25 (2014): 158–159.

35. John Paget, *Meditations of Death* (Dort, 1639), 238–239.

# INDEX

Abbot, George, Archbishop of Canterbury, 118
Achinstein, Sharon, 104, 167, 169
Actor-network theory (ANT), 8–10, 69, 191–92n29
Adams, David R., 28
Adrian VI, Pope, 66
Advanced Research Consortium, 184
Ahnert, Ruth, 10, 106
Ahnert, Sebastian E., 106
Airports: degree distribution, 72, 75 (fig.); hubs, 25, 72
Aitzema, Leo Van, 155
Amsterdam: books printed in, 120–21, 123–24; English Protestants in, 187; Rijksmuseum, 54, 184
Ansell, Christopher K., 148
ANT, see Actor-network theory
Anwykyll, John, 52

*Areopagitica* (Milton), 68, 131–32, 151, 162, 168–69
Artistic prints, 54
Aspley, William, 54
Assarino, Luca, *La Stratonica*, 113
Atlas of Early Printing, 177, 181
Authors: agency and influence, 63–64, 105, 142; betweenness centrality, 109 (fig.), 109–10; female, 103–4, 114; highest-degree, 108, 108 (fig.). *See also individual names*

Bacon, Francis, 51–52, 79, 177, 181, 198n18
Bacon, Kevin, 7, 51
Baillie, Robert, 169
Banks, Thomas, 109
Barabási, Albert-László, 2, 6, 25, 26
Barker, Robert, 113

# INDEX

Barnard, John, 134
Baron, Sabrina A., 28
Barrows, Christopher, 99, 100
Bastwick, John, 96
Bavelas, Alex, 5
Bawcutt, Nigel W., 100
Baxter, Richard, 108, 109
Beale, John, 136
Beard, Thomas, *Theatre of God's Judgments*, 41–42
Beaumont, Francis, 158, 164, 171, 173
Beer, Anna, 167
Berger, Jonah, 2
Betweenness, defined, 105
Betweenness centrality: of authors, 109 (fig.), 109–10; Bavelas on, 5; of Calvert, 134; of Cary, 14–15, 114–15, 129–31, 141–42, 177; of Davies, 14–15, 114–15, 124 (fig.), 125, 128, 142, 177; defined, 39; relationship to degree, 39, 105 (fig.), 105–6; of stationers, 106; of texts, 14–15, 111, 112 (fig.), 112–15; of women, 106–7
Bible: Daniel, 117; printers, 141; Psalms, 92
Bibliographic databases, 19–20, 30–31, 103–4, 181, 182–83. *See also* English Short Title Catalogue
Big Data Visualization Application (BigDIVA), 184
Blair, Ann M., 65, 179
Blayney, Peter W. M., 36, 49–51, 81–82, 91
Bloom, Harold, 15, 143
Books, *see* Texts
Booksellers: authority records, 22–23, 34; as hubs, 65, 67, 77 (fig.), 97, 134; use of term, 35–36. *See also* Calvert, Giles; Sparke, Michael; Stationers
Bourke, Evan, 107
Boyle, Robert, 107

Brennan, Timothy, 178
Brewster, Thomas, 142
Brill Tagger, 31–32
British Library, 18, 20–21, 151. *See also* English Short Title Catalogue
British Museum, 54
Brooke, Christopher "Kit," 116–17
Brooks, William, 99, 100
Brown, Cedric C., 156
Browne, John, 97, 100
Bruno, Giordano, 51–52
Bulkley, Stephen, 113
Bullard, Paddy, 30
Burre, Walter, 32, 35
Burt, Ronald S., 147, 148
Burton, Benjamin, 167, 169
Burton, Henry, 96, 101
Busa, Roberto, 179
Busby, John, 88–89
Butler, Samuel, "The Elephant in the Moon," 180
Butter, Nathaniel, 32, 86, 87–88

Callon, Michel, 8, 9, 155
Calvert, Giles: books sold by, 112; Cary and, 129, 130, 134, 140, 141, 142; English print network and, 125, 134, 135 (fig.), 161, 164, 177; social network, 141
Carew, Thomas, 165, 171–72, 173
Caricchio, Mario, 141
Cary, Mary: authorial identity, 139–40, 142; betweenness centrality, 14–15, 114–15, 129–31, 141–42, 177; English print network and, 129–31, 133–36, 141–42; *The Glorious Excellencie of the Spirit of Adoption*, 139, 214n118; historians on, 104; *Little Horn's Doom* and *A New and More Exact Mappe*, 132–39; married name, 135–36, 142; as publisher, 134–39; publishing strategies, 15;

*Resurrection of the Witnesses*, 137, 139, 142; *Twelve Humble Proposals*, 114, 129–30, 130 (fig.), 134, 140–42; *A Word in Season*, 139; writings, 128–34, 139, 140–41
Catholics, 15, 66, 86, 93, 99, 141. *See also* Henrietta Maria, Queen; Religious controversies; Sales, Francis de
Caxton, William, 46, 52, 53
Censorship: in Elizabethan era, 205n52; enforcement, 94–95, 99, 100, 101; evasion of, 91; licensing regulations, 167, 169; of political satire, 159; religious, 67, 121, 131; by Star Chamber, 159–61
Chapman, George, *Whole Works of Homer*, 32, 33 (fig.)
Chapman, Livewell, 142
Charles I, King: Davies's prophecies and, 117, 119, 124; *Eikon Basilike*, 66, 125, 129, 165, 170; *His Majesties Declaration*, 113; judges, 115; marriage, 93, 117; order by, 160
Charles II, King, 110
Chernaik, Warren, 171
Chettle, Henry, 57, 70, 71–72, 76–77
Christakis, Nicholas A., 2
*Chronicle of Higher Education*, 178
Civil War, English: histories, 103; Milton and, 166–67, 169–71, 173; printed works, 112–15; royalists, 111, 113, 117, 125, 165, 167, 172–73; women's roles, 103, 104, 120
Clegg, Cyndia Susan, 91, 205n52
CLS (Computational Literary Studies), *see* Digital humanities
Coe, Jane, 139, 142
Cohen, Jeffrey J., 8
Coiro, Anne Baynes, 150–51
Coke, Edward, 32, 41, 86–87
Coker, Cait, 103

Coldiron, A. E. B., 52–53
Collings, Richard, 141
Collins, Randall, 148
Comenius, Jan Amos, 133, 140
Communication networks, 1, 2, 3, 5, 45
Como, David R., 113–14
Computational Literary Studies (CLS), *see* Digital humanities
*Comus* (*A Maske*) (Milton): copies, 217n44; first printing, 150, 151–53, 155, 158, 162, 163, 216–17n37; music, 162, 171, 173; performances, 124; real-world models, 123; significance, 125
Cope, Esther S., 104, 126
Cornell University, 185
Cotes, Richard, 112
Cotes, Thomas, 158, 159, 218n61
Cotton, John, 108, 109, 116
Council of State, 129, 137, 139, 141
Court of High Commission, 94–95, 121–22, 160
Cowley, Abraham, 164–65, 173
Creede, Thomas, 35, 36
*Critical Inquiry*, 181
Cromwell, Elizabeth, 138
Cromwell, Oliver, 129, 137
Crooke, Andrew, 61, 109
*Cultural Analytics*, 186

Da, Nan Z., 178, 180–81
Dacres, Edward, 68
Dane, Joseph A., 23
Daniel, Drew, 8
Danter, John, 61, 62 (fig.), 63
Databases: bibliographic, 19–20, 30–31, 103–4, 181, 182–83; Linked Open Data, 17, 30, 183–86; network analysis using, 181–86. *See also* English Short Title Catalogue
Dati, Carlo, 144, 156–57
Davenant, William, 153, 158, 164

Davies, Eleanor: *The Appeal to the Throne*, 126; betweenness centrality, 14–15, 114–15, 124 (fig.), 125, 128, 142, 177; brother, 123–24; epitaph, 128; ESTC records, 19; *The Everlasting Gospell*, 120–21; historians on, 104; influence, 115, 119, 124, 126; *The Lady Eleanor Her Appeal*, 118; life of, 115–23, 125–28; network maps of works, 121, 122 (fig.), 124 (fig.), 125; prophecies, 117–20, 127, 128; publishing strategies, 15; *Strange and Wonderfull Prophesies*, 114, 124 (fig.), 125; *A Warning to the Dragon and All His Angels*, 117–18; weak ties, 126, 127; Winstanley and, 126–28
Davies, John, 115, 116, 117, 118–19
Davies, Stevie, 104
Davis, Natalie Zemon, 7
Degree distribution, 26, 64, 72–74, 73 (fig.), 75 (fig.)
Dekker, Thomas, *Lanthorne and Candlelight*, 36, 37 (fig.), 39
Deleuze, Gilles, 8
Dering, Edward, 119
Devereaux, Robert, 113
Diggers, 15, 115, 125, 126–27. See also Winstanley, Gerrard
Digital humanities: challenges, 11, 183–84; critiques, 10–11, 178, 180–81; development of field, 10, 12, 178–79, 183; future of, 16, 182–84, 186–87; methods and tools, 17, 179–80, 183–86; projects, 181–83, 184–86; scope, 182. See also Network analysis
Diodati, Charles, 144, 150, 155
Diseases: epidemics, 7, 47, 48 (fig.), 65–66, 68, 69; infectious, 1, 7; measles, 47; plague, 47
Dobranski, Stephen, 150, 151, 165

Donne, John, 40, 79, 116, 119, 158, 164
Douglas, Archibald, 119–20, 123
Drucker, Johanna, 10–11
Ducarel, Andrew, 185
Duncan-Jones, Katherine, 62, 63, 83
Dury, Dorothy Moore, 107
Dury, John, 107

Early English Books Online (EEBO), 19–20
Early Modern Letters Online (EMLO), 16, 177, 181–82, 185
ECCO, *see* Eighteenth Century Collections Online
Education reforms, 133, 140
Edwards, Thomas, 169
EEBO, *see* Early English Books Online
Egerton, Alice, 123, 124
Eichmann, David, 30
Eighteenth Century Collections Online (ECCO), 19, 20
*Eikonoklastes* (Milton), 125, 129, 149, 170
Eisenstein, Elizabeth L., 7, 45, 46
Eld, George, 51, 54, 88
Elizabeth I, Queen, 60, 205n52
EMLO, *see* Early Modern Letters Online
English Broadside Ballad Archive, 181
English print network: agency and influence of actors, 82, 142; average degree, 26, 39–40; average degree per year, 27, 27 (fig.); clusters, 40–42, 41 (fig.), 124 (fig.), 125; continental print networks and, 52–54; degree distribution, 74 (fig.), 74–76, 75 (fig.); growth and spread, 53–54; high-betweenness of texts, 111, 112 (fig.), 112–15, 177; highest-degree members, 78 (fig.), 78–79, 108, 108 (fig.), 134, 163–65, 165 (fig.); highest-degree texts, 14, 110–12, 111 (fig.), 114; Milton

and, 150–57, 165–66, 167–75, 177; network analysis results, 3, 43, 176; oppositional, 91, 151, 157–58, 159, 161–63, 167–70. *See also* Betweenness centrality; Phase transition

English print network maps: 1557–1640, 25–27, 26 (fig.), 36–38; 1588–1589, 56 (fig.); 1589–1590, 58–60, 59 (fig.); 1590–1600, 49, 50 (fig.); 1593–1594, 61–63, 62 (fig.); 1600–1616, 40–42, 41 (fig.); 1630–1637, 158–59; 1641–1660, 121, 122 (fig.), 124 (fig.), 125; Calvert's connections, 134, 135 (fig.); Cary's *Twelve Humble Proposals*, 129–30, 130 (fig.); Davies's *Strange and Wonderfull Prophesies*, 124 (fig.), 125; generation of, 36–38, 52; hubs, 76–78, 77 (fig.); implications, 64–65; of Milton and works, 162 (fig.), 162–63, 164 (fig.); phase transition, 49, 50 (fig.)

English Short Title Catalogue (ESTC): as data source, 13, 17–19, 22–29; data structure, 31; data translation, tagging, parsing, and extraction, 29–36; description, 17–18; EEBO database and, 19–20; ESTC 21, 181; history of project, 13, 17–18, 20–22; limitations, 18–19, 20, 21–22, 23, 34; missing data and metadata, 23–25, 28 (fig.), 28–29, 158–59, 218n61; scope, 18, 21, 23; Shakeosphere project, 23, 30–36, 43, 177, 178, 184, 185–86. *See also* English print network

Epidemics: metaphors, 65–66, 68, 69; phase transitions, 7, 47, 48 (fig.); small-world networks and, 64

*Epitaphium Damonis* (Milton): autobiographical elements, 150; first printing, 29, 151–55, 152 (fig.), 154 (fig.), 156–57, 161–62, 216–17n37; Italian inspiration, 157; network map, 162 (fig.), 162–63; poetic ambitions, 149

Erasmus, 69

Erdős, Paul, 3

Erne, Lukas, 34, 61, 88–89, 173

ESTC, *see* English Short Title Catalogue

Europeana Labs, 184

European print networks: artistic prints, 54; digital bibliography, 182; English network and, 52–54; histories, 7, 8; in Renaissance, 65–66

Eyers, Tom, 178, 180, 181

*Faerie Queen* (Spenser), 3, 60–61, 83

Farmer, Alan B., 24

Faulkner, Francis, *The Jests of George Peele*, 88

Feake, Christopher, 137–38

Field, John, 112

Field, Richard: career, 85; as network hub, 83; Okes and, 62, 83–84; publications, 32, 61–63, 83–84, 115; Shakespeare and, 51, 61–63, 62 (fig.), 83, 87; shared work, 85

Fifth Monarchists, 117, 137, 142

Fire: metaphors, 14, 65–66, 67–68, 69; tree density and spread of, 47, 48 (fig.)

Fisher, Edward, *The Marrow of Modern Divinity*, 113–14

Flescher, Miles, 158, 218n61

Forsyth, Neil, 144

Fowler, James H., 2

Fox, George, 129

Foxe, John, "Book of Martyrs," 106

Francini, Antonio, 157

French, J. Milton, 172

Gadd, Ian, 19, 155
Gale State Papers Online, 181–82
Garrard, George, 101
Gatekeepers, 4–5
Geiger, Brian, 181
Gephi software, 42–43
Gerbils, see Great gerbils
Gill, Alexander, 155, 158
Gillespie, Katharine, 125, 128–29
Global Renaissance project, 186
Granovetter, Mark, 5–6, 145–46, 163
Great gerbils (*Rhombomys opimus*), plague outbreaks and burrow occupancy, 47, 48 (fig.)
Great Tew Circle, 107
Green, Jonathan, 24
Greenblatt, Stephen, 55
Greene, Charles, 109
Greene, Robert: connection to Bacon, 52; death, 55–57; English print network and, 46, 56 (fig.), 55–57, 64; life and career, 55–58, 64; *Pandosto*, 40; *Perimedes the Blackesmith*, 57–58; publications, 55–58; Shakespeare and, 63
Grinnell College, 186
Grismond, John, 94, 165
Guattari, Félix, 8

Haan, Estelle, 156
Haas, Christina, 68–69
Hall, John, 166
*Hamlet* (Shakespeare), 10
Harper, Charles, 32
Harper, Thomas, 32, 158, 159, 218n61
Harrington, John, 62, 83
Harris, Jonathan Gil, 9
Harrison, John, 61, 87, 204n39
Hartlib, Samuel: circle of, 15, 107, 141; *Clavis Apocalyptica*, 134; on educational reform, 140; female writers and, 15, 115, 128–29, 132, 133, 136; linguistic reforms, 133; Ranelagh and, 107
Harvard University, 185
Henrietta Maria, Queen, 15, 93, 115, 119
Henry VIII, King, 34
Herrick, Robert, 171, 173
Heylyn, Peter, *A Coale from the Altar*, 151–53, 160, 216–17n37
Heywood, Thomas: on Okes, 89–90; *Rape of Lucrece*, 87–88, 204n38
Heywood, William, 97, 99, 100, 101
Hie, Brian, 42
Hill, Christopher, 103, 136
Hills, Henry, 129, 130, 141, 142
Hinds, Hilary, 103, 133
Hirsch, Rudolf, 24
Hobbes, Thomas, 129
Hobby, Elaine, 103, 104
Holland, see Amsterdam
Hollar, Wenceslaus, Laud trial engraving, 97, 98 (fig.), 207n74
Honigmann, E. A. J., 79
Hooks, Adam, 61, 63
Howell, James, 110
Hubs: airports, 25, 72; betweenness, 106; booksellers as, 65, 67, 77 (fig.), 97, 134; in English print network, 4, 65, 67, 72–79, 83, 163–65, 165 (fig.), 176–77; high-degree texts, 110–12, 111 (fig.); network maps, 76–78, 77 (fig.); printers as, 76, 77 (fig.), 78, 83, 90; publishers as, 76, 77 (fig.), 78; stationers as, 76, 77 (fig.), 78–79, 83; ten most connected, 78 (fig.), 78–79, 83
Humanities, see Digital humanities
Husband, Edward, 112

Ibbitson, Robert, 109, 128
IBM, 179
"IDEA: Isabella d'Este Archive," 182

*Index Thomisticus*, 179
Internet: phase transition in connectivity, 49; as small-world network, 7, 64; social media, 1; Wikipedia pages, 73 (fig.), 74
Internet Movie Database (IMDb), 7
Ireton, Bridget, 138–39
Ireton, Henry, 138–39

Jacob, Lady Mary, 115–17
Jacob, Robert, 116
Jacobson, Miriam, 9
Jaggard, William, 24, 32, 89–90, 204n29
Jagodzinski, Cecile M., 12
James I, King, 84, 86, 93, 115, 119
James II, King, 141
Jessey, Henry, 128, 137
Jockers, Matthew L., 11
Johns, Adrian, 46, 67
Johnson, Gerald D., 88
Jonson, Ben: *Alchemist*, 32, 35, 36, 37 (fig.), 39, 40; connection to Bacon, 51; friends, 116; on Okes, 96, 97; poetry, 171, 173; publishers, 79; *Volpone*, 116; *Works*, 40, 61

Karian, Stephen, 29–30
Kastan, David Scott, 46
King, Edward, 107
*King Lear* (Shakespeare), 3, 79–81, 87, 88
Kirkman, Francis, 61
Kirschenbaum, Matthew, 181
Knappett, Carl, 9–10

Lady Eleanor, *see* Davies, Eleanor
Lambe, John, 99, 128, 160
Latour, Bruno, 8, 9, 10, 69, 176, 217–18n45
Laud, William, Archbishop of Canterbury: conspiracy charge, 96; Davies and, 121, 124; execution, 97; Okes and, 14, 96–100, 101; on Sparke, 67; trial, 82, 97–100, 98 (fig.); Williams' book and, 159–61
Law, John, 8, 155
Law, Matthew, 36
Lawe, Thomas, 35
Lawes, Henry, 125, 150, 151, 153, 162, 171–72
LD4L, *see* Linked Data for Libraries
Leake, William, 61
Lee, James, 186
Lesser, Zachary, 88
Letters: Medici Archive, 16, 177, 182; network analysis using, 24–25; of Protestants, 106. *See also* Early Modern Letters Online
Library of Congress, 185
Lichfield Cathedral, 118, 125–26
Lincoln, Matthew D., 54
Linked Data for Libraries (LD4L), 185
Linked Open Data, 30, 177, 183–86
Linked Reading, 186
Link Grammar Parser, 32
Literary studies, network science applications, 7–10, 12–13, 16, 177–78, 181–87. *See also* Digital humanities
Liu, Alan, 183
Lodge, Thomas, 55
Loewenstein, David, 131
Loewenstein, Joseph, 12
London: as global city, 45; literary scene, 55; Map of Early Modern London, 20, 30, 34, 177, 181, 185
Love, Christopher, 110
Love, Harold, 7, 46, 155
Lownes, Humphrey, 95
Lownes, Matthew, 95
Luther, Martin, 66, 83–84

Mack, Phyllis, 103, 115, 140
Manoff, Marlene, 179

## INDEX

Mansion, Colard, 52
Manso, Giovanni Battista, 157
Manuscript circulation, 7–8
Map of Early Modern London (MoEML), 20, 30, 34, 177, 181, 185
Maps, *see* English print network maps; Network maps
Marlowe, Christopher, 41, 52, 55, 72
Marotti, Arthur F., 7–8, 46
Marriot, John, 94, 95
Marshall, William, 66, 172
*Martine Mar-Sixtus*, 69
Marvell, Andrew: *Paradise Lost* preface, 15, 143–44; Ranelagh and, 107; *The Rehearsal Transpros'd*, 101
Mary, Queen, 49, 51
Mathewes, Augustine, 93, 94, 95–96, 151–53, 157–62, 167, 216–17n37, 218n61
Matthew effect (rich-get-richer effect), 4, 54, 76, 165
McCabe, Richard A., 8, 12
McGann, Jerome J., 12
McIntyre, Frank, 24
McKenzie, D. F., 12, 134
McKitterick, David, 22, 46
McLuhan, Marshall, 7, 45
Mead, Joseph, 119
Measles, 47
Medici, Cosimo de, 148
Medici Archive, 16, 177, 182
Melnikoff, Kirk, 8
Merton, Robert K., 4
Methods: data sources, 13, 17–19, 22–29; data translation, tagging, parsing, and extraction, 29–36; NetworkX software, 42–43, 180; timeframe, 23; visualization and analysis, 36–43. *See also* English Short Title Catalogue
Middleton, Thomas, *The Puritan*, 88
Milgram, Stanley, 7

Millington, Thomas, 61
Milton, John: *Areopagitica*, 68, 131–32, 151, 162, 168–69; close relationships, 144, 155; *Defense of the English People*, 170; *The Doctrine and Discipline of Divorce*, 161, 167–68; Dury and, 107; early works, 150, 151–55, 161–62; *Of Education*, 140; on educational reform, 133, 140; *Eikonoklastes*, 125, 129, 149, 170; influence, 15, 143–44; "Lycidas," 107; marriage, 144, 167; network in book trade, 15, 150–57, 165–66, 167–75, 177; network maps, 162 (fig.), 163, 164 (fig.); *Paradise Lost*, 3, 15, 143–44, 150, 167, 174–75; *Poems* (1645), 151, 153, 155, 157, 161, 171, 172; poetry, 150, 171; *Prolusion* VII, 144; Ranelagh and, 107; *Reason of Church Government*, 131, 166; social isolation, 144, 149–50; *Tenure of Kings and Magistrates*, 129, 170; *Tetrachordon*, 161; tracts on church reformation, 166; weak ties, 6, 15, 144–45, 149, 155–57, 162–63, 165–66, 170–75, 177. *See also Comus*; *Epitaphium Damonis*
Moeller, Christine, 34
MoEML, *see* Map of Early Modern London
More, Thomas, 66
Moretti, Franco, 10, 11, 180
Moseley, Humphrey, 61, 113, 153, 158, 163–65, 170–73
Mulholland, Paul, 84, 89

Nashe, Thomas, 55, 57, 69
National Union Catalogue of Manuscript Collections (NUCMC), 16
Needham, Paul, 24

INDEX    233

Network analysis: digital, 1–2, 6–7, 10–12, 42, 177–78, 181–87; future applications, 16, 177–78, 182–87; of letters, 24–25; missing data challenges, 28–29; weighted edges, 39 (fig.), 39–40, 41 (fig.). *See also* Betweenness centrality; Degree distribution

Networking Archives, 177, 181–82

Network maps, 2, 10–11, 36–38. *See also* English print network maps

Networks: actor-network theory, 8–10, 69, 191–92n29; complex, 4, 25, 68; degree distribution, 26, 64, 72–74, 73 (fig.), 75 (fig.); density effects, 54; edges, 36, 39–40; epistolary, 24–25; linked, 177–78; nodes, 2, 9–10, 36–38; printing and publishing, 7; random, 25, 72, 73 (fig.); resilience, 25, 68, 72, 76; scale-free, 25, 72–76, 73 (fig.), 202n3; small-world, 44–45, 64, 71, 176; vulnerability to attacks, 76–78. *See also* Betweenness centrality; English print network; Phase transitions

Network science: history, 2–7; literary studies applications, 7–10, 12–13, 16, 177–78, 181–87. *See also* Network analysis

NetworkX software, 42–43, 180

Newcomb, John, 161

Newcomb, Lori Humphrey, 58

*New York Times Book Review*, 178

Nodes, 2, 9–10, 36–38. *See also* Betweenness centrality; Hubs

Norbrook, David, 93

North, Sir Thomas, 62

Northampton, Earl of, 93

NUCMC, *see* National Union Catalogue of Manuscript Collections

O'Callaghan, Michelle, 116–17

ODNB, *see* Oxford Dictionary of National Biography

Okes, John (father of Nicholas), 82

Okes, John (son of Nicholas), 84, 97, 99

Okes, Mary, 99

Okes, Nicholas: authors and, 205n48; betweenness centrality, 106; career, 82–90, 91–93, 102; connection to Bacon, 52; controversies, 91–101; critical appraisals, 79–82; ESTC records, 18, 85; Jonson's criticism of, 96, 97; Laud's trial and, 97–100; as network hub, 14, 79, 81–82, 91–92, 97, 100–102, 177; printing quality, 84–85, 89–90; printing shop, 14, 84–90, 102; Shakespeare works printed, 79–81, 87, 88, 204n39; shared work, 85, 86; training, 13–14, 62

Okes, Peter, 83

Oldenburg, Henry, 136

O'Neill, Lindsay, 10

Ong, Walter J., 7, 45

Online networks, *see* Internet

*Othello* (Shakespeare), 79, 186

Overbury, Thomas, 58

Overton, Henry, 139, 142

Overton, Richard, 28

*Oxford Dictionary of National Biography* (ODNB), 78, 79

*Oxford English Dictionary*, 181

Ozment, Kate, 103

Padgett, John F., 148

Paget, John, 187

Paine, Thomas, 161, 163, 167

Palmer, Herbert, 168

Pantzer, Katherine F., 20

*Paradise Lost* (Milton), 3, 15, 143–44, 150, 167, 174–75

Parker, William Riley, 158–59
Parliament: authors and, 110; James I and, 93; petitions to, 101; printers, 112, 128, 129, 164; publishing regulations, 68, 94, 167, 169. *See also* Civil War, English
Parse trees, 32, 33 (fig.), 34
Parsons, Marmaduke, 160, 161
Pateman, Carole, 104
Patronage networks, 2, 12, 60–61
Peele, George, 55, 88
Peeples, Matthew A., 29
Peters, Hugh, 137–38
Phase transition, English print network: central authors, 55–64; connected component, 47–49, 50 (fig.); effects, 3, 51–52, 69–70, 71–72, 176; factors in, 49–51, 54
Phase transitions: defined, 3, 47; in epidemics, 7, 47, 48 (fig.); in social networks, 54
Pito, Richard, 32
Plague, 47
Pollard, Alfred W., 20
Ponsonby, William, English print network and, 59 (fig.), 59–60, 61
Poole, Alex H., 11
Preferential attachment principle, 76. *See also* Matthew effect
Pricket, Robert, 86
Printers: agency and influence, 82, 171, 173; authority records, 22–23, 34; female, 139, 161, 181; as hubs, 76, 77 (fig.), 78, 83, 90; of Milton's works, 151–53, 157–62, 166, 167, 175; names on title pages, 34–35; of official publications, 129, 141; to Parliament, 112, 128, 129, 164; piracy, 88, 91, 94; production, 84, 203n28; royal, 113, 141; shared work, 85, 86, 204n29; of unlicensed works, 14, 91, 159, 169;

use of term, 35–36. *See also* Okes, Nicholas
Printing presses, 45–46, 53
Print revolution, 45–46, 65
Privy Council, 99, 100
Prophets, female: constraints, 139–40; influence, 5, 104–5; as mediators, 114–15, 128, 132, 142; Trapnel, 130, 131, 136. *See also* Cary, Mary; Davies, Eleanor
Protestants: exiles, 187; letter networks, 106; Luther, 66, 83–84; Presbyterians, 113, 125, 167, 168, 169; printers, 51; Puritans, 108, 109; Reformation, 46, 66. *See also* Wither, George
Prynne, William: *Canterburie's Doom*, 99; *Four Serious Questions*, 68, 201n69; Laud's trial and, 96, 99, 100, 101; publications, 125
Publishers: authority records, 22–23, 34; as hubs, 76, 77 (fig.), 78; use of term, 35–36. *See also* Booksellers; Printers; Stationers
Puritans, 108, 109

Quakers, 129, 134

Raffield, Paul, 86–87
Raleigh, Walter, 60, 79
Rand, John, 136
Rand, William, 136
Rande, Mary, *see* Cary, Mary
Random graph theory, 3
Random networks, 25, 72, 73 (fig.)
Ranelagh, Viscountess, 107
*The Rape of Lucrece* (Shakespeare), 62, 83, 87, 204n37, 204n39
Ratcliffe, Thomas, 164
Raworth, John, 161
Raworth, Richard, 86
Raworth, Ruth, 161

Raymond, Joad, 12–13
Redgrave, G. R., 20
Reese, Terry, 31
Reformation, 46, 66. *See also* Protestants
Religious controversies: lay preaching, 131–32; Milton and, 166–71; printed works, 14, 66, 68–70, 83–84, 86, 91–92, 96–100, 102. *See also* Catholics; Laud, William; Prophets, female; Protestants
Renaissance: digital humanities projects, 182, 186; information volume and spread, 65–66, 69; print revolution, 45–46, 65
Rényi, Alfred, 3
Rhodes, Neil, 53–54, 65
*Rhombomys opimus*, *see* Great gerbils
*Richard II* (Shakespeare), 86
*Richard III* (Shakespeare), 35
Rijksmuseum, 54, 184
Rip, Arie, 155
River systems, 77
Roberts, Rosemary A., 23
Robinson, Humphrey, 153, 158, 163, 171
Rolle, Henry, 139
Rolle, Margaret, 138–39
*Romeo and Juliet* (Shakespeare), 63
Rood, Theodoric, 52
Rothwell, John, 166
Rupert, Prince, 113

Sales, Francis de, 91; *An Introduction to a Devout Life*, 96, 97, 100–101
Sawday, Jonathan, 53–54, 65
Scale-free networks, 25, 72–76, 73 (fig.), 202n3
Scientists, networks, 4, 107
Semantic Web, 183
Shaaber, M. A., 34, 35
Shakeosphere project, 23, 30–36, 43, 177, 178, 184, 185–86

Shakespeare, William: Bacon and, 51; Chettle and, 70; *Cupid's Cabinet Unlock't* attributed to, 173; English print network and, 46–47, 61–63, 62 (fig.), 64; Field and, 61–63, 62 (fig.), 83, 87; first folio, 61, 155; Greene and, 55; *Hamlet*, 10; *King Lear*, 3, 79–81, 87, 88; Okes and, 79–81, 87, 88, 204n39; *Othello*, 79, 186; *Poems*, 171, 173; printers and, 61–62, 63, 87, 88, 90, 186; *The Rape of Lucrece*, 62, 83, 87, 204n37, 204n39; *Richard II*, 86; *Richard III*, 35; *Romeo and Juliet*, 63; second folio, 150, 156, 162; sonnets, 54; sources, 62–63, 83; *Titus Andronicus*, 63; *Troilus and Cressida*, 185; *Venus and Adonis*, 62, 83, 204n37; *Winter's Tale*, 58
Shawcross, John T., 144, 151, 216–17n37
Sheppard, William, 112–13
Shirley, James, 164, 171–72, 173
*Short-Title Catalogue of Books Printed in England, Scotland, and Ireland, and of English Books Printed Abroad, 1475–1640* (STC), 20, 21, 22, 24
Sidney, Philip: *The Countess of Pembroke's Arcadia.*, 58–60; death, 59; English print network and, 46, 58–61, 59 (fig.), 64
Simmons, Matthew, 149, 161, 163–64, 167–70, 173
Simmons, Samuel, 175
Simon, Herbert A., 4
Sireniacs, 116
Six Degrees of Francis Bacon, 51–52, 177, 181
"Six Degrees of Kevin Bacon" game, 7, 51
Six degrees of separation, 7, 44, 51–52, 198n18

Small-world networks, 44–45, 64, 71, 176
"Small world" phenomenon, 7, 44–45, 52
Smith, Nigel, 103, 128
Snodham, Thomas, 32, 35, 38–39, 79
Snowdon, George, 84, 85
Snowdon, Lionel, 84, 85
Snyder, Henry L., 18
Social networks: defined, 1; in early modern England, 2, 3, 45; gatekeepers, 4–5; phase transitions, 54; strong ties, 6, 144, 145, 146; triadic closure, 146, 147 (fig.). *See also* English print network; Networks; Weak ties
Sparke, Michael: betweenness centrality, 106; English print network and, 14, 67, 177; ESTC records, 19; fire metaphor, 14, 66, 67–68, 97; Hollar and, 207n74; as hub, 67, 97; Laud's trial and, 14, 97, 98 (fig.), 99; publications, 67–68, 125; wholesale book sales, 66–67, 70, 97
Spenser, Edmund: English print network and, 46, 58, 59 (fig.), 60–61, 64; *Faerie Queen*, 3, 60–61, 83; "Muiopotmos," 2
Stafford, John, 109
Stahmer, Carl, 181, 184
Stanford University, 177, 185
Stanley, Anne, 123–24
Stanley, Elizabeth, 123–24
Stapylton, Robert, 172
Star Chamber, 68, 99, 100, 115, 159–61
Stationers: betweenness centrality, 106; as hubs, 76, 77 (fig.), 78–79, 83. *See also* Booksellers; Okes, Nicholas; Printers
Stationers' Company: Court, 91, 92; English Stock, 67, 92; history, 34, 49–51; Milton and, 169; Okes and, 84, 92, 94–95; power, 49–51, 63, 93, 96; registers, 35, 88, 93, 94, 161; regulations, 34; royal charter, 49, 51; royal patents, 92; Wither and, 159

STC, *see* Short-Title Catalogue
Stern, Tiffany, 87
Strong ties, 6, 144, 145, 146
Suckling, John, 120, 134, 164, 171, 172
Sutherland, John, 7
Svensson, Patrik, 11

Tabor, Stephen, 20, 21
Technologies: printing, 8, 45–46, 53; software, 42–43, 180; textual, 12. *See also* Digital humanities; Internet; Network analysis
Teskey, Gordon, 174
Texts: betweenness centrality, 14–15, 111, 112 (fig.), 112–15; bibliographic databases, 19–20, 30–31, 103–4, 181, 182–83; burned, 99, 100, 101, 115, 118, 119–20, 121; exchanged by friends, 155–56; high-betweenness, 111, 112 (fig.), 112–15, 141–42; highest-degree, 14, 110–12, 111 (fig.), 114; loss rates, 23–24; novels, 113; official publications, 112, 113, 129; title pages, 18, 21–22, 28, 34–36, 52
Thomas Aquinas, 179
Thomason, George, 167
Thorpe, Thomas, 54
Title pages, 18, 21–22, 28, 34–36, 52
*Titus Andronicus* (Shakespeare), 63
Touchet, Mervyn, Earl of Castlehaven, 123–24
Tourneur, Cyril, *Atheist's Tragedy*, 36, 37 (fig.), 39, 40
Translation and the Making of Early

Modern English Print Culture project, 181
Transportation: in early modern England, 45; networks, 3. *See also* Airports
Trapnel, Anna, 130, 131, 136
Treadwell, Michael, 35
Tree density, fire spread and, 47, 48 (fig.)
Triadic closure, 146, 147 (fig.)
*Troilus and Cressida* (Shakespeare), 185
Trollope, Anthony, 24
Trussell, Thomas, 94–95

Underhill, Thomas, 166, 168
Universal Short Title Catalogue (USTC), 16, 182–83
University of Iowa: Atlas of Early Printing, 177, 181; Linked Data for Libraries initiative, 185; Shakeosphere project, 23, 30–36, 43, 177, 178, 184, 185–86
University of Montreal, Translation and the Making of Early Modern English Print Culture project, 181
Ussher, James, 110
USTC, *see* Universal Short Title Catalogue

*Venus and Adonis* (Shakespeare), 62, 83, 204n37
Vicars, John, 97–99
Vickers, Brian, 79–81, 82, 83
Viral transmission, *see* Epidemics
Visualization methods: adjacency matrices, 36, 37 (fig.); clusters, 40–42, 41 (fig.); Gephi software, 42–43; projections, 38 (fig.), 38–39, 39 (fig.), 40, 110; value, 10–11. *See also* English print network maps; Network maps

Von Maltzahn, Nicholas, 168

Walker, George, 68
Walkley, Thomas, 94
Waller, Edmund, 171–72
Walwyn, William, 161
Wase, Christopher, 170–71, 172
Watson, Thomas, 179
Watts, Duncan J., 2, 6
Weak ties: as bridges, 145–49, 148 (fig.), 163, 164 (fig.), 165–66, 171–73, 174–75; of Davies, 126, 127; defined, 145; Granovetter on, 5–6, 145–46, 163; intellectual innovations and, 148–49; of Milton, 6, 15, 144–45, 149, 155–57, 162–63, 165–66, 170–75, 177; structural holes and, 147–48, 148 (fig.)
Weaver, Edmund, 93
Weiss, Adrian, 80
Westminster Assembly, 68, 113, 164, 168, 169
White, Edward, 61
White, Robert, 142
Wikidata, 20, 30, 184, 185
Wikipedia pages, degree distribution, 74, 75 (fig.)
Williams, John, *The Holy Table*, 159–61
Wing, Donald G., 20, 21, 23
Winstanley, Gerrard, 15, 115, 118, 125, 126–28
*Winter's Tale* (Shakespeare), 58
Wise, Andrew, 35
Wither, George: *Abuses Stript and Whipt*, 93; *Collection of Emblemes*, 31, 159; *Preparation to the Psalter*, 92; printers of works, 91, 92–93, 158; *Schollars Purgatorie*, 96; *Wither's Motto*, 93–96, 159

Witmore, Michael, 9
Women: authors, 103–4, 114; betweenness centrality, 106–7; overlooked by historians, 103, 104, 107; printers, 139, 161, 181; in Protestant letter networks, 106; readers, 58. *See also* Cary, Mary; Davies, Eleanor; Prophets, female

Women in Book History Bibliography, 103–4, 181
Woodward, Hezekiah, 169
WorldCat, 183
Wotton, Henry, 155, 217n44
Wright, John, 54

Yonge, Walter, 101
Young, Thomas, 155, 166

STANFORD
TEXT TECHNOLOGIES

Series Editors
Ruth Ahnert
Elaine Treharne

Simon Reader
*Notework: Victorian Literature and Nonlinear Style*

Yohei Igarashi
*The Connected Condition: Romanticism and the Dream of Communication*

Elaine Treharne and Claude Willan
*Text Technologies: A History*

The authorized representative in the EU for product safety and compliance is:
Mare Nostrum Group
B.V Doelen 72
4831 GR Breda
The Netherlands

www.ingramcontent.com/pod-product-compliance
Lightning Source LLC
Chambersburg PA
CBHW070314240426
43661CB00057B/2642